NATIONALISM IN PORTUGUESE AFRICA

NATIONALISM IN PORTUGUESE AFRICA

Dr. Surya Narain Yadav

Dr. Indu Baghel

JNANADA PRAKASHAN (P&D)

NEW DELHI

Published by :
JNANADA PRAKASHAN (P&D)
4837/2, 24, Ansari Road, Daryaganj
New Delhi-110002
Phone : 011-23272047
Mobile : 9212137080

Assisted by :
TEXT BOOK PROMOTION SOCIETY OF INDIA
4837/2, 24, Ansari Road, Daryaganj
New Delhi-110002
Phone : 011-23272047
Mobile : 9212137080

Edition: 2010

Nationalism in Portuguese Africa

ISBN 978-81-7139-371-8

Typesetting by :
Vardhman Computers
New Delhi-110017

Published by Mrs. S. Chowdhary for M/s. Jnanada Prakashan (P&D) Daryaganj, Ansari Road, New Delhi-110 002 and printed at Balaji Offset, Navin Shahdara, Delhi-110032.

Preface

Portugal has been the oldest colonial power in Africa and, remarkably, also the last colonial power to leave Africa. The book entitled "Nationalism in Portuguese Africa" critically investigates the basic nature and characteristics of the Portuguese colonial policy in Africa, with a particular focus on Angola. Penetration of Portugal in Africa is an important issue in the study of the colonial history. As a result, a separate chapter has been devoted to this particular area.

Economic factor has always been an important consideration in the colonisation of Africa. A thorough examination of the economic conditions prevailing in Portugal as well as Africa, particularly Angola makes it abundantly clear that economy has been the dominant consideration in the Portuguese African policy.

Rise of anti-colonial movements in the Portuguese Africa, especially after the Second World War has been examined in details. All the three leading Angolan liberation movements constitute the significant part of this book. Impact of Angolan liberation movements on the political, economic and socio–cultural milieu of Angola is the specific part of this study.

The book is the original, comprehensive and critical analysis of the emergence of nationalism in Portuguese Africa, in general and Angola in particular. The authors are fully convinced that it would provide an entirely new direction to the study of colonialism and nationalism.

Acronyms

AASA	African Association of Southern Angola
ACOA	American Committee on Africa
ALIAZO	Alliance des Ressortissants de Zombo
CONCP	Conferencia das Organizacoes Nacionalistas das Colonias Portuguesas
FNLA	Frente Nacional Liberacao Angola
FRELIMO	Frente de Liberacao de Mozambique
GRAE	Angolan Government in Exile
LNA	Angolan National League
MPLA	Movimento Popular de Liberacao de Angola
OPVDC	Provincial Organisation of Volunteers and Civil Defense
PAIGC	Partido Africano da Independencia de Guinea e Cabo Verde
PCA	Angolan Communist Party
PCP	Portuguese Communist Party
PDA	Partido Democratico de Angola
PIDE	International Police for the Defense of the State
PNA	African National Party
PSP	Public Security Police
UD	Independent Dominion
UNITA	Uniao por Total Independencia of Angola
UPNA	Union of the Peoples of Northern Angola
ZANU	Zimbabwe movement in Rhodesia

Contents

1

Introduction

While often depicted as a progressive and modernising force, colonialism, in fact, was based on autocratic and frequently oppressive foreign rule. Ironically, the conquest and partition of the African continent took place at a time, when major European powers such as Britain and France were moving towards greater implementation of democratic principles at home.

Although, the European occupation of Africa was well under way by 1870, the year 1885 is a useful date to mark the beginning of the colonial era because of the historic importance of the Berlin Conference of 1884-85, which legitimised the "Scramble for Africa" by formally sanctioning the partition of the continent among several European powers. This study is primarily concerned with the impact of colonial policies and indigenous responses during the autocratic phases of colonial rule (1885-1945), when Africans had few political and civil rights.

Partition of Africa among European Powers

The nature of the relationships between Europe and Africa began to change with the abolition of the slave trade and the expansion of commodity exports. The Industrial Revolution spurred Britain and other European countries to intensify their trade with the non-Western world. The requirements of an expanding world capitalist system dominated by the the key industrial nations were major factors underlying the subjugation of Africa and other parts of what has come to be known as the developing world.

Technological and Military Supremacy of Europe

While superior technological and military strength allowed Europe to conquer and occupy the African continent, the essential causes for colonisation were political and economic.[1] Political factors, such as nationalist rivalries and balance of power politics among the leading European nations and a quest for national glory, heightened the desire for colonies. Imperialism was also stimulated by the need of the major industrial powers to acquire and control new markets and sources of raw materials in areas of the globe, which Europeans considered economically "backward."

In many instances, Africa was not as highly valued as other parts of the world. Britain, for example, was at first more concerned with maintaining and developing its Asian possession than with acquiring an African empire. Thus, the military intervention and occupation of Egypt in 1882 began primarily as a measure to protect sea routes to the Middle East and Asia by ensuring British control over the Suez Canal.

Military Supremacy of Britain

As the leading military and industrial nation in Europe, Britain obtained the most valuable colonial possessions in Africa. Encouraged by Germany, France also acquired a large number of colonies on the continent, to compensate for the provinces of Alsace and Lorraine, lost to Germany during the Franco-Prussian War of 1870-71. Germany became an imperial power by establishing colonies in German East Africa, South-West Africa, Togo, and Cameroon. However, all these were lost following Germany's defeat in World War I.

Portugal, a close ally of Britain and the European nation with the longest historical ties to Africa, acquired more territory in Angola, Mozambique, and Portuguese Guinea. Belgium emerged as a colonial power largely through the efforts of King Leopold II, who established the Congo Free State, which became the Belgian Congo (now Zaire) in 1908. Italy gained colonies in Libya and Somalia, and Spain acquired holdings in the Spanish Sahara and in equatorial Africa. The only two African states to retain their sovereignty during the colonial era were Ethiopia and Liberia, the latter founded in 1821 by freed African American slaves. Even Ethiopia lost its independence for a time in the 1930s, when it fell under the domination of Italian fascism.

With the exceptions of Algeria, Senegal, Portuguese enclaves in Angola, Mozambique, and Guinea, and South Africa, where the Afrikaners had pushed inland from the British-controlled Cape Colony to establish their own autonomous republics, most of the continent remained under African control until the last two decades of the nineteenth century.

Characters of African Societies

At the time of the colonial conquest, many African societies were in a state of flux. Morocco, Tunisia, and Egypt in North Africa were Muslim states whose monarchs had begun to modernise their countries before the occupation by France and Britain. In West Africa, Europeans had to deal with highly structured, well-established states such as Dahomey, Asante, and the Mossi empire, as well as numerous Muslim states including the Emirates of Northern Nigeria, Fouta Jalon, and newly created empires built by nineteenth-century Islamic reformers and military leaders such as Umar Tall and Samori Toure. Among the more prominent states in northeast and East Africa were the ancient Christian kingdoms of Ethiopia and Buganda and the Arab sultanate of Zanzibar. However, the great diversity of peoples and political units scattered throughout the continent at the time of colonial conquest included not only large-scale states but also smaller chiefdoms and decentralised societies, reflecting different levels of political, social, and economic development.

The military conquest of Africa was precipitated by the terms of the Berlin Conference, which insisted that European powers had to "effectively occupy" a territory before they could claim sovereignty over it. Although, Europeans portrayed themselves as liberators, the process of occupation was often violent, conducted by mercenaries concerned primarily with enriching themselves and their employers. Perhaps, the most notorious case of brutality and greed occurred in the Congo Free State, which came under the personal rule of Leopold II after the Berlin Conference. Under Leopold's rule, the pillaging and abuse of the indigenous populations reached such proportions that the pressure of world opinion obliged him to transfer control of the colony to the Belgian government. With the tacit support of their governments. empire-builders and adventurers such as Cecil Rhodes, George Goldie, and Sir Harry Johnston (all British), Carl Peters (German), and Savorgnan de Brazza (who worked for the French) organised personal armies and expeditions which brought large areas under European rule. France relied primarily upon its regular military forces to carve out a vast empire in West and equatorial Africa and Madagascar, while military conquest was also the principal means used by Germany, Portugal, and Italy in acquiring colonies.

Although, resistance to colonial conquest was widespread throughout the continent, Menelik II's success in preserving Ethiopian independence in the face of European imperialism proved to be the exception rather than the rule. Samori Toure organised one of the most spectacular examples of resistance to the imposition of European rule, using guerrilla tactics which delayed the completion of France's occupation of French West Africa for nearly two decades before his defeat and capture in 1898. Armed resistance was also fierce in other Muslim-controlled areas of West Africa, among the desert peoples of the Sahara, the

Baoule of the forest areas of Cote d'Ivoire, the Hehe, who kept the Germans at bay for seven years in German East Africa, and the Yao, who fought the Portuguese in Mozambique. After brief periods of resistance, other African states and peoples capitulated, realising that European technological superiority gave the invaders a decisive edge over conventional African armies, whose tactics and weaponry were ill suited to modern warfare.

Policy of Divide and Conquer

However, not all African leaders saw Europeans as enemies. In some instances weaker rulers allied themselves with Europeans to escape the hegemony of more powerful neighbours. Moreover, imperial forces often included large numbers of African troops recruited from conquered territories or provided by African allies. In retrospect, it is clear that the strategy of "divide and conquer," taking advantage of traditional political and ethnic rivalries, proved to be extremely successful in undermining local efforts to form effective alliances for the common purpose of resisling the invader.

The conquest period proved to be a shattering experience for many. Although, the imposition of colonial rule eventually led to the abolition of slavery and the establishment of peace, it also meant the end of African political, economic, and cultural autonomy, the transformation of elites and masses alike into colonial subjects with few political and civil rights, foreign economic domination, and the decline and denigration of traditional authority and values.

African Responses to Colonial Rule

Africans responded to colonialism and the accompanying social and economic transformations in a variety of ways. These often led to new ethnic, gender, and class relationships.

Ethnicity continued to be a primary force in shaping identity and expressing social solidarity.[2] In towns, for instance, new ethnic identities emerged where none had existed before. Such was the case with the Bangala of Léopoldville in the Belgian Congo, who had not existed as a distinct rural society in the precolonial period. The explorer-journalist Henry Morton Stanley first gave the name to people living in a string of villages between the Congo and Ubangi rivers. It was then appropriated by workers from that region in order to distinguish themselves from their neighbours in the eyes of whites, who perceived the "Bangala" as industrious and reliable. Subsequently, those migrating to find work in Léopoldville from a large area of the Upper Congo came to be known as the "Bangala," and the language which they spoke, a new *lingua franca,* as Lingala. When political competition intensified in Belgian Congo in the 1950s, the "Bangala" were major rivals of another broad group from the Lower Congo that had developed a politicised ethnicity, the Bakongo. In the Copperbelt towns of Northern Rhodesia (Zambia), a similar process took place as people from the same region but sharing no real sense of common ethnicity took over labels which enhanced their social solidarity in the trying urban conditions experienced under colonial rule. These included the Bemba and Ngoni. Other examples of previously dispersed autonomous communities with linguistic affinities adopting an ethnic identity for social, political, or economic ends can be found all over Africa.

In West Africa, the Igbo of Nigeria and the Diola of Senegal also exemplify this process. The identity of the Igbo was reinforced when they went to the towns or other regions of Nigeria or abroad to study. Building on their tight ethnic identity, the Igbo organised various self-help voluntary associations and ethnic unions in Lagos and other Nigerian towns and promoted education for their upward mobility. Their ethnic identity became highly politicised and pushed them to play a major role in Nigerian colonial politics. In 1966, ethnic considerations led to a bitter civil war in Nigeria, with the Igbo demanding their own nation-state, Biafra.

In some areas, colonial rule favored one ethnic group over another, thus, creating the basis for intense ethnic conflict and competition in late colonial and post-colonial politics. For example, in Guinea, the French favored the Fula over the Mandinka, Susu, and forest societies, and gave Fula aristocrats the best posts in the *chefferies.* Following World War II, Sekou Toure, the Mandinka leader who had led the resistance to French rule in the late nineteenth century, organised an anti-Fula alliance which brought him to power. After independence, hundreds of thousands of Fula fled Guinea as a response to the Toure regime's hostility to this group.

African Women during the Colonial Era

The status of women throughout much of Africa declined under colonialism, as colonial policies often reinforced patriarchal authority.[3] In precolonial Africa, women in some areas had served as chiefs, for example, among the Mende of Sierra Leone as village leaders among the Tonga in Northern Rhodesia; and as female officials such as the Iyalode in Yorubaland, who represented women's concerns in male-dominated political councils. Under colonial rule, white officials whose perceptions of female roles were based on their European experience worked almost exclusively through male traditional authorities and ignored female candidates for chiefships in areas where this would have been feasible. For example, in Igboland in Nigeria, where a female counterpart of the male chief *(obi)* existed, only the male *obi* became a salaried official.

Under colonialism, women also saw a decline in their access to land and labour and their share of household income, particularly in the rural areas. Men took control over cash crops and most of the income derived from the sale of their crops. In response. many enterprising women moved to the new towns, where they earned a living as market women, petty traders, and domestics. While some earned enough money to become urban property owners or organised mass-based women's interest groups such as the Lagos Market Women's Association in western Nigeria, others were forced into illegal activities such as prostitution and beer brewing.

Colonial rule also disrupted other pre-colonial social relations. In Senegal, the defeat of the Wolof states was accompanied by the elimination of the warrior caste, who had to return to the land to make a living. Many of them became followers of Amadou Bamba, the founder of the Mouride Brotherhood in Senegal. Elsewhere in francophone Africa, slaves liberated by the French organised their own villages. On the other hand, the institution of slavery survived in Mauritania and serfdom among the Fula of Fouta Jalon in Guinea.

Many African artisans, such as blacksmiths, jewelers, weavers, woodworkers, and musicians, also saw a decline in their economic status as imported European goods replaced their own products. The destruction of precolonial states undermined formerly wealthy African rulers. The artisans who were previously dependent on them responded by doing more farming or going to the towns, where they often assumed occupations which resembled their former ones. Thus, blacksmiths became mechanics. Throughout much of Africa, opportunities for social mobility were few during the colonial era because of the slow pace of economic development. Education was a key factor influencing the transformation of class and gender relations.

Racial and Cultural Domination under Colonialism

Notwithstanding different patterns of European rule throughout the continent, colonialism was essentially a system of political, economic, and cultural domination forcibly imposed by a technologically advanced foreign minority on an indigenous majority. As a system, colonialism justified itself largely through ideologies which asserted the superiority of the colonizer and the inferiority of the colonised.

Much of the rationale justifying the conquest and colonisation f Africa had been based on evolutionary theories of history influenced by the ideas of Darwin, Spencer, Morgan, and Marx. Such theories maintained that societies organised within the framework of the nation-state and industrial capitalism represented the most advanced human forms of organisation. Apologists for European colonialism and imperialism argued that it was the right, indeed the duty, of the "higher" civilisations to conquer the "lower" civilisations in order to bring prosperity and "progress" to all parts of the world. Such claims, often expressed in terms of the "White Man's Burden," or what the French referred to as their "civilising mission," were reinforced by racial theories which asserted the biological superiority of the "white race."

The dogma of the innate moral inferiority of the indigenous populations was widely shared by many Europeans living in colonial Africa and was used to rationalise the master-servant relationships between Europeans and Africans. The demeaning concept of "the native" implied that Africans, as inferior creatures, were not fit to rule themselves. In his powerful polemic against colonialism, *The Wretched of the Earth,* Frantz Panon bitterly described the image of "the native" held by the colonizer: "As if to show the totalitarian character of colonial exploitation the settler paints the native as the quintessence of evil. The native is declared insensible to ethics; he represents not only the absence of values, but the negation of value."[4]

The Europeans who came to live and rule in Africa invented new traditions to promote their self-esteem and respectability.[5] White settler farmers who came from lower-middle-class backgrounds perceived themselves as "gentleman farmers" and attempted to imitate the style of the upper classes and aristocracy back home. Colonial administrators also adopted gentlemanly styles, particularly in the British colonies, where colonial officials radiated pride in God, king, and country. The new traditions reflected a feudal, patriarchal ethic rather than the capitalist ethic which had been so instrumental in transforming European social structures.

The Europeans also invented traditions about the unchanging nature of customary Africa. Sometimes these traditions were used to criticise African backwardness and reluctance to modernise. At other times, they were used to praise the "traditional" Africans who knew their place, kept their own customs, and did not aspire to become like Europeans. On the other hand, Africans who sought equal status with Europeans and agitated for political and economic reforms were often viewed as rootless troublemakers who had lost touch with their "tribal" origins.

Social Implications of Colonial Policy

The racial character of the colonial system was reflected not only in the ideologies of the day but also in colonial social structures. Thus, in most colonies, European officials, businessmen, farmers, and missionaries constituted a privileged ruling caste open only to those of European birth. The principle of racial hierarchy was most developed in South Africa, particularly after 1910, when Britain transferred all of its prerogatives as a colonial power to a white settler minority government. One interesting feature of the colonial caste system was the relatively privileged but ambiguous status of the Euro-Africans, who constituted a small Westernised elite midway between the European rulers and the African masses in the colonial racial hierarchy. In the rare instances when political and civil rights were accorded to "nonwhites," these were generally granted to Euro-Africans such as the Creoles in Sierra Leone, the *metis* in Senegal, and the *mesticos* in Portuguese Africa.

Although, the colonial system was often justified in terms of its "civilising mission," few regimes were willing or able to provide the Western education deemed necessary to transform the "native" into a "civilised" person. Until the end of World War II, education was made available to less than five per cent of the school-age population. Girls were largely excluded. During the early phases of colonial rule, Catholic and Protestant missions provided the main opportunities for schooling. Whether at government or mission schools, children learned that European culture and civilisation were superior and were taught to reject their former religious practices and cultural traditions. The limited education offered to a small minority of Africans did not attempt to make them the equal of the European; it prepared them only to occupy subordinate positions within the colonial system.

While Euro-Africans and educated elites sought political and social equality for themselves, they often regarded the indigenous African masses as backward and not ready for full political and civil rights until they acquired a modicum of Western education and values. Liberal Europeans were willing to grant some rights to Westernised Africans. The greatest resistance to African equality came from the relatively large white settler populations of South Africa, Kenya, Southern Rhodesia (Zimbabwe), Portuguese Africa, and Algeria, where relationships between Europeans and Africans most closely approximated the master-slave model depicted by Fanon.

Metropolitan Policies towards Africa

The broad outlines of colonial policy were formulated in London, Paris, Brussels, and Lisbon, primarily in terms of the needs of the metropole. Colonial policies were affected more by the political climate at home and by international events than by what was taking place in Africa. Because of France's numerical inferiority in relation to Germany, the French government adopted a colonial policy which treated the African territories as a reservoir of troops for the French army. Germany ceased to be a colonial power not because of revolts in its African colonies but because it was the loser in World War I. During the interwar period 1919-39) the triumph of fascism in Portugal in 1926 perpetuated repressive colonial policies in Portuguese Africa, while the victory of the left-wing Popular Front in France in 1936 led to significant colonial reforms.

Metropolitan governments and public opinion were generally indifferent to colonial matters, which they regarded as less important than domestic issues and foreign policy. Although, colonial questions were significant in British politics because of the vast size of the empire, Britain was generally more concerned with events taking place in Asia, such as the rise of Indian independence movements under the leadership of Gandhi and the emergence of Japan as a world power. Smaller European colonial powers such as Belgium and Portugal were more involved with their African possessions than were Britain, France, Italy, and Germany, which were preoccupied with big power politics in Europe. Portugal Portugal looked to its African colonies as a means of restoring the grandeur of the past. Despite the fact that Portugal was a fascist state while Belgium was a bourgeois parliamentary democracy with a constitutional monarch, both nations pursued paternalistic colonial policies which stressed the spiritual mission of the colonizer, centralised decision making in the metropole, and denied political representation to both Europeans and Africans in the colonies.

While some commentators on French and British colonial policy have contrasted French "Cartesianism" with British "Empiricism."[6] these differences may have been overstated. "Cartesianism" implies a uniform approach based on a clear-cut set of rules which are universally applied; yet French colonial policies and practices were far from uniform, since France, like Britain, responded pragmatically to the various political, economic, and cultural realities in different parts of Africa. Thus, French policy in North Africa bore little resemblance to that practiced in Black Africa. In North Africa, the French regarded Algeria as an integral part of the metropole and totally destroyed indigenous political structures. On the other hand, in Tunisia and Morocco, which were governed as protectorates, the French maintained existing political and social structures, particularly in Morocco, where the sultan remained a prominent political figure throughout the colonial period.

Colonies in French West and French Equatorial Africa were organised within a highly centralised federal framework headed by a governor-general who supervised and coordinated the activities of the territorial colonial governors. Although, France practiced a policy of Direct Rule which insisted upon the legitimacy of only one sovereign authority, that of France, its colonial policy in Black Africa was nonetheless flexible enough to preserve and work through preexisting political structures in territories such as Mauritania, Upper Volta, Chad, and Niger, where the limited French presence necessitated a greater use of indigenous authorities.

Britain's reputation as a "liberal" colonial power was based largely on its policies in West Africa, whereby a small number of Africans could vote and participate in modern representative institutions even during the earlier phases of colonial rule. Each British colony in West Africa was divided into a "colony," whose inhabitants were governed by British law and granted political representation in municipal councils, and a "protectorate." Unlike the "colonies" centered on coastal towns such as Bathurst, Freetown, Lagos, and Accra, the "protectorates" in the interior were administered through traditional African leaders and institutions or through newly constituted "native administrations," often organised along ethnic lines and headed by traditional chiefs. The absence of a white settler population and the opportunities for African farmers to be integrated into the colonial export economy on relatively favorable terms made British colonial rule in West Africa less heavy-handed and oppressive than in East and Central Africa, where white settlers expropriated large tracts of communal lands and denied Africans political representation.

Colonial State

Colonial state in Africa was an overseas extension of the metropolitan state, run by a relatively small number of European colonial administrators whose loyalty was to the metropole. In the name of the metropole, the colonial state exercised sovereignty over often vast territories whose boundaries had been drawn up in Europe. The colonial state was not designed to lay the foundations for the development of a modern African nation-state. It had more modest goals: to maintain law and order, to foster obedience and loyalty to the colonial authorities, and to defend and promote the political and economic interests of the metropole.

The colonial state was autocratic, not democratic. While colonial rule has often been described as a "School for Democracy," this image did not reflect the realities of political life in Africa. Before 1945, less than 1 per cent of the African population had full political and civil rights or access to modern democratic institutions. Instead, most Africans were ruled by autocratic bureaucracies with little interest in promoting democratic ideals.

While the establishment of European colonial governments imposed a new political order in Africa, the impact of the colonial state on African societies should not be exaggerated. The European presence in many territories was, in fact limited to small numbers of administrators, merchants and missionaries concentrated primarily in the colonial capital and in the major trading centers. In many areas of rural colonial Africa, the people rarely came into direct contact with European officials. As late as the mid-1920s, there was only one British administrator for every 100,000 persons in northern Nigeria. In some parts of Africa, the colonial state was not able to impose its rule permanently and had to rely on periodic military expeditions to "pacify" the area. Thus, in the desert regions of several French colonial territories such as Algeria, Mauritania, Mali, and Niger, the Tuareg and other desert peoples managed to maintain a considerable degree of autonomy because their areas were largely inaccessible and ungovernable.

Because of the small, number of European personnel, limited financial resources, and an undeveloped communications infrastructure, the colonial state had to rely heavily upon traditional African rulers, chiefs, and religious authorities to help govern the vast areas and populations under its control. Where the Europeans did not find local rulers, they often created their own chiefs to administer an area or named strangers or people of low social status to fill the role.

The French, for example, who had less respect for traditional authority than did the British, would often name an interpreter, a guide, or even a cook as canton chief to replace a local authority when the latter's loyalty to France was in question. The system of Indirect Rule permitted rulers and chiefs to govern certain areas under the careful supervision of the Europeans. The survival of traditional authority did not alter the fact that rulers and chiefs were clearly subordinate to the colonial power structure and could be deposed if they did not follow the dictates of the colonial administration. The ideal chief under the colonial system was loyal, accepted the hegemony of the colonizer, maintained order collected taxes for the colonial regime, encouraged his people to produce cash crops for the export economy, and provided forced labour for public works projects and cheap wage labour for European enterprises.

As long as they complied with the demands of the colonial authorities, traditional rulers and chiefs retained a privileged position within the colonial system. Thus, because of his collaboration with the Belgian colonial administration, a traditional chief such as the father of Moise Tshombe, the leader of the unsuccessful Katanga secession movement after independence and prime minister of Zaire in the early 1960s, could become a millionaire in his own right. In other instances, the colonizer permitted rulers and certain ethnic groups to preserve and even enhance their hegemony over other peoples, as was the case in Rwanda, where the Tutsi continued their domination of the Hutu, a situation that has led to bloody genocidal conflict since independence. Many of the ethnic and regional cleavages which plague contemporary Africa had their roots in the administrative politics of the colonial era, which favored certain traditional authorities, regions, and ethnic groups over others.

Powers and Functions of Local Chiefs during the Colonial Period

The integration of chiefs as subordinate cogs in the colonial bureaucracy, performing unpopular tasks such as collecting taxes and recruiting forced labour, undermined chiefly authority throughout much of colonial Africa. The people came to regard them as agents of the colonizer rather than representatives of African interests. This was particularly true in France's Black African colonies and in the Belgian Congo, where the *chefferies* were clearly creations of the colonial state and had few roots in the African past. On the other hand, indigenous authority tended to persist in colonial areas under indirect rule such as eastern and western Nigeria, where the British successfully modernised traditional authority structures while reinforcing the prestige of chiefly authority.

The colonial state usually relied on educated Africans to run the lower echelons of the colonial bureaucracy as clerks, bookkeepers, and minor officials. With few exceptions, Africans rarely rose to high positions within the administration. Europeans felt no compulsion to Africanise the colonial state, since it was assumed that colonial rule would be more or less permanent.

The army and police force were important components of the colonial state and were used to preserve order. While commanded by European officers, they were composed largely of local recruits. The French and British also used African troops to put down revolts in other parts of their empires or to fight in European wars. The French conscripted tens of thousands of Africans in their West African colonies to fight in World War I and continued to conscript thousands during the interwar period (1919-39), a policy which led many young Africans to flee to nearby English colonies. African soldiers serving in the colonial armies were expected to give their full loyalty and allegiance to the metropole. The British in East Africa, for example, developed elaborate regimental rituals and symbols to cement their troops' loyalty to the British monarchy.

For the masses, the colonial state was a foreign institution which operated according to unfamiliar rules and norms. The official language of the colonial state was a European language unknown to all but a tiny minority of the colonised population. And few European officials spoke any of the indigenous languages. Within a single territory, the administration brought together many different ethnic groups which were obliged to coexist and to live according to the rules of the colonizers, who did little to unite their subjects or to promote nationalist sentiments. On the contrary, they preferred to keep the various groups apart and to prevent any alliances which might be used to challenge their rule.

The limited opportunity that Africans had to Africanise the colonial state before attaining independence, the illegitimacy of the colonial state with the African masses, and its failure to promote a sense of common national identity among the diverse peoples living within the boundaries of the colony were important features of the colonial legacy. All these have contributed to the political instability and fragility of many African nations since independence.

Politics of White Settler

White settler politics consisted primarily of efforts by Europeans to perpetuate their political and economic supremacy over colonial populations. In the multiracial societies of Kenya, the Rhodesias, and Tanganyika (Tanzania), white settlers fought to restrict the suffrage of the Asian and Arab populations and to limit their representation in the legislative councils which were set up after World War I. In Kenya, white settlers not only expropriated the best farmlands but also won their battle to prevent Asians from obtaining equal political, economic, and social rights. The white settlers of Southern Rhodesia gained the right to govern themselves in 1923 and used their power to maintain white supremacy.

Settler influence on colonial administrative policy was not as great in Nyasaland (Malawi) and Tanganyika, where climatic conditions and fewer economic opportunities attracted much smaller European populations. Despite the presence of significant numbers of settlers, European political life was less intense in Belgian and Portuguese Africa, which had no representative political institutions. Colonial administrators generally had a freer hand in colonies with small European populations.

An unusual blend of democratic and totalitarian politics emerged in South Africa. For the Europeans, there was a highly competitive and democratic form of electoral politics which pitted a predominantly English-speaking party against a predominantly Afrikaans-speaking party; for the so-called Cape Coloureds and the Asians, there was limited political representation and an inferior political, social, and economic status; for Africans, there was almost no representation and, over the years, a steady deterioration of their civil rights.

In Algeria, the sizable French population enjoyed all the political prerogatives of metropolitan citizens, including representation in the French parliament, which they used to prevent the passage of colonial reforms aimed at enfranchising Muslims. Ironically, white settler tyranny over the indigenous populations was often greatest in territories such as Algeria, South Africa, Southern Rhodesia, and Kenya, where Europeans insisted on exercising all the rights of citizens living in democratic societies while denying these same rights to Africans. Hence, it was not surprising that African hostility to colonial rule and European domination tended to be most intense in these territories. The Mau Mau rebellion in Kenya, the Algerian revolution, and the wars of national liberation undertaken in Portuguese and southern

Africa were, to a large extent, the fruits of the white settler politics of the colonial era.

African Participation in Democratic Politics

Before World War II, the main centers of modern African political activity could be found in colonial protectorates such as Morocco, Tunisia, and Egypt and in West Africa, where colonial policies permitted limited African participation in electoral politics.

In North Africa, radical nationalist parties emerged, such as the Neo-Destour Party in Tunisia led by Habib Bourguiba, as well as more tradtionalist nationalist movements which rallied around the banner of Islam in Egypt and Libya or around the persons of the monarch, as in Morocco with Muhammed V. The French harshly repressed North African nationalist movements which challenged French sovereignty especially in Algeria. which was considered to be an integral part of Egypt. The British continued to occupy Egypt, despite its nominal independence, until 1936 and intervened frequently to protect pro-British monarchs and governments from being overthrown by nationalist opponents.

Unlike the mass nationalist politics practiced in North Africa, African political activity in West Africa during the colonial era was restricted to a small, educated African elite which was primarily concerned with gaining full rights for educated Africans, increasing the power of representative political bodies in the colony, and widening the scope of African participation in the political process. In British West Africa, educated leaders sought to improve their position by constitutional means. This meant petitioning for more African representation on the legislative councils and demanding less representation by chiefs appointed by the colonial administration or by European officials themselves, who often constituted a majority of the members.

The elite of British West Africa resented the system of Indirect Rule practiced in "protectorates," which treated the chiefs as the authentic representatives of the people. The establishment of "native administrations" and the preservation of precolonial entities such as the Emirates of Northern Nigeria often frustrated the aspirations of the new elite to provide leadership in the colony. Yet, those with Western education and the chiefs were not always in conflict; blood and marriage ties often bound them together, and some of the chiefs were themselves highly educated by colonial standards. Moreover, the modern elite defended the prerogatives of the chiefs on many occasions, especially on questions concerning the expropriation of communal land by the colonial administration.

Policy of Assimilation

African participation in French West Africa was largely confined to Senegal's so-called Four Communes of Dakar, Goree, Rufisque, and Saint Louis, where they enjoyed the rights and privileges of "citizens." Senegal was the only Black African colony where the French ideal of "assimilation" was actually practiced. The principle of assimilation called for giving the overseas colonial populations the same kind of education and rights extended to the French, representation in metropolitan assemblies, and local political institutions patterned on those found in France. Senegal was perhaps the only colony in tropical Africa during this period in which Africans and Europeans competed and worked together in politics on an equal and integrated basis. Like their counterparts in British West Africa, the African elite of "citizens," led by such men as Blaise Diagne and Galandou Diouf, were more concerned with asserting the rights and prerogatives of the "citizens" in the "Pour Communes" than with extending these rights to the "subject" populations of the interior, who constituted more than 95 per cent of Senegal's total population.

Elsewhere in French West and Equatorial Africa and in Madagascar, Western-educated Africans resented their subject status and sought to gain the same rights enjoyed by Senegal's citizens. Despite France's assimilationist ideals, French colonial officials resisted efforts to increase African participation in democratic institutions and made it extremely difficult for even well-educated African subjects to become naturalised French citizens. It was not surprising that French colonial policy totally excluded African women from participating in electoral politics, since French women in the metropole also did not have the right to vote.

Participation of African Elites in Colonial Politics

In other parts of colonial Africa, African elites, such as *assimilados* in Portuguese Africa, *evolues* in the Belgian Congo, and the mission-educated in British East and Central Africa, were not permitted to engage in electoral politics. In these territories, Africans learned most of their modern political skills through their activities in various ethnic, cultural, and religious associations.

Although, less than one per cent of the African population directly participated in the limited democratic politics of the colonial era, there were other ways in which the African masses could express their political views. These responses to colonial rules and policies varied from violent rebellions and protest to accommodation and collaboration.

During the early colonial period, rebellions were frequent throughout the continent, often touched off by repressive land, labour, and tax policies. Thus, in South Africa, the Zulus in Natal rebelled in 1906 after the imposition of oppressive poll taxes; in Tanganyika, the Maji-Maji insurrection against German rule in 1905 was put down only after a bitter struggle in which tens of thousands of Africans lost their lives; and in Liberia, the Kru revolted against the black American-Liberian government. With the consolidation of colonial rule, large-scale rebellions became less frequent during the interwar period (1919-39).

In areas where Africans had few formal political outlets to express themselves collectively, political protest was often organised through millennarian religious movements and separatist churches which affirmed African values and world views. Kimbanguism in the Belgian Congo, the Watchtower movement in British Central Africa, the Black Zionist churches in South Africa, and the Muslim Hamallist movement in French Soudan are prominent examples of mass dissatisfaction with European rule expressed in a religious form. On the other hand, Islamic movements often gained more headway when they made their peace with the colonial authorities. Such was the case in Senegal, where the Muslim Brotherhoods thrived.

Although, they were excluded from the political process, African peasants, workers, and women did not remain passive in voicing their sentiments about colonial economic policies and employment practices. Miners in South Africa and Northern Rhodesia, for example, launched illegal strikes to protest low pay and poor working conditions, while the railway workers in West Africa were among the first group of African wage earners to organise trade unions. Asante cocoa farmers initiated the Cocoa Holdup of 1939 to protest the low prices they were getting for their crops. In the rural areas, tax evasion was widespread, particularly among herders, who moved frequently to avoid paying the cattle tax. Market women in Dahomey and Nigeria also rioted to protest against high taxes and harassment by colonial administrators. Africans often expressed their dissatisfaction by voting with their feet and moving across the border into neighbouring territories, where they hoped for better conditions which they did not always find.

Despite the unpopularity of colonial rule, most Africans wound up accepting the authority of the colonial state. Indeed, some leaders and societies collaborated very closely with the colonizer in exchange for certain privileges within the colonial system, while others welcomed the colonizer, at least initially, for liberating them from slavery and rule by other ethnic and religious groups. Moreover, many Westernised Africans saw colonialism in Africa as a progressive and "civilising" force which, despite its many abuses, had eliminated slavery and internecine warfare while providing opportunities for those with modern skills to rise socially and economically regardless of previous low social status.

Africans could also vent their feelings about colonial rule on a personal level, expressing hostility, for example, in popular songs which made fun of the colonizer.[7] Others who identified with the power or the culture of the colonizer wore Western suits and ties and emulated European mannerisms and customs.

Economic Perspectives of Colonialism

As an economic system, colonialism bound the peoples of Africa more closely to the international capitalist system in general and to the metropolitan economy in particular. The colonial situation gave the metropole the power to monopolise economic policy and impose a system of "enforced bilateralism." In practical terms, this meant that international trade was generally oriented toward the metropole, that nationals of the metropolitan power controlled the most important sectors of the colonial export economy, and that colonial development policies reflected the interests of metropolitan banks, import-export houses, shipping firms engaged in colonial trade, mining companies which exploited the mineral resources of the colonies, and the white settler population. The colonial system provided the metropole with outlets for its manufactured goods, raw materials for its industries, and tropical products for metropolitan consumers on terms that were advantageous to the colonizers.

Although, colonial economic policies clearly stimulated economic growth, this growth was often achieved at the expense of the indigenous populations. From the African point of view, colonial rule meant the expropriation of traditional communal lands, the transformation of many Africans into an uprooted and poorly paid urban and rural proletariat, and a labour system which kept Africans at the bottom of the economic scale and prevented them from effectively competing with European farmers. Economic exploitation, like political oppression, was most pronounced in territories containing relatively large numbers of white settlers in need of cheap African labour.

During the colonial era, the white settler population was primarily concerned with acquiring land and access to cheap labour. Economic exploitation was most systematic in South Africa. There, Europeans took the best land and established a Native Reserve system and an economic "color bar" which forced Africans to work for low wages while legally preventing them from holding the same jobs as whites. Appropriation of vast tracts of land by European settlers was also widespread in Kenya, Southern Rhodesia, Portuguese Africa, the Belgian Congo, and Algeria, and carried out on a smaller scale in Cote d'Ivoire, Tunisia, Libya, and Cameroon.

The development of mining and the rapid expansion of plantation agriculture stimulated an enormous demand for African labour, which was generally supplied from the poorer and usually more densely populated regions in the territory or else imported from neighbouring colonies. In most instances, the labour-supplying region had no solid economic base of its own and lacked a source of cash income to pay the taxes levied by the colonial government. Thus, to pay taxes, it was necessary for Africans in Mozambique and Nyasaland, for example, to seek work in the mines of South Africa and on the farms of Southern Rhodesia. In West Africa, Upper Volta became a major reservoir of labour for cocoa plantations in Cote d'Ivoire and the Gold Coast.

The subordinate position of Africans within the colonial economic system was also maintained by discouraging local initiatives which might result in competition for whites in the modern sectors of the colonial economy. Thus, European import-export companies thwarted the development of a modern entrepreneurial class in places such as Senegal by withholding credit from what had been a flourishing class of African traders and middlemen before 1900. European firms and the colonial administration further stifled African competition in the modern sectors of the economy by using nonindigenous groups as middlemen, including the Lebanese in West Africa and the Asians in East Africa. Colonial economic policies also made it difficult for Africans to compete with Europeans in agriculture. Thus, the British in Kenya did not permit African farmers to grow coffee and other cash crops produced by the white settlers, while the French administration in Cote d'Ivoire discriminated against African cocoa producers by offering higher prices to French planters.

In West Africa and Uganda, where colonial policies precluded large-scale European settlement and seizure of African communal lands, rural farmers, though increasingly vulnerable to fluctuating world market conditions, nevertheless enjoyed economic opportunities as producers of cash crops such as cocoa, coffee, cotton, peanuts, and palm oil for European markets. The main beneficiaries of economic growth in the rural areas tended to be notables, chiefs, and religious leaders who could transform their traditional prerogatives over the allocation of communal land and local labour into wealth derived from cash crops.

The development of cash crops had a negative effect on the economic status of women and widened the gap between men and women in many parts of colonial Africa. Male family heads tended to produce the cash crops and to pocket the proceeds from selling them, while women continued to produce the staples for household and local consumption. Colonial economics also adversely affected the status of young males, who often had to serve on forced-labour gangs or leave their village to find work to earn money to pay taxes and the bride wealth. Colonial patterns of development which generally favored coastal areas over the interior and cash crops over food crops widened economic gaps between regions and ethnic groups.

In the urban areas, educated Africans who occupied wage-earning jobs, such as bookkeepers, clerks, civil servants, and school teachers, also profited materially from the patterns of change fostered by the colonizer. On the other hand, for menial laborers working in colonial capitals and mining towns, life was generally harsh and living conditions were difficult. Africans responded to urban life by creating various associations based on ethnicity, place of origin, economic activities, and class. These might take the form of savings associations, burial societies, market women's associations, and craft guilds.

Many regions and territories continued to remain largely untouched by modern economic forces and modes of production, however. This was particularly true of the desert, Sahelian, and forest zones, which lacked modern roads and railways to facilitate the evacuation of tropical products. In territories such as Mauritania and northern Nigeria, precapitalist modes of production and exchange continued to persist as most of the people remained largely outside the colonial economic system. In areas where the colonial economy did not replace traditional African products with European imports, African artisans and merchants continued to supply most of the needs of the local populations in goods and services and to control the traditional long-distance trade in cattle, dried fish, cola nuts, salt bars, and other products.

The colonial situation clearly made it more difficult for Africans to enjoy the full fruits of whatever economic growth took place during this period. However, one should not overstate African economic dependency on the colonizer or understate the ability of Africans to take economic initiatives and to adopt survival strategies which helped them to cope with economic disruptions and to take advantage of new economic opportunities. The diverse patterns of economic development and their consequences for Africa, especially as they relate to the economic problems of the postindependence period.

The Second World War marked the beginning of the end of the colonial era and its autocratic rule. The war discredited the racist ideologies which had served as the original rationale for European colonisation, heightened African aspirations for self-government, and seriously weakened the capacity and the will of the major colonial powers to maintain their overseas empires, thereby setting the stage for the era of political decolonisation which was to follow.

NOTES AND REFERENCES

1. There are two principal contending interpretations of the causes and motivations underlying modern European imperialism. One school of thought, associated with the names of such historians as Brunschwig and Gallagher and Robinson, gives the primacy to political factors, while the other school of thought, associated with such names as Hobson and Lenin, gives the primacy to economic factors. For a useful discussion of these schools of thought and excerpts from their main proponents, see George H. Nadel and Perry Curtis, *Imperialism and Colonialism* (New York: The Macmillan Company, 1964).
2. For an excellent discussion of the development and strengthening of ethnic identity in colonial Africa, Charles W. Anderson, Fred R. von Mehden, and Crawford Young, *Issues of Political Development,* 2nd ed. (Englewood Cliffs, N.J.: Prentice-Hall, 1974). Also Leroy Vail, ed.. *The Creation of Tribalism in Southern Africa* (London: James Currey, 1989).
3. For a thorough discussion of the declining status of women under colonialism, Jane L. Parpart, "Women and the State in Africa," in Donald Rothchild and Naomi Chazan, eds., *The Precarious Balance: State and Society Africa* (Boulder, Colo.: Westview Press, 1988), pp. 208-15.
4. Frantz Fanon, *The Wretched of the Earth* (New York: Grove Press Inc., 1968), p. 41.

5. Terence Ranger, "The Invention of Tradition in Colonial Africa," in Eric Hobsbawm and Terence Ranger, eds.. *The Invention of Tradition* (London: Cambridge University Press, 1983), pp. 211-62.
6. Thomas Hodgkin's classic *Nationalism in Colonial Africa* (New York: New York University Press. 1957).
7. Leroy Vail and Landeg White, "Forms of Resistance: Songs and Perceptions of Power in Colonial Mozambique," *American Historical Review* 88, no. 4 (October 1983): 883-919.

FURTHER READING

Balandier, Georges. "The Colonial Situation." In Pierre Van Den Berghe, ed., *Africa: Social Problems of Change and Conflict,* pp. 36-57. San Francisco: Chandler Publishing Company, 1965.

Crowder, Michael. *West Africa under Colonial Rule.* London: Hutchinson, 1968.

Delavignette, Robert. *Freedom and Authority in French West Africa.* London: Cass, 1968.

Gellar, Sheldon. *Structural Changes and Colonial Dependency.* Senegal, 1885-1945. Beverly Hills: Sage, 19.76.

Newitt, Malyn. *Portugal in Tropical Africa: The Last Hundred Years.* London: C. Hurst and Company, 1981.

Rotberg, Robert I. *Imperialism, Colonialism and Hunger: East and Central* Africa. Lexington. Mass.: Lexington Books, 1983.

Schmidt, Elizabeth. *Peasants, Traders, and Wives: Shona Women in the History of Zimbabwe,* 1870-1939. London: Heinemann, 1992.

Suret-Canale, Jean. *French Colonialism in Tropical Africa, 1900-1945.* London: C. Hurst and Company, 1971.

2

Portuguese Penetration of Africa

Political leaders in Portugal are fond of describing themselves as a "mixed-blooded people," and refer to their history to explain their non-racist attitudes and policies. Africans, of course, would hotly contest their claim to being nonraist. An examination of the history of Portugal and its behaviour in Africa makes it apparent that, despite the seeming contradiction, both views are correct.[1]

Background

Roderick, the last Visigoth king in what is now Portugal, was defeated in 711 by the Moors. His kingdom collapsed. During the next 300 years, Islam spread over the Iberian peninsula, across the Pyrenees, and throughout the southern shore of the Mediterranean beyond the Caspian Sea. For the next 100 years, from 1055 onward, Portuguese royalty of the houses of Braganza and Burgundy began to reestablish Portugal as a Christian country, finally taking Lisbon In 1147. During another century of warfare against the Moors, the Portuguese dynasty began colonising the land and establishing law, language, and institutions.

Nor did the Portuguese stop with driving the Moors from Portugal itself. In a series of wars they pursued the Moors to fight and lose at Tangiers. The Portuguese royalty then formed shaky alliances through marriage and common cause with the houses of Castile, Leon, and Aragon. The Portuguese fear that, unchecked, the Spanish influence would extend to conquest and subjugation, proved justified: Spain dominated Portugal for nearly 100 years.

In the thirteenth and fourteenth centuries, there were major alliances between Portugal and England. The first of these, a commercial treaty enacted in 1294, initiated Portuguese naval activity under Genoese and Venetian guidance. In 1386, by the Treaty or Windsor, England and Portugal became permanently allied, and King John of Portugal married Philippa, the daughter of England's John of Gaunt.

In 1433, the Portuguese navy, under King Henry the Navigator, first rounded Cape Bojador to a long series of explorations along the coast of Africa. Soon afterward Portuguese became the first Europeans to import slaves from the west African coast. They begun almost inadvertently. Moslems held North Africa, and the Portuguese wanted not only to secure the products of the Sudan, but also to gain allies there for an attack on Islam from the flank and rear. When, in 1441, the two captains of the expedition which reached Cape Blanc, Tristao and Goncalvos, captured 12 Africans to take back as trophies to Lisbon, Lisbon merchants recognised the commercial value of the slave trade and for that purpose financed Portugal's subsequent expeditions.

Before the century ended, traders and explored Cape Verde, sailed south across the equator, were at the mouth of the Congo, and sailed a round the Cape or Good Hope and up the cast coast to India. By 1510, by conquest, threat, and treaty, 2,000 miles of the cast African coast had been brought under Portuguese hegemony. On the west coast the Portuguese had established forts and trading posts from Cape Blanc to what is now Angola. By the mid-1500s slave traffic was so heavy that it is estimated that slaves comprised 10 per cent of Lisbon's population.[2]

The exploration and conquest of the New World set up further demands for the slave and mining wealth of Africa. The Spanish, who were precluded from the slave trade by a series of papal bulla mid treaties in the latter part of the fifteenth century, were in urgent need of manpower for their colonies. Since Indians had not proved satisfactory slaves, they commissioned the Portuguese to provide them 4,000 African slaves a year. Until the latter part of the sixteenth century, when other countries entered the market, the Portuguese had a virtual monopoly on the trade. The West African slave trade spanned a period of 400 years, during which the Portuguese government—through a royal monopoly—profited directly from the trade on a per unit basis. With the discovery of gold and diamonds and the growth of sugar industries in Brazil, that country alone imported 10,000 slaves a year.

In four centuries, Portugal shipped estimated 5 million slaves to the Western Hemisphere.[3] The Guinea Coast, Angola, and the adjacent Congo, the most fertile region in Africa, was, through the Portuguese exploration and exploitation, the ethnic source of most of today's Afro-Americans. It is both appropriate and ironic that on the last weekend of July 1974, a ship named after Henry the Navigator carried hack to Portugal the first 1,100 Portu-guese colonists leaving the new nation state of Mozambique.

The course of expansion brought the people of Western Europe into contact with peoples of vastly different cultures. Those hostile contacts provided a base for feelings of competitiveness and superiority. In the Iberian peninsula, on lands reconquered from the Moslems, free Christian peasant communities were encouraged by grants of greater land freedoms than existed in the northern lands from whence they came. Side by side with them were Islamic communities subjected to almost slave conditions. This servitude was the model for that later imposed by Spanish and Portuguese conquerors on the Indians of the New World, and was quite in keeping with the conditions of warfare between Christian and Islamic countries during the medieval period. Besides the enslavement of each other by conquest, other groups had already enslaved Africans for domestic labour.

Mercantilism and Racism

Even while the Portuguese were involved in the exploitation of Africans through the slave trade, mercantilism rather than racism was the motivating influence. Only later, when the Portuguese began to push inland and colonise in Africa, did the basis for racism become evidenced, to order to justify the extension of Portuguese civilisation on the African territory. The Portuguese had to perceive their culture superior and themselves as a race capable of bringing order and profit out of the "chaos" and primitiveness of the territory. Racism is a widely used and variously defined term. Dante Puzzoi's description is instructive:

> Racism [he says] is new modern conception. Prior to the sixteenth century there was nothing in the life and thought of the West that can be described as racist. To prevent misunderstanding a clear distinction must be made between racism and ethnocentrism.... The moral self sufficiency of the nation state proved of salient importance. For, in the circumstances engendered by the struggle for empire, it gave powerful impetus to the natural tendency of nationalism to become chauvinism. And chauvinism, perverting to its uses the new sciences, could become and where conditions were propitious, did become racism. The interaction between colonialism and this nationalism provided the necessary milieu for the emergence and development, of racism.[4]

Native Policy of Portugal in Africa

The object of Portuguese native policy in Africa was to produce assimilated Portuguese out of the African natives. This, not unlike the earlier objectives of the English in Ireland, is the typical goal of colonial racism, which denies the legitimacy and integrity of indigenous cultures and political systems in order to legitimate their subjugation.[5] William Minter says about this:

> To become an assimilado involved, until shortly after the beginning of the war in Angola, a considerable procedure. An applicant had to prove his ability to speak and write correct Portuguese; show that he had a certain income, submit a number of documents and certificates and finally, pay a fee.... The Portuguese settler who might be illiterate and unable to satisfy the requirements himself did not have to worry about such a test: he was already a Portuguese citizen.[6]

There is no question that the racialism of Portuguese Africa is manifested most particularly in the economic sphere, and that despite Caetano's belated attempt to apply the Nazi eugenic thesis in his warning to his fellow Portuguese in Africa, skin color has not had a particularly strong social impact on the metropolitan Portuguese in terms of miscegenation, entrance info professions, and housing. In that sense, there has always been less racist overtone in Lisbon than in New York, Chicago, or London. In the African colonies themselves, it has been commonplace for the white Portuguese settler to engage in sexual relations with native African women, and the children of such matches are brought up in the socioeconomic class and household of the father regardless of the marital status of the parents. The Portuguese settler, in fact, takes some pride in his mistos children. One told me, "I have planted my seed in the soil of this place and it will grow and continue here long after I myself am gone.[7] If the settler is economically successful, his mistos children as well as his other children are likely to return to Portugal itself for their education. If he is less successful, all of his children will receive their education in the African province.[8]

Marcelo Caetano, Salazar's hand picked successor, was Minister for the African Colonies in 1945. In repeated visits to those colonies, his speeches reflected a degree of racism comparable with that of Rhodesian and South African leaders:

> On one point only should we be rigorous with respect to racial separation: namely, marital or casual sexual mixing of blacks and whiles, die source of serious disturbances in social life, and of the

> serious problem of race mixing. Serious I say, if not from the biological point of view, so controversial and on winch it's not for me to take a position, then al least from the sociological point of view.[9]

It is apparent that despite the prolonged and continuous struggle for democracy in metropolitan Portugal itself, despite the Portuguese tradition of individualism and humanism, despite the mixture of bloods which characterised the Portuguese people ethnically, it is the tradition of imperialism, racism, fascism, despoliation, and corruption which has most often characterised the Portuguese presence in Africa.

Portuguese Democracy and Dictatorship

As members of the Armed Forces Movement are fond of pointing out, Portugal and the Portuguese people have a tradition of freedom and democracy. Even more relevant to their revolution, they claim, is the tradition of individualism and humanism which is in contrast to that of their neighbours, the Spaniards. This tradition, however, has been obscured by 50 years of dictatorship, which make the April 25, 1974 revolution and its subsequent events so much of a shock and puzzlement to Western political analysts. Here I want to outline that lost tradition.

The nineteenth century in Portugal saw a series of attempts to achieve a constitutional republic. These attempts made the period from 1820 to 1861 one of ongoing civil strife.

Under King Louis I in the 1860s, the country was ruled in a pseudo parliamentary system by two political parties, the Conservative and the Liberal, which held office in rotation. In 1881 the formation of the Republican Party marked the real beginning of a system of elected representation and party politics. Sporadic revolts, strikes, and conspiracies during the reign of Carlos I led to his appointment of a prime minister, Joao Franco, who in 1906 oppressed the parliamentary government, gagged the press, and punished all opposition to his dictatorial regime.

On February 1, 1908, the king and the crown prince were assassinated in the streets of Lisbon, and although the new king put an end to Franco's reign, he was forced to flee to England when, in October 1910, insurrection flared up again in Lisbon.

On October n, 1910, a provisional government proclaimed the Republic of Portugal, which proceeded to a frontal attack on the Catholic Church. Religious orders were expelled, their property was confiscated, and religious teaching in the primary schools was forbidden, in 1911 there were enactments separating church and state, and the constituent assembly adopted a liberal constitution and elected a president, Dr. Manuel de Arriaga. Royalist plots, however, created unrest among the workers, who wore disappointed when the revolution failed to bring them relief from long hours and low wages. In January 1912, a serious general strike broke out in Lisbon. The city was put under military rule and thousands of syndicalists were imprisoned. The radical outbreaks continued.

Portugal, Britain and France *Vs.* Germany

On November 28, 1914, the Portuguese' National Assembly voted to join Great Britain and France in war against Germany, but General Pimenta de Castro, representing a pro-German faction in the army, led an insurrection which lasted until May 1915. At that point President Arriaga resigned and Dernardino Machado became president. In 1916, Germany declared war on Portugal after the Portuguese had seized German vessels in port at Lisbon, m 1917, another general sympathetic with the German cause, Sidionio Pais, led an insurrection, deposed the president, and took office himself. One year and ten days later he was assassinated and the democratic regime was reestablished.

In a land which was still 65 per cent illiterate, the democratic system could hardly be expected to function smoothly, and throughout the early years of the century the average duration of governments was about four months. Insurrections and coups were as numerous as changes in the cabinets, and the already perilous economic situation went from bad to worse. During the 1920s, unrest provoked a succession of changes, and in 1926 an army movement inspired by Mendes Cabecadas and led by General Gomes da Costa overthrew the democratic regime. Machado (again President) and the cabinet of Antonio Mara da Silva were thrown out, political parties were broken up, and parliament was again dissolved.

In February 1927, insurrection against the military dictatorship broke out in Oporto and Lisbon. The uprising was described as "Communist" but was really inspired by a group of intellectual reformers. It was, in any case, defeated. In 1928, General Antonio Oscar de Fragosa Carmona was elected president. His regime proved little different from its predecessors, except that it was led by the military rather than by civilian politicians. On April 27, a 40-year-old professor of economics, Antonio de Oliveira Salazar became Minister of Finance with extraordinary powers. the solved the financial muddle by economy and strict accountancy, and before long was the dominant figure in Portugal.

The National Union Party was founded in 1930, the only party allowed by the government. On July 5, 1933, Salazar became Premier and virtual dictator. In 1935, a new constitution provided that a president would be elected for a seven-year term, a cabinet would be selected by the president and responsible to him alone, a national assembly would ho elected by heads of families possessing a certain degree of education, and there would he a corporate chamber with advisory powers representing occupations.

In January of the following year an insurrection led by the General Confederation of Libor and the Communists was suppressed and the leaders were imprisoned. The first national assembly of the new regime met on January 10, 1935. Salazar, to achieve stability by employing massive systems of repression, remained in office for 40 years. His system was then maintained under the dictatorship of his former associate, Marcelo Caetano.

The 48-year history of the fascist state and the resistance movements which took various actions against it is a picture of an ongoing action and reaction, repression and rebellion, and continual political maneuvering. Viewed in this perspective, the MFA revolution was neither outside the context of Portuguese history, nor an improbability in the context of Portuguese political sophistication.

African Labour under Colonialism

Forced labour was the characteristic system for the exploitation of the African population in Portuguese Africa. It is most specifically tills system which exemplifies the economic racism of that society and which became the basis of disaffection through which the liberation movements gained masses of adherents. The Labour Regulation of 1899 put it like this:

> All natives of Portuguese overseas provinces are subject to the moral and legal obligation of attempting to obtain through work the means that they lack to subsist and to better their social conditions. They have full liberty to choose the method of fulfilling this obligation, but if they do not fulfill it, public authority may force a fulfillment.[10]

By making unemployment a crime, the regime was able to legislate forced labour on plantations and industries, thus providing cheap, noncompetitive labour not only in the Portuguese provinces, but also in the mines and plantations of Rhodesia and South Africa. The export of cheap labour, in fact, was so widespread that an American reporter remarked in 1958, "Something like two-thirds of the mature, able-bodied men of Southern Mozambique are employed in foreign territories."[11]

A final element of the relationship between Portugal and her overseas provinces is the economic sphere. Minter contends that metropolitan Portugal has a consistent trade deficit which is offset primarily by a strong surplus with the overseas provinces. He goes on to say:

> The income created for Portugal by Angola and Mozambique comes mainly from export of primary commodities and African labour; secondarily from their role in transport for South Africa, Bhodesia, Zambia and the Congo. Angola exports coffee, diamonds, iron ore and oil to world markets. Mozambique's most important exports are all agricultural: cashew nuts, sugar, tea, sisal.
>
> Portugal profits not only from the income gained by Angola and Mozambique but also from the pattern of trade established with them.
>
> But, these advantages for particular Portuguese interests depend on cooperation with particular interests from other Western countries. The Benguela Uailroad and the Angola Diamond Company are under the control of British, South African and Belgian financial interests.... In Mozambique, Sona Sugar Estates, the largest producer of sugar in the country, is British owned.... Indeed, in Portugal itself there is substantial foreign command of the economy. The largest producer of Wolfram is a former British company, recently acquired by the Angola American Corporation of South Africa. The main producer of tires is controlled by General Tire and Rubber of Ohio. The public transport system of Lisbon is run by a British company; SACOR, which runs the principal petroleum refinery in Portugal, is two thirds controlled by French interests.[12]

Guinea-Bissau

Guinea- Bissau, the first independent nation state born out of the Portuguese African colonies, was also the oldest of the colonies. It was perhaps, the first of the provinces to manifest the cumulative after-effects of the peculiarly Portuguese brand of racism, and its liberation movement was the model for the other liberation movements. The lender of that movement, Partido Africano da Independencia de Guinea e Cabo Verde (PAIGC), was Amilcar Cabral, who showed a precise understanding of the economic issues involved in liberation:

> If we wish to place the fact of imperialism within the general trajectory of the evolution of the transcendental factor which has changed the face of the world, namely, capital and the process of its accumulation, we can say that imperialism is piracy transplanted from the seas to the dry land, piracy reorganised, consolidated and adapted to the him of exploiting the natural and human resources of our people.[13]

PAIGC was first organised in Bissau in 1956 with its principal support among urban workers leadership came from a group of assimilados wire formed a larger percentage of the population here than in the other two colonies. Organisation of the workers resulted in several strikes, the bloodiest of which was a dock strike that took place in August 1959 and paralysed the port or Bissau. It was broken with extreme brutality by the Portuguese military, and although no casualty figures were ever released, Cabral estimated them to be very high.

Cabral was born in Bafata, Cape Verde Islands, of mixed African and Portuguese ancestry. Educated as an agronomist in Lisbon and later employed as a census officer for the Portuguese colonial government, he organised PAIGC and dedicated himself to guerrilla warfare.

Cabral's anticapitalist convictions did not reflect an uncritical adaptation of Marxist theory and strategy. the recognised its shortcomings when applied to the nature of peasant society in Guinea. In a way which was to become characteristic of the other Portuguese African liberation movements and of the MFA itself, Cabral understood that "the people are not fighting for ideas. They are fighting for material benefits, to live better in peace, to see their lives go forward."[14]

Among the 36,000 troops required to maintain control of the one-third of Guinea-Bissau not under PAIGC control by 1970 were many future leaders of the MFA. It was in Guinea that General Spinola, who became the first president of the provisional government, obtained his major experience in governing a colony during its liberation struggle. Out of his experiences in that colony, he wrote the book that went farther than any other publication had gone before criticising Portuguese colonial policy and the conditions of the armed forces. It was through his experience in Guinea, also, that Spinola was to develop his political thesis for the evolution of the colonies into a kind of partnership status with Portugal. Other MFA leaders, while posted in Guinea, did academic studies of the movement and had interactions with PAIGC leaders—either while the latter were imprisoned or in the process of negotiations. The effectiveness of Cabral's instruction, then, extended far beyond his African constituency, and well into the forces of oppression originally marshaled to subdue them.

Cabral was in close touch with the leaders of Movimento Popular de Liberacao de Angola (MPLA) and Frente de Liberacao de Mocambique (FRELIMO Mozambique). In addition, in 1961 he had played an important part in the development of Organizacaos Nacionalistas das Colonlas Portugueses (CONCP), which coordinated the nationalist movements. PAIGC was organised so effectively that, even after the arrest of its leaders in Bissau commencing on March 13, 1962, the network of organisation continued to extend throughout the country.[15]

PAIGC had the constant support of Conakry, which borders Guinea on one side, and limited support from Senegal, bordering on the other side. In 1973 systematic guerrilla warfare began in the north, where dense forests and numerous waterways made guerrilla action feasible. By 1905 half of Guinea was under PAIGC control, and local institutions for food production, education, health services, and trade had been established by the organisation. By 1970, PAIGC claimed control of three-fifths of Guinea, although aerial bombardment and counterattack by Portuguese military was frequent. Exports of rice and palm oil helped pay for the import of necessary trade goods, and by 1970, 20,000 students wore enrolled in the schools. Like the other African colonies. Guinea under PAIGC had a voice and impact in the Organisation of African Unity, relations with its neighbouring African stales, and contacts for weapons and training in North Africa and Eastern Europe.[16]

Between April and July of 1972, elections had been held in the liberated area of mainland Guinea. With the minimum voting age at 15,600,000 eligible voters were registered. They elected regional councils which then selected a third of their number to sit with members nominated by PAIGC in the National Council. Cabral set the (Into for announcement of independence of mainland Guinea for early 1973. There was an opposition party as well a s local opposition groups.

The first Mozambiquan nationalist movements had been organised among the exiles who were exported as workers to surrounding countries.

Frente de Liberacao de Mozambique (FRELIMO) formed as a coalition of Unido Nacional Democratica de Mozambique (UDENAMO), organised in Rhodesia in 1900; Mozambique African National Union (MANU), formed in East Africa along the models of the Tanganyikan and Kenyan parties, TANU and KANU; and Unlto Africana de Mozambique Independent (UNAMI), organised in Malawi. When Tanganyika Ix-came independent in 1901, nil three parties setup headquarters in Dares Salaam. The three movements merged in 19G2, met in a congress and worked out a program of action, political organisation, training, and mobilisation of world opinion.

FRELIMO objectives were to form an independent government representing the majority of the population, which was African and colored.

The first group of 250 guerrilla fighters was trained in Algeria. FRELIMO began education programs among the refugees in Tanzania and sent largo scale of scholarship students abroad. Its first, action was on September 24, 1904, will attacks in four provinces. FRELIMO forces remained in two of those provinces fighting and living in the jungle. Soon they began training Inside Mozambique itself, and by 1967 FRELIMO had approximately 8,000 troops armed and active. Minter says:

> From 1967-70, FRELIMO forces in Cabo Delgado and Niassa provinces moved to larger scale attacks on Portuguese posts and air bases. Mueda, the site of the massacre years before and now one of Portugal's major airbases in the area, was hit several times.... Heavier weapons and pre-experienced fighters as well as control of base areas inside Mozambique, made possible such intensification of the combat.
>
> In the liberated areas production of food crops increased, while the forced cultivation of cotton was abandoned. People marvelled at having enough to eat. Some cash crops such as cashew nuts and peanuts were cultivated, and traded by FRELIMO across the border for farm tools, cloth and other necessities. FRELIMO nurses and medical aides set up a system of first aid posts and clinics; primary schools were set up inside Mozambique and in the refugee camps. Administrative structures for the liberated areas were established for the Portuguese to play on latent tension between northerners and southerners and the contradiction between those who understood the necessity of a protracted war of liberation and those who expected an immediate victory. In March, 1968, a new front was opened up in Tete province, adjacent to Zambia, a front of crucial strategic importance. In July, 1968, the second party congress, held inside Mozambique... solidified the direction and unity of the movement.[17]

FRELIMO, along with MPLA and PAIGC, drew support from a variety of organisations and states. In 1970, at an international conference in Rome, they received support from the Vatican. The various Black African countries surrounding the Portuguese colonies (Congo, Tanzania, Zaire, Zambia) and the Zimbabwe movement in Rhodesia (ZANU) participated and supported the movement by raising issues in the international arena. U.S. groups as diverse as the Black Panthers and the Congressional Black Caucus took favorable positions and offered one or another kind of support.

In addition, the massacre of whole villages and the tortures and penalties imposed on the native population generated support from sources which normally take a dim view of leftist revolutionary movements, among them various Roman Catholic and Protestant missionaries, many of whom were expelled from Mozambique for their outspokenness in denouncing atrocities committed by government troops against the native population:

> The missionaries also had severe criticism to make as regards the compromise policies of the Mozambican hierarchy: "The Church in Mozambique renounces its prophetic mission, since it fails to proclaim openly that the people in that country is fully entitled to its own Identity. It also fails to proclaim basic human rights and permits missionaries to be bound by laws agreed upon by the Holy See and the Lisbon government, according to which their activities must correspond with the African country's complete nationalisation (the policy of 'Portugalisation'). Nor does the Church speak out against the socioeconomic system in effect in Mozambique, nor against the stealing of land from the Africans, the huge landed estates and the privileges. Nor docs it denounce violence and war, thus submitting to the view of the Portuguese (government) Instead of acting as a middle man between the two parties, as it ought to do." Other expelled missionaries spoke on Italian radio. They told of villages that had been "wiped out" by acts of war and reprisal: "Virinno, Juvano, Viola and Chillmani are now nothing but names that recall huts consumed by flames, children burned alive, girls raped, men pitilessly murdered, women disembowelled." They described the means employed in perpetrating these atrocities: airplanes, helicopters, chemicals that destroy harvests, flamethrowers to burn the forests—in order to drive out the guerrillas.
>
> In addition there arc the tortures perpetrated in the prisons, called "places of political regeneration," where all those who express disagreement with the government are locked up. At Macailba,

> for instance, 35 Protestant pastors were imprisoned; two of them died from the tortures they had to endure.
>
> "The more sensitive, more educated and more politically aware sector of the population has justly rebelled," the missionaries stated. "And so was formed the Front for the Liberation of Mozambique."[18]

The fact that diverse tribes and adverse terrain were united under a democratic leadership first into a nonstate nation and then into a nation state, suggests great efficiency. The matter was accomplished, moreover, within 13 years of the commencement of organisation. Furthermore, the organisation developed Institutions and structure and is not a novice to government as it commences its nationhood.

We Stay! (FICO), a right-wing political party, emerged in Mozambique after 1974; a white Portuguese newspaper owner and millionaire businessman of Beira, Mozambique, Engineer Jorge Jardin, is the organiser. Born in 1918, he qualified as an agronomist at Lisbon University. Beginning in 1946, he served in a number of increasingly important posts under the Salazar regime. After quarreling with Salazar, he moved to Beira 22 years ago and built up newspapers and a model farming estate. Since then he has acted as a go-between with Dr. Banda of Malawi, President Kaunda of Zambia, and the Swaziland government. He was also involved in a plot to overthrow President Nyerere of Tanzania.

Jardin states his goals as the defeat of FRELTMO and the creation of a conservative, capitalist, multiracial society in Mozambique, or on Independent Dominion (UD) for the whites in Mozambique. He is trying to mobilise the flechas (arrows), the black soldiers recruited to fight FRELIMO. He estimates there are between 30,000 and 50,000 of them, some of whom are deserters from FRELIMO, others of whom participated in the massacres at Wirriyamu. In addition, he is recruiting mercenary officers of the Fifth Commando Unit who had experience in the Congo against Lumumba and a group railed the Dragons of Death composed of former paratroopers and commandos. Prospects are good for support and even direct aid from the governments of Rhodesia and South Africa; both of which have expressed wariness about new nations on their doorsteps. With such a powerful reactionary figure at work, FRELIMO may not yet have fought its last battle.

Angola

The war for liberation came to the attention of the world through events in Angola in 1961. The struggle here is also the last to be resolved. For one thing, there are more Portuguese settlers involved in Angola, greater economic stakes, and three different competing and often conflicting liberation groups.

The Movimento Popular de Liberacao de Angola (MPLA) was the largest of the three Angolan liberation movements, and the oldest. Dr. Agostlnho Neto, an intellectual, led the movement for a decade. Daniel Chipenda, former professional soccer player in Portugal who has the friendship of heads of state in Zambia, Zaire, Tanzania, and Congo, contested Neto's leadership in 1974 and in 1975 organised his own splinter group which then wined with Uniao por Total Independencia of Angola (UNITA). The other group, Frente Nacional Liberacao Angola (FNLA), formed and headquartered in Zaire, is led by Holden Roberta.

It would be comforting to think that the knottiest colonial question of all, Angola, had been resolved by the January 15, 1975 Independence Agreement worked out between the president and prime minister of the provisional government (both MFA leaders) and the leaders of the three Angolan liberation movements. It climaxed eight months of intensive fighting among these liberation groups, which had intensified even after Admiral Rosa Coutinho, the MFA leader, had taken the place of the former Salazarist administrator. Marques.

The racial connotations of the Angolan struggle are the product of the past 20 years. They are typified by the division of Luanda, the capital city, which is divided into two sections, the "Asphalt" (white) and the "Red Clay" (black) sections. In the last 20 years, the black unskilled population of Luanda has gradually moved to the outskirts of the city—70 per cent of the inhabitants of Luanda live in musseques (suburban ghetto shantytowns). The whiles who had lived in these musseques were merchants, they were expelled and their shops robbed and burned.

Many of the Angolans now leading the liberation movements were among the young intellectuals of the late 1950s who expressed their patriotism and leftist idealism in literature. They founded the magazine Mensagem, which was subsequently suppressed by the authorities. Then, when the Sociedade Cultural of Angola welcomed the membership of this element, it too was suppressed. Between 1959 and 1964, PIDE stepped up its activities and any legal expression of dissent became impossible, and in 19G4, the governor closed the cultural society, the Association of Natives of Angola, and the Portuguese Society of Writers.

In 1956 the MPLA was founded clandestinely with the support of whiles and blacks, some connected with the Communist party and some with the progressive Portuguese movements. In 1901 Galvao hijacked the Santa Maria and announced that he would head for Angola, there to prepare the liberation of Portugal. On February 4, a group of 20 Angolans assaulted the prison of Sao Paulo de Luanda to set free the prisoners that were scheduled to be sent to the concentration camp of Terrafal. Many were killed and a wave of repression followed.

The year 1961 really marks the beginning of the armed struggle in Angola. The MPLA opened its first political military region in the north and Holden Roberta, heading the Unitae dos Povos de Angola (UPA), began a wave of terrorism in the region of the coffee plantations and extended it to the zone of the cotton plantations. The MPLA had had support and freedom of movement in neighbouring Congo. However, in 1963 they were expelled from the Congo and began operating from Zaire with increasing success. They were particularly effective in Luanda.

From its initiation, MPLA attempted to bring the conditions of Angolan exploitation and the contradictions enacted by the colonial authorities to the attention and action of the international arena. For this reason, operations have been aimed at maximal publicity and issues of international law.[19] For instance, in February 1961 their raid on the central prison in Luanda coincided with the presence of large numbers of foreign journalists gathered to report on Galvao's seizure of the Santa Maria. The combined incidents raised international legal issues and finally caused the United Nations Security Council, at the request of Liberia, to place Angola on its agenda. In the meeting of March 15, 1961, a draft resolution was introduced calling on Portugal to introduce reforms in conformity with the previous year's resolution on the granting of independence to colonial countries and peoples. The Security Council resolution also mandated a subcommittee to study the situation. The resolution failed with six abstentions from Latin American and European countries against five positive votes. Including that of the United States.

The same day that the Security Council voted, Holden Roberta (FNLA) and his group attacked the Portuguese in northern Angola. Fighting continued with savage reprisals. On April 20 the General Assembly passed Resolution 100:$ (XV) by a vole of 73 to 2, with 9 abstentions, reaffirming the Security Council resolution of the previous month. In June the Security Council voted again and adopted the resolution by a vote of 9 to 2 with 2 abstentions.

> The Special Committee on Territories under Portuguese Administration completed its report in August 1962. It declared "that the danger lies, on the one hand, in Portugal's insistence

> there can be no change in its relationship with the Territories which it considers are integral parts of its national territory, and, on the other, in the complete disregard for the legitimate aspirations of its indigenous populations." As representatives of the African nationalist movements had expressed willingness to negotiate with Portugal over the terms and timing of independence, the Committee concluded that the onus for lack of any peaceful solution fell on Portugal.... The Committee also concluded that the arms furnished to Portugal by her allies were of aid to her in suppressing the people of Angola. It, therefore, recommended that the General Assembly "should consider and adopt measures aimed at immediate discontinuance of such assistance and a complete embargo on further sales and supplies of such weapons."[20]

MPLA had made an effective impact in the international arena through relationships formed with the governments of surrounding nations and through advocates in the United Nations. Their battle for independence did not consist of terror tactics in Lisbon, and it had involved only one incident, in the early part of the campaign, of international skyjacking. It did involve maintaining coordination with underground political dissidents in Portugal and abroad and developing institutions to nationalise and educate the native population to join the struggle in the territory itself. Perhaps, the single major impediment to success was the split between MPLA and the oilier Angolan movements, which delayed recognition by the Portuguese Provisional Government until the end of January 1975.

Holden Roberta, who organised UPA in 1961, wont on to form the Angolan Government in Exile (GRAE), a government-in-exile recognised in 1963 by the Organisation of African Unity. American and other supplies were funneled through the armies of Morocco, Tunisia, and Congo to FNLA, his guerrilla movement, fn 1968 the Military Commission of the Organisation of African Unity withdrew recognition of GRAE's status as a government in exile and Jonas Savimbi broke away and formed UNITA. Initially, GRAE's great impact was not only on other

African stales, *but* also on America and North African Arab countries. It was dissolved after the formation of UNITA and had no official part in the new provisional government.

Jonas Savimbi (former Minister for Foreign Affairs of Holden Roberta's GRAE, from whom he says he separated because of lack of accomplishment of democratic objectives),[21] organised UNITA. Savimbi, son of a Protestant pastor, received a degree in political science in Lausanne, but chose to live near his people and to fight by their side in the Liso region. His prestige and popularity are vast. He established himself there ten years ago and only left in October 1974, in order to visit some African capitals for conferences with the leaders of the other liberation movements, Agostinho Neto and Holden Roberta.

Savimbi was accused by the magazine Afrique Asie of treason, of attachment to and complicity with the Portuguese colonial armed forces in their combat against the MPLA. UNITA called the charge a maneuver of its enemies, including the MPLA and "its Soviet friends."

UNITA, which arose as a movement open to all Africans, developed primarily in Luso and Silva Porto, counted also on the support of certain tribes from southern Angola. It proposed the organisation of a government of African majority, the purposes of which would be to organise general elections in the spirit of the Universal Declaration of the Rights of Man for a national constitutional assembly elected through direct and secret vote of all citizens older than 18; to promote an authentically African and Angolan culture and to tight "against obscurantism" to energetically combat tribalism as a latent enemy of national unity; to guarantee the emancipation of Angolan women; and to guarantee the equality of all Angolans before the law without any discrimination.[22] Its basic thrust was for national independence without dependence on external aid. As a result Savimbi refused foreign aid for fear of outside control—which, UNITA claims, happened with the FNLA aid, and in certain circumstances, with the MPLA.

UNITA is essentially a movement of farmers and country people who are more concerned with pragmatics and reality than with revolutionary theory. Today it includes many white elements from among the small and medium bourgeoisie: merchants principally, for whom UNITA stands as a guarantee of peace and security. As time passes, UNITA proposes to defend the interests of the less protected classes, and it has with time moderated its attitude toward capitalism. On the other hand, UNITA attacked the provisional government for proposing its own participation in security and policing, stating that security is a job of the liberation movements themselves.

Holden Roberto organised the FNLA after the dissolution of his Uninao de Africa Portuguese (UPA) organisation. Many whites chose at the last minute to be part of this movement to guarantee their interests as a privileged class. FNLA resulted from a division of the former UPA over issues of foreign involvements. It has always defined itself as an African and rightist movement, and is supported indirectly by the United States, via Mobutu in Zaire.[23]

Holden Roberta denounced (in the magazine Noticia) "tendentiously Soviet maneuvers in the interior of Angola" and stated that the "FNLA already lias at this moment forces of combat and sufficient means to provoke a military defeat to the demoralised Portuguese Army, but we have agreements of peace which we will respect as long as the Portuguese government respects them too."[24] Force of arms is the great argument of the FNLA. Its representative in Luanda, Val Neto, claims they have 20,000 well-armed, well-trained, disciplined men ready to fight.

FNLA reputedly receives help from China, Romania, and Zaire,[25] and it avoids references to aid from the United States. Of nil delegations that were opened in Luanda, the FNLA office seems to he the most militarily defended. Yet, FNLA claims that it brought to Luanda only the necessary number of soldiers for the protection of its headquarters. Moreover, because most FNLA soldiers speak French, suspicions have been raised that the group employs foreign mercenaries. According to some observers, the FNLA was the initiator of many disturbances which occurred in Luanda since April 25, 1974. The FNLA communicated from Kinshasa through tin' radio program "Vez do Angola Livre," and announced in Luanda: "The junta has before it three alternatives: either punish the extremists, assuming their responsibilities; accept our petition of formation or brigades in order to restore peace, security and order, or declare itself incapable and resign."

Race and Nationalism

Racial policy and nationalisation of resources arc two of the major problems facing Angola. The population is believed to include 350,000 to 450,000 white Portuguese settlers of whom over 200,000 arc leaving. About 25 per cent of them wore born in Angola and the others are long-time residents. It is the second largest European population (next to South Africa's) on the continent. As of spring 1975, no more than 20,000 Angolans had left; many of them, after a brief time in Lisbon or Brazil, returned to Angola. The Europeans, consistent with colonial policy, have been the technicians, managers, or financiers who have made the sophisticated capitalist economy operative.* How will the new government deal with this population?

None of the leaders of the three movements have been calling for radical economic reforms. They sec progress in agriculture as being best promoted by cooperatives rather than collectivisation.

---

* The estimates on emigration of whites from the former colonies vary considerately. There is no doubt that the pace of emigration out of Angola quickened in April 1975 and by mid-June estimates ran to 80,000 emigrants from Angola alone. By the end of August, over 100,000 emigrants were already taxing the limited resources of the Provisional Government in Lisbon. Another 200,000 white Angolans are estimated to be seeking transportation back to Portugal or to Brazil.

But, it is expected that Dr. Augustinho Neto will be in favour of nationalising the rich oil fields of Cabinda, the diamond mines, and the coffee plantations.

Because of the nature of the war in Angola, the extensive involvement of foreign capital (to be discussed further in Chapter 3), and the involvement of foreign military support, the prospects for developing a workable coalition government—even in accordance with the January 1975 agreements—seem gloomy.

Perhaps, the vital symbiotic relationship between the struggles of the liberation movements in Guinea-Bissau, Mozambique, and Angola with the development of a viable liberation movement in metropolitan Portugal had gone unnoticed because scholars and journalists tended to study and/or report either one or the other end of the related entities. There is a tendency to view the link between a European Center power and its colonial periphery as a unilateral direction line, rather than the umbilical cord-like connection which transmits change in two directions simultaneously.[26]

NOTES AND REFERENCES

1. D. M. Abshire and M. A. Samuels, eds., *Portuguese Africa: A Handbook* (New York: Praeger, 1969); deOliveira Marques, *History of Portugal*, vol. 1 (New York and London: Columbia University Press, 1972); James Duffy, *Portugal in Africa* (Baltimore, Md.: Penguin African Library, 1903).
2. de Oliveira Marques, *op. cit.*, says: "In truth there is no reliable source for evaluating the impact of slaves on the growth of population (in Listen), yet it seems improbable that slaves ever exceeded one-tenth of the total population...." (p. 167).
3. H. V. Livermore, *A New History of Portugal* (London: Cambridge at the University Press, 1967).
4. Dante A. Puzzo, "Racism and the Western Tradition," *Journal of The History of Ideas* (1.9G4): 579-86.
5. Leonar B. Liggio, "English Origins of American Racism" (Paper presented at the Columbia University Symposium on Irish Studies, February 1974).

6. William Minter, *Portuguese Africa and the West* (London: Penguin African Library, Penguin Ltd., 1972), p. 20.
7. Communication from confidential interview with an Angolan colonist returned to Portugal in 1974. Similar statements were made by returned Mozambiquan colonists in interviews by the author in Lisbon in 1974 and 1975. At an early time, miscegenation had been official policy in the colonies.
8. Communication from returned colonists substantiated by David Abshire, *op. cit.*, pp. 101-303.
9. Marcelo Cactano, *Alguns Discorsose Relaturios: Viegen Ministerial a Africaem 1945* (Lisbon: Agenda Geral das Colonias, 19-16).
10. *African Labour Regulation issued in 1899.* Tin's decree and its aftermath are discussed at length by Henry W. Novison, A Modern Slavery (London and Now York: Harper and Brothers, 1906). The decree was countermanded in 1960, but the latter was never enforced. Cf. Minter, *op. cit.*
11. Marvin Harris, *Portugal's African Wards* (New York: American Committee on Africa, 1958), p. 29.
12. Minter, *op. cit.*, pp. 32-33.
13. Quoted by Basil Davidson, *The Liberation of Guinea: Aspects of an African Revolution* (Baltimore, Md.: Penguin, 1969), p. 83.
14. *Ibid.*, p. 83.
15. Communication through interviews with MFA officers by author in 1974 and 1975. These officers had been stationed in Guinea and Mozambique prior to the April 25, 1974 revolution. My impression is that this circumstance was more characteristic of the interaction and effect of Cabral's PAIGC and Mondlane's FRELIMO than it was related to the Angolan groups. In fact, MFA officers tended often to quote from the writings of these two leaders.
16. Lars Rudebeek, *Guinea-Bissau: A Study of Political Mobilisation* (Uppsala: Scandinavian Institute of African Studies, 1974).
17. Minter, *op. cit.*, pp. 68-69.
18. *IDOC/IPS International news service*, published out of New York, with offices in Buenos Aires, Rome, and New York. May 1974 issue. These statements were made during the period just prior to

the revolution in Portugal, when considerable world opinion had been focused on the debate about whether an entire Mozambiquan village had been destroyed, or, as the Caetano government claimed, such a village had never existed in the first place. The missionaries in this account had been imprisoned and subsequently expelled for having made public statement about the atrocities they had witnessed in that and other similar episodes.

19. "Angola on the Eve of Independence, " *Vida Mundial,* December 26, 1974.

20. Minter, *op. cit.,* pp. 79-80.

21. Vida Mundial, *op. cit.*

22. *Ibid.*

23. *Ibid.*

24. Noticias (Lisbon), December 1974.

25. Vida Mundial, *op. cit.*

26. Phillippe Sehmitter, writing on the April 25 1974 revolution in Portugal, said, for instance:

> To my knowledge no scholarly or journalistic observer of Portugal foresaw the overthrow of Marcelo. Caetano, least of all the rapid and complete collapse of authoritarian rule in Portugal. Quite the contrary, the mini-boom in Portuguese studies of 1972-73 produced several supposedly objective and documented essays by North American social scientists which emphasised the dynamic, reformist and presumably viable qualities of the Caetano regime. Marxist and/or radical scholars despite their more critical scrutiny of the data and their more or less perennial wishful thinking about the imminent maturation of contradictions also failed to predict the overthrow of Caetano, much less the extent and profundity of political change which has so far accompanied it....

"Retrospective and Prospective Thoughts About the Liberation of Portugal," paper prepared for the Mini-Conference on Contemporary Portugal, Yalp University, March 28-29, 1975.

3

Economic Perspective of the Portuguese Colonial Policy

Close on half a century ago, in 1924. Vicente Ferreira, who was one of the most experienced and influential of Portuguese colonial administrators, wrote that in economist might consider the whole colonial enterprise of Portugal absurd. but that mystic or simpleton might describe it as a miracle. A generation later, the Brazilian sociologist Gilberto Freyre was to attribute the miracle to unique Portuguese ability to create a *luso-tropical* civilisation, largely through miscegenation. This explanation would not have satisfied Ferreira, for whom miscegenation was at best a 'necessary mistake' to he avoided in the future; it was apparently at his instance that the white settlers in the government's new agricultural colony at Cela in Angola, started in 1952, were forbidden to employ African labour.

The critical period, between 1885 and 1910, in establishing Portugal's African empire within its present boundaries was one in which miscegenation was in some degree officially frowned on; and though current Portuguese governmental thinking—in contrast to the views of Ferreira and the nineteenth-century proconsul Antonio Enes (Ennes)—emphasizes the multi-racial character of the overseas territories, current settler practice tends in the opposite direction. White women are no longer rarities in Luanda, the capital of Angola, as they were as recently as the beginning of the present century.

It is not necessary to invoke miraculous explanations of the continued Portuguese presence in Africa, even though that presence breaks the rules that historians of modern imperialism have conic to think of as normal. Portugal, at the time of the nineteenth-century scramble for Africa, held title to a few hits of African seaboard and title besides: no industries seeking overseas markets, no middle class seeking overseas fortunes, no capitalists seeking overseas investments no large military forces seeking overseas employment. Portugal was a net importer of capital. As late as 1900, 78 per cent of Portuguese adults were reckoned as unable to read; fifty years later the figure was still 40 per cent. There was indeed continual emigration, mainly from the north of Portugal and of pool, illiterate peasants; not, however, save in a trickle, to Africa, but to Brazil. Such as went to Africa, wrote Antonio Enes in 1893, were 'useless people without a trade, led astray by the belief that in Africa one digs gold with one's fingernails'.

It was the remittances of emigrants to Brazil that until 1890, when an economic crisis in Latin America reduced them to vanishing point, kept the Portuguese balance of payments in equilibrium. The failure of remittances helped to drive Portugal off the gold standard and to compel an arbitrary reduction in interest on its foreign debt (June 1892). The decisive years when it established itself in Mocambique were years when the kingdom was an un-discharged bankrupt; not until 1902 was nil agreed settlement reached with the foreign creditors, who were chiefly French and German.

The fact that the foreign-debt negotiations were allowed to linger over ten years suggests that the governments in question were anxious to do nothing that would threaten the existence of monarchy in Portugal (and consequently in the Iberian peninsula);

an abortive Republican revolution did break out in Oporto on 31 January 1891. For more than a year, during the protracted negotiations between Portugal and Great Britain that followed the British 'ultimatum' of January 1890. counsels of moderation had been urged on the British government by the crowned heads of Europe.[1]

The territorial settlement that ensued in 1891 fell far short of the expectations of opponents of Portugal in Africa like Cecil Rhodes, just as the territory included in Angola after the Berlin West African Conference of 1884-5 had been huge compared with that over which the Portuguese could claim effective authority. In each instance the moderation displayed by governments that could readily, had they wished, have put Portugal out of business as an imperial power rested largely on the belief that there was no need to hasten the inevitable. It was the impatience of one government, that of post-Bismarck Imperial Germany, with the slow process of inevitability that led to the notorious secret Anglo-German treaties of 1898, providing for a contingent partition of the Portuguese colonies. These treaties, however, constituted an aberration from the generally indulgent altitude of the powers towards Portugal.

What might have been expected to end Portuguese dominion overseas before long was the sheer expense and difficulty of the (asks—establishing boundaries, ensuring settlement and promoting economic development—that were implicit in the new rule on 'effective occupation' laid down at the Berlin West African Conference.[2] Until then, the Portuguese empire had consisted mainly of a series of isolated coast communities, dating back for many centuries, and inhabited (apart from a handful of officials) by Africans, persons of mixed Portuguese and African blood, and criminals exiled from continental Portugal. The primary purpose of these posts, centuries earlier, had been to serve as stages on the sea route to the Indies; they had been chosen for their merits as harbours and for their case of defence against local tribesmen, rather than for trading with the interior. Several of them—Bolama in Portuguese Guinea (Guiné), Ibo, and Mocambique in Mocambique—were on offshore islands. As early as the sixteenth century also, the Portuguese had established settlements well up the Zambezi, at Sena and Tele; in the seventeenth century, they had added a number in the Cuanza river basin behind Luanda, and in the hinterland of Benguela.

These settlements have persisted to the present day. It is evident that continuity. particularly in those up-country, was often tenuous and even broken for years at a time. It is evident also that even at the height of Portuguese influence, the number of while men in Africa cannot have been more than a very few thousand. When historians speak of the Angolan wars of the seventeenth century they mean not wars between European and African but wars between African and African in which Europeans joined: sometimes, as with the Portuguese and the Dulch there, on opposite sides. The Portuguese settlements in Africa rested at bottom on a *modus vivendi* with the surrounding African tribes. In Mozambique there was a further clement: Indians from Goa, who were more adaptable to the East African climate than Europeans, and who came to dominate the great estates (*prazos*) of Zambézia as early as the seventeenth century.

The basis of this modus vivendi was, of course, the slave-trade, for which Brazil provided a principal market and the Arab countries a secondary one. Nothing useful can be said about the slave-trade from the economic point of view by people who forget that it, as a member of the British Foreign Office wrote in 1888, was 'a slate of things founded on religion, custom, profit, and taste, and handed down from time immemorial'.[3] Slaves appear to have been the only African export that had: for hundreds of years, a consistent large-scale market; they were hence the only means by which Africans could obtain imports they desired or needed; their capture required little capital investment; and they were not only sell-transporting to seaboard, hut might serve as porters for another valuable export—ivory. To say as has been said, that the development of Portuguese Africa over centuries of slave-trading was hindered by the existence of the trade seems perverse; it implies that there was some unrealised alternative export that would have provoked greater development. Yet, quite apart from the environmental obstacles in Africa itself—climate, disease, absence of skilled labour, want of transport—there was no sizeable market abroad for anything new that might be produced there, except the precious metals. Again and again this point has been ignored by promoters of development schemes. It is inconceivable, for instance, that the Zambézia *prazos* could at any time before the present century have found an export market for substantial quantities of cultivated crops. Yet, the mistaken belief that their original purpose had been agricultural underlay the ineffective *prazo* legislation of Lisbon from the mid-eighteenth century onwards.

It would be truer to say, therefore, that the economic development that occurred in Portuguese Africa before the nineteenth century and that is reflected in the buildings that survive in some of the coast towns, came either from the slave-trade or from without—from the silver and gold of Brazil, which from about 1700 onwards replaced the Indies as a source of treasure for the Portuguese kingdom. These buildings beat witness to another long-standing (rail of Portuguese settlement: the export to Africa of numbers of craftsmen and artisans, trained to build in the European style. The un-African appearance of towns like Luanda, Mocambique and Bolama was remarked upon by nineteenth-century travelers, who frequently went on to note, however, that the buildings were in decay.

The process of economic decline appears to have begun, at any rate in Zambézia, a century at least before the abolition of the slave-trade, which was itself a relatively unprofitable substitute for the acquisition of the precious metals that had originally been hoped for. On the west coast, there had never been any substantial alternative to the slave-trade, and the economic history of Angola and Portuguese Guinea in the second half of the nineteenth century can be read in terms of an effort to find one. Only painfully and gradually did it come to be recognised that economic development in Portuguese Africa, as elsewhere in the 'underdeveloped' world, called in the early stages for capital investment disproportionate to the immediate financial reward that might be expected from it.

The settlement of Portuguese families in the African provinces to engage in farming had been a recurrent will-o'-the-wisp for centuries. It had been pre-scribed in such early *donatarias* as that to Paulo Dias de Novaes (Luanda, 1575) aind was implicit in the decree of 1760 that sought (vainly) to limit the renewed of the Zambézia *prazos.* In the second quarter of the nineteenth century a renewed attempt was made. In 1840 the *presidio* of Mocamedes was established on the and southerly coast of Angola: in 1845 that of Huila. inland on the healthy southern plateau; and in 1854 that of Porto Alexandre, south of Mocamedes. Both Mocameds and Porto Alexandre succeeded in becoming permanent, though small, civilian settlements whose economies were based, not on agriculture but on the rich fisheries oil the coast.

The Fishing industry was analogous to peasant proprietorship in that its labour, as well as its meagre capital, was exclusively white. About the same time, the ports of Angola became bases for whaling, carried on mainly by Americans. The settlement at Huila, however, was abortive; not until the 1880s did which men (mainly at first Boers) establish themselves as farmers there. In 1857, an unsuccessful effort had been made to plant a farm settlement at Pemha Bay in northern Mozambique. Contemporaries put down these failures to poor, 'Utopian' planning; bill it is questionable whether the conditions for success were ever present. It is perhaps worth mentioning that native African opposition was not held responsible for any of these failures.

How insignificant, economically the possessions in Angola and Mozambique were a century ago can the judged from the colonial budgets of the 1860s: the revenue and expenditure figures for the tiny enclave of Portuguese India considerably exceeded those of Angola, which in turn were nearly twice those of Mozambique. Some progress was registered in Angola in the 1870s. Between 1865 and 1875, for instance, the Banco Nacional Ultramarino (founded 1864), whose Luanda branch was managed by a British citizen, multiplied its cash turnover there ten times. A line of river steamers under Anglo-American management began operations between Luanda and Dondo, two hundred miles up the Cuanza liver, in 1867, but its traffic amounted to only a few thousand tons a year. Even so, exports from Angolan ports in the early 1870s were valued at twice what they had been half a century earlier when, of course, they consisted almost exclusively of slaves.

In 1886, work began on a railway inland from Luanda the title of which, Grand Trails-African Railway, reflected a current Portuguese preoccupation: that with establishing a belt of territory across Africa from Angola to Mozambique in accordance will the claims on the 'rose coloured' map, published that same year. There were hopes that the new line would encourage large increases in plantation agriculture. It received a heavy government subsidy that guaranteed its *gross* revenues per kilometre, so that it was encouraged to be roundabout (when it came to be rebuilt in the 1920s it was shortened by 100 km, or one-fifth) and to keep its (rallies, and hence its expenses, as low as it dared.

Twenty years later, the quantify of products reaching Luanda annually by rail was no more than had been carried by the Cuanza steam-boats the railway had superseded: less than ten thousand tons. The subsidy, as a governor-general of the time wrote, was being used for 'pulling a muleteer's load on wheels... the less traffic the more profits'. By that time the railway had readied Amhaca, about two hundred miles inland. It was subsequently extended to Malange, a further hundred miles or so. and has not been extended since, though there are plans to do so.

Contemporary critics pointed to the Amhaca railway guarantee as a typical example of the restrictive practices that, they implied, were strangling the growth of Angola. On every side, indeed, such practices were evident: the national shipping line, enabled by flag discrimination to keep its rates high; the Banco Nacional Ultramarine, likewise a monopoly dial could gel on quite well without actively promoting trade and agriculture; the Mocamedes Company (formed in 1894 under mainly French auspices to develop the extreme south of Angola), which sixteen years later was reported to he completely inactive. The question is whether these altitudes were not it reflection as much as a cause of Angolan economic stagnation. Time and time again, there had been hopes of some commodity development that would replace the slave-trade and make the colony's fortune. At the time of the American Civil War, there had been cotton; in the eighties and early nineties, coffee and wild rubber successively formed the principal exports; hut the tonnages were all hut insignificant even at their peak. The rubber boom in the late nineties was held responsible for generating another mushroom industry: the production of sugar for making into ruin. the favourite barter object of the African gathering rubber or beeswax for export. The mm industry had teen made profitable by a series of increases in import duties on spirits, introduced partly as a result of the Brussels Convention (1890) aimed al discouraging their use by black Africans, but not matched, as they logically should have been, by rises in excise duties.

By 1899, imports of gin into Angola had been all but wiped out, but production there of *aguardente* had risen to 15 million litres a year. At this point, an additional excise tax was imposed on the industry, the proceeds ol which were eventually used to extend the Ambaca railway to Malange. The pressure of world humanitarian opinion, however, made it impossible for the

Portuguese to allow the industry to continue; and after some years of fruitless tinkering the decision was taken to prohibit distilling outright. There was left an industry producing raw cane sugar for export, which competed for the small protected metropolitan market with the older-established industry in Mozambique. The colonial sugar surplus that resulted began to disappear only in the 1950s, when rising consumption in Portugal itself al length caught up with supplies.

The predominance of spirituous drinks in the economy of early twentieth-century Angola could he matched in Marques]'. 'The measure of the state of trade |of Louicnco Marques]', wrote Antonio Enes in his *Relatorio* of 1893, 'is the importation of intoxicants'; the favourite occupation of immigrants from Portugal was that of innkeeper. Alcoholic drinks were the only commodity for which the natives' demand was unlimited; they would distil or ferment them themselves if they could not get them otherwise. In the coastal areas near Quelimane and Mocambique town, where the cashew tree grows wild, there had long been annual saturnalia on liquor made from the fruit, which was sold to the natives in 'small drinking houses usually kept by [Portuguese] convicts'. Mocambique south of the latitude 22°S (roughly, south of the Save river) was, moreover, outside the application of the anti-alcoholic rule prescribed by the Brussels Convention. A law was actually enacted for Mocambique in 1902, in the supposed interest of wine-growers in continental Portugal, prohibiting distilling and the brewing of 'fermented Kaffir drinks' such as *sopé* and *sura.*

But, the imported substitute, fortified grape wine, proved unacceptable; Africans declined to work for white men who could not supply them with their customary drinks; and in the end the law had to he abandoned. As late as 1919 it was asserted that the majority of white farmers in Southern Mozambique lived by glowing sugar-fane, the juice of which they fermented and sold to the blacks. The sale of liquor was said In he virtually the only commercial activity engaged in by Portuguese, petty trade in oilier things being, as it had been for centuries, in the hands of Indians.

This situation was irksome to believers in colonial development. The economic stale of Angola, wrote Governor-General Paiva Couceiro of the period 1997-9, was the same as if the first stone monument *(padrao)* set up by Diogo Cao in 1482-3 had been established yesterday. Oilier colonial writers pointed out that the very existence of a colonial budget surplus was evidence that much-needed development had not been undertaken. Colonial budget surpluses, except in Mozambique and the tiny 'cocoa province' of Sao Tome, were not indeed the rule in the last years of the monarchy; hut the greater part of the deficits, mostly in Angola, were accounted for not by development hut by military expenditures. The chief exception was the subsidy to the Trails-African railway. Even these were below the optimum for swift and effective pacification of the remote interior; it was not the strength of African opposition so much as the want of Portuguese financial and military resources Ilial delayed the coin plete conquest of southern Angola, northern Mocambique and Portuguese Guinea until the second decade of the twentieth century. But, until complete conquest was attained, the funds available from a bankrupt central government for development had to he law. What is doubtful is whether, had funds been more plentiful, the rate of development would have been substantially quicker.

The only territories in Portuguese Africa, except for the extreme south of Mocambique, that showed any substantial signs of economic development under the monarchy were the tiny volcanic islands of Sao Tome and Principe in the Gulf of Guinea. These were uninhabited when the Portuguese occupied them, about 1485, and by the late nineteenth century had acquired a small hut heterogeneous population: owners, some white and some *mestico* of large estates; a substantial number of tenant farmers and peasant proprietors; a number of *Angolan's,* descended from the survivors of a slave-ship wrecked centuries before, who lived in a village of then own apart from the remainder of the population; and a large contingent of former slaves, emancipated in 1876. None of these people was willing to work regularly on plantations for wages, and such was the natural fertility of the islands that men could live without doing more than an occasional job of work.

Slavery and Colonial Economy

The ending of slavery and of the slave-trade had destroyed the economic base on which the little province, as a statutory port of call *en route* for Brazil, had lived for centuries. Labour on the islands for the new crops of coffee and cacao became unavailable over night; and it was in these circumstances that the shipment of contract labourers (*servicaes*) from the Angolan mainland was started, in 1877. For a generation, these shipments continued, and after 1890 their numbers sharply increased, thanks to the growing demand for Sao Tome cocoa; moreover, no *servical* who went from Angola to the islands was ever known to return. Anxiety was already being shown in Angola about the traffic, which was causing a shortage of plantation labour there, and measures were being taken at least on paper to deal with it before Henry Nevinson by his articles in *Harper's Magazine,* let loose the humanitarians of the world on the Portuguese government.[4] From the subsequent boycott of Sao Tome cocoa the industry never completely recovered; though cocoa still institutes some three-quarters of exports by value, it accounts for only per cent of world production. Only a quarter of the crop is absorbed by Portugal.[5]

It was, of course, true that as late as the outbreak of the First World War, investment there, both Portuguese and foreign, had been concentrated in the port and railway of Lourenco Marques, which, as Governor-General Freire de Andrade indignantly wrote, were 'tied to the destinies of the Transvaal'.[6] But, everything, not least the surplus that the province contributed to the total colonial budget during the last decade of the monarchy, points to an economic justification for this policy. By contrast, the chartered companies that had come into existence in Mozambique in the i89os were a disappointment to their shareholders no less than to the Portuguese government that had counted on them to promote land settlement. Neither the Mozambique nor the Nyassa Company fulfilled the intent of its charier that. in phraseology redolent of the *donataria* given to the founder of Luanda in 1575, provided that it should establish one thousand Portuguese families within its territory within five years.

The Nyassa Company never built a mile of the railway, some 400 miles long, it was charged with building from Porto Amelia to Lake Nyasa. The failure of these companies to come up to expectations was only partly, if at all, due to bad management; it was due. rather, to over-sanguine expectations that, for instance, precious metals might he found, or to overconfidence in the ability of ports and railways to generate development by themselves. One cannot say too often that the provision of economic infrastructure in any country is a necessary, but not a sufficient, condition of economic development.

Such provision had not indeed, gone very far in cither Mozambique or Angola by the time the monarchy was overthrown in 1910. By far, the most important developments were the port and railway of Lourcnco Marques, which continued to he the preferred mule for Transvaal transit trade in spite of British efforts to divert it to less convenient ports under their political control. The Portuguese were able to exploit the need of the Transvaal gold-mines for Mocambique labour so as to secure a guarantee of a minimum proportion of rail traffic for the Lourcnco Marques route; and the 1909 treaty with the Transvaal to this effect was specifically incorporated in the British Act of Parliament establishing the Union of South Africa, passed later the same year. It is of some technical interest that the agreement was formally unconstitutional in monarchical Portugal though as events turned out this proved to he of no importance.[7]

Other colonial railroads were comparatively insignificant. That from Umtali (Rhodesia) to Beira had been completed, though initially only in narrow (two-fool) gauge, at the turn of the century: but the development of Rhodesia, and hence the transit traffic, disappointed expectations when the massive gold finds forecast by Rhodes failed to materialise, and that of the Mozambique Company's territory was no less disappointing. The management of this territory was almost exclusively in the hands of the British: 'saints' days and Portuguese festal days arc not observed in Beira', wrote an indignant Portuguese observer in 1898. It was, indeed, only the Anglo-German secret treaties of 1898 which would have called for an equivalent concession to Germany that prevented moves towards acquisition of the Mozambique Company by close allies of the 'Chartered', the British South Africa Company of Cecil Rhodes. The Benguela Railway in Angola, started in 1904, proved so difficult and expensive to build that its promoters, also former associates of Rhodes, ran out of capital at the end of 1908 and construction was halted for a time. By 1911, however, it had readied Huambo (later Nova Lishoa) on the central plateau.

The first year of the republic was marked by little economic progress in either Angola or Mocainbique. The level of colonial administrative competence was lowered by the exile or retirement from public life of a number of leading loyalist figures, such as Aires de Ornelas; Freire de Andrade was almost alone in continuing to serve under the republic. The principal preoccupation of the governor-general of Angola in these years, Norton de Matos, was with the glowing boldness and insolence of German designs on the territory, designs encouraged by the complaisance of the British Foreign and Colonial secretaries, Sir Edward Grey and 'Lulu' Harcourt. Actions like the German demand for low transit duties on goods passing through Angolan ports *en route* for South-West Africa, and the foundation in that colony of the *Angola Bund,* with the proclaimed purpose of creating in Angola an indispensable complement to German South-West Africa, naturally alarmed the Portuguese. The governor-general was convinced that these and other activities were preliminaries to a military invasion: a view that was borne out, after the First World War had started, by the discovery in September 1914 of a series of clandestine depots in Angola, containing food for men and horses, along the routes which an invader would take from the southern frontier to the Benguela Railway.

A German invasion of Angola, however, would have been practicable only with the acquiescence of the British. Once general war had broken out, the German African colonies were isolated from Germany: first by British naval supremacy in the South Atlantic and Indian oceans, secondly by British control of the submarine cable-telegraph systems at a time when radio-communications were in their infancy. South-West Africa's only hope of survival alter 1914 lay in the possible neutrality of the Union of South Africa, and this was in the end denied it. So too in East Africa the outbreak of the First World War alone prevented the Niassa Company from coming under German control; but there was no possibility of a permanent conquest of Mozambique by German forces. The fantastic exploits of von Lettow-Vorbeek, who responded to defeat in German East Africa by invading Mozambique will) his askaris in November 1917, penetrated as far south as Quelimane, and was still undefeated, on Northern Rhodesian soil, when the Armistice was signed in Europe a year later, were a military irrelevance that was made partly possible by incompetence on the part of the Portuguese defenders of the province.

Military glory so persistently eluded the Portuguese forces, whether in southern Angola, northern Mozambique or on the Western Front in Europe, as to make highly questionable the arguments of those Portuguese who had urged that the government declare war on Germany. In the end, it is true, it was the Germans who declared war on Portugal, in February 1916; but even so, the dispatch of troops to the Western Front, where they constituted no more than an embarrassment to their allies, might well have been avoided. The Portuguese delegation to the Peace Conference of 1919 was, partly if not wholly in consequence of the poor military performance of its troops, subjected to a series of slights; the only reward for belligerency was the tiny Kionga triangle in northern Mocambique, which had been taken from the Portuguese by the Germans in 1894. A Portuguese request for a colonial mandate, prompted by the award to Belgium of Ruanda-Urundi, was not taken seriously by the remaining Allies.[8]

The Peace Conference, in fact, provided an opportunity for the other Allies to lecture the Portuguese on their failure to develop Angola and Mozambique, and to suggest that their continued possession of the territories might turn on their ability to develop them. Such assertions were, of the in line will) the spirit of the time's, as expressed in the establishment of League of Nations mandates for the conquered German territories: a system that some would have liked to extend to those of Portugal. They were not accompanied by any serious analysis of the problems dial Portuguese colonial development presented or by any acceptable proposals that would help Portugal to deal with them.

It is indeed difficult to believe dial the oilier powers, and particularly the 'ancient ally'. Great Britain, had any real interest in developing the Portuguese colonies, for it must have been clear to anyone giving thought to the question that Portugal lacked the resources to develop them itself and would have to rely on foreign help: that it would leave Item undeveloped rather than allow foreign developers and foreign capital to act as Trojan horses for a foreign conquest; and that a guarantee of continued possession, rather than vague threats of dispossession. was therefore essential if foreign capital were to he let into Mocambique and

Angola. It does not, of course, follow that if more capital investment had been permitted and forthcoming it would have been fruitful. One can argue that too much. not too little, capital had been put into African infrastructure around the turn of the century—witness the five separate railways from the Transvaal to the coast, any one of which could have carried all the traffic, and those to Luanda and Beira which were likewise under-employed.

In any event, the disorganised political and financial condition of Portugal in the decade between the Armistice and the appointment of Dr Oliveira Salazar as Minister of Finance in 1928 was such as to discourage any foreign investment in its overseas territories. That this condition did not result Iron anything except had administration is demonstrated by the case, technically speaking, with which Salazar was able to deal with a situation that his predecessors had thought insoluble without a League of Nations loan. His financial miracle was produced, not by brilliance as an economist, but by single-minded determination hacked by military force. In the long term it has undoubtedly assisted Portugal to secure a modicum of foreign investment, both at home and in the overseas territories. But, in the short run it produced painful results, particularly in Angola.

Angola rather than Mozambique tended to receive the greater solicitude from Portuguese governments under the republic, for a number of reasons: its greater need for economic help, in the absence of a large source of invisible exports comparable to the ports and railroads of Lourenco Marques and Beira; its more exclusively Portuguese character, in the absence of the sizeable influence of Great Britain and the Union of South Africa on Mozambique; and the greater suitability of its central and southern plateaux, compared with any part of Mocambique, for settlement by Portuguese peasants. There were sometimes complaints of discrimination in favour of Angola, notably by the (partly British-owned) cane-sugar industry of Mozambique, which by itself was capable of supplying metropolitan Portugal's requirements and found its output artificially restricted to make room for sugar produced by the former rum industry of Angola.[9] The long-standing custom of relieving Angola's budget deficits from the surpluses in the budgets of Sao Tome and Mozambique had been an earlier source of criticism.

The period when attention was most sharply focused on Angolan economic problems was the 1920s. The decade had begun auspiciously: the diamond held in the district of Lunda, discovered just before the First World War, had proved sufficiently important to justify the grant of a mining monopoly to an *ad hoc* associate of the De Beers organisation in South Africa, the Companhia de Diamantes de Angola (Diamang). For the next two decades, diamonds were to be Angola's leading export and a substantial contributor to provincial revenues; they are still important fifty years later. Diamang is reputed to be a model employer, and its provision for education and health among its African employees is said to the noteworthy. But, its operations are confined to one remote inland corner of the province that, if the boundaries of 1885 had been settled on ethnic grounds, might well have been included in the Congo Free Stale. Its influence on the mass of the Angolan population is negligible.

In 1922, a British writer published a hook—*Angola, a coming colony*—that radiated optimism about the province's future.[10] In 1923 the Mocamedes Railway readied Sa da Bandeira, on the plateau. Thereafter, however, everything began to go wrong. Norton dc Mates, who had been governor-general in the immediate pre-war years and afterwards the principal instigator of Portugal's ill-starred military activity on the Western Front in Europe, was sent back to Angola for a second term, this time as high commissioner, with his mind full of devices for economic and social development. In principle some or these made sense. But, in Portugal in the mid-twenties there was neither the money to finance them nor the trained men to carry them out; the want of qualification of Norton de Males' recruits for Angola became a national laughing-stock. Severe parliamentary criticism, led by the formidable Cunha Leal, followed; and in June 1924 the light commissioner resigned, leaving a legacy of unfinished projects, financial confusion and commercial depression.

It was in this situation that one Alves Reis conceived a scheme for bringing prosperity to Angola and fortune to himself by founding a new bank—the Angola e Metropole dial would break the banking monopoly of the Banco Nacional Ultramarine in Angola and remedy the shortage of capital there. The new bank's initial capital was obtained in a unique way: a forged letter from the Bank of Portugal to its bank-note printers, the highly reputable British firm of Waterlow and Sons. On the strength of this. Alves Reis and his fellow-conspirators obtained the printing and personal delivery of $5 million worth of 500-cscudo notes that, being printed from the same plates, were indistinguishable, except for a secret printer's mark from the genuine article. It had been represented to Waterlow's that the notes would he overprinted 'Angola' before issue—a point that should have aroused suspicion, inasmuch ;is the sole hank of note issue for the Portuguese colonies was not the Bank of Portugal hut the Banco Nacional Ultramarino.

In June 1925, the new bank received its official charier and began to open offices in Angola and to lend money. The false notes—not or course, overprinted—began to he circulated in Portugal itself, where alone they could escape detection. The bank's activities began to arouse gossip and hostile criticism in least one influential Lisbon newspaper; but the bubble was burst in December through the individual activity or a single, completely obscure citizen of Oporto, who read the newspaper articles and jumped to the conclusion that tile new bank's notes were forged. His views readied the Bank of Portugal's Oporto office, which examined the 500-escudo notes in its possession and found that they were will apparently genuine, but that some had duplicate numbers. There was nothing for it hut to call the whole issue in replacing it all by genuine notes of oilier kinds. The Bank of

Portugal eventually sued Waterlow for damages in the British courts and won. though not without going as far as the House of Lords, and then only by a vole of three law lords to two: the minority held that because the notes had no gold backing, the Bank of Portugal had failed to prove loss beyond its printing hill. Allowing for the assets of the defunct Banco Angola e Metropole and the part ol the false note issue that had not found its way into circulation, the total damages were rather more than $2 million. Efforts have since been made, though without any attempt at proof, to represent Alves Reis (who was given a long prison sentence by the Portuguese courts) as a Keynesian before his time.[11]

It is not clear how far this bizarre episode, reflecting on the methods of British business rather than those of Portuguese government, was responsible for the next move. in 1926: the transfer of the rights of note issue and commercial banking in Angola away from the privately owned Banco Nacional Ultramarine to a newly created semi-public body, the Banco de Angola, and the replacement of the heavily discounted Angolan escudo by a new currency unit, the angolar of a nominal par value with the metropolitan escudo but, like its predecessor, not freely exchangeable against it or directly into foreign currency. It is not easy to see why this measure was expected to help with the chronic problem of Angolan currency between the two world wars—shortage of metropolitan and foreign exchange because this was inherent in the province's trade situation, and not to he remedied by any administrative device.

Unless an undeveloped country has some extremely valuable export in quantity, such as gold or diamonds in South Africa al the end of the nineteenth century, it will seldom if ever he able to pay out of export earnings for the imports it needs for development. In Angola's case, even with the earnings of Diamang, there was often difficulty in converting into escudos current demands in angolares, such as those represented by funds belonging to persons returning to Portugal from spells of duty. It was rare for such people to settle permanently in Angola, or to wish to keep their surplus funds there. Currency transfer continued to he a cause of complaint, along with the banking monopoly of the Bank of Angola to which it was linked, throughout the inter-war period. Indeed, as late as 1960 an informed critic wrote that the main result of exchange control in Angola had been to promote illegal exchange transactions, speculation and flights of captal.[12] These problems were less consistently troublesome, perhaps, in Mozambique, but policy have persisted there also.

Complaints from the overseas territories became more vociferous when, after 1928, the extravagances of the Norton de Matos era were suddenly replaced by the budget austerities of Salazar, the like of which had never been experienced in Portugal. The Salazar remedy for financial extravagance—an insistence that the annual budget for each province, at least in appearance, be in balance or surplus, an insistence that was, moreover, written into the new 'corporative' constitution—did nothing in the short run for colonial economic development. Nor was the austerity made easier to accept in the overseas territories by the fact that at no time in his forty years of virtually unchallenged power did Salazar visit a single one of them. It is easy to understand why the series of budget surpluses overseas immediately before the outbreak of the Second World War should have been pointed to with pride. On a longer view, however, the who referred to these 'housekeeper's balances' as 'merely the privilege of theorists in the study, adherents of a narrow-minded fiscal policy' and called for a positive policy of help for Angola, were surely in the right.'[13]

Nevertheless, without the administrative discipline that the budgetary reforms embodied, it might have been hard for Portugal to retain Angola and Mozambique at all, particularly alter 1933 when the Germans were clamouring for colonial territories. The dilemma remained inescapable right up to the Second World War: cither keep control in the hands of Portugal, which though now financially solvent had insufficient resources in capital and skilled labour to develop even its metropolitan territory; or the control slip into the hands of foreign-controlled and foreign-financed companies and thence, at least indirectly, into those of foreign governments.

It is, let it be repeated, by no means certain that economic development would have been more extensive or more rapid under different political control. As in many other economically backward regions, such as southern Italy and much of Latin America, the return on investment was inadequate, the skilled and literate manpower required for industrialisation absent, and the market for increased agricultural and other production remote, inaccessible or non-existent. In any case, the ban on foreign investment in Portuguese Africa was not absolute, nor would that investment have been substantial in the economic climate of 1929-39.

One large enterprise was completed in Angola during this period: the building of the Benguela Railway, which reached the border of the Belgian Congo in 1925 and the Kalanga copper mines, the prime object for which it was built, in 1931. Its completion coincided with the worst of the world slump and a fall in the price of copper to $25 a ton. The Renguein Railway was yet another example of unprofitable, because premature, colonial railway investment. Grossly underestimated in cost; forced, for the first and most difficult phase of its construction, to import East Indian coolie labour from Natal in default of local labour; compelled to resort to the costly rack-rail system (since replaced by the normal adhesion system) for the steepest part of its climb to the plateau; unable to raise extra capital in Great Britain before 1914 by reason of the Anglo-German secret agreements of 1898. and halted completely in building during the First World War. The line did not pay a dividend until 1948, more than folly-five years after the grant of its ninety-nine-year concession.

Between the world wars, the economy of Mozambique continued to he dominated by the transit trade with the Union of South Africa and Southern Rhodesia. The agreement tying a minimum quota of trade through Lourenco Marques to a regulated supply of labour for the Rand mines was renewed with minor modifications in 1928. In 1935, a two-mile long railway bridge over the Zambezi at Sena was completed, the principal engineering work on the mainly British-owned Trans-Zambézia Railway, linking the Beira-Uintali line at Dondo with Nyasaland (now Malawi).

In 1938, a Cotton Export Board (Junta de Exportacao dc Algodao) was set up to promote cotton-growing by Africans, mainly in the northern part of the province, for export to Portugal. There appears to be no doubt that the introduction of an unaccustomed cash-crop, together with an organised system of road transport to bring it to market. brought about a 'general economic awakening' of northern Mozambique." Bill the compulsion on Africans to grow cotton, coupled with the fixing of a buying price well below the world price, was to arouse much foreign criticism in the 1950s. These arrangements could not have been brought into full being but for the disappearance, with the expiry of its concession in 1929, of the Nyassa Company, which had inconspicuously failed to develop the northernmost part of the province over a forty-year period. It was to he followed into obscurity twelve years later, in 1941 by the somewhat more successful Mocambique Company based in Beira, once thought of as the vehicle by which disciples of Cecil Rhodes might attain British control over the whole of Mocambique.

Portuguese neutrality in the Second World War made possible by the disappearance in 1919 of the German African colonies, ensured that Angola and Mozambique did not once again become the scene of military operations. Moreover, in the later years of the war exports of tropical products from the Portuguese territories were not subjected to the bulk- operations of the Allied Combined

Food Board, but left as an uncontrolled source of supply for neutral countries. The provinces appear to have prospered during the war years, and they shared in the post-war economic boom. Financial revenues were sufficient, and tax revenues buoyant enough, to justify the authorities in launching a series of development schemes.

The scale on which these schemes were launched and the confidence with which the government embarked on them were something new in Portuguese history. The confidence can be explained partly by twenty years of political and financial stability, partly by awareness that the outcome of the Second World War had removed, at long last. any European threat to the Portuguese African dominions. The character of the schemes, however, was not new: it combined the long-standing—and very necessary—attention to economic infrastructure with an even longer-standing aim that elsewhere in tropical Africa had never been attempted—namely, the settlement of European peasant fanners on the land. By this means the Portuguese intend to permeate Angola and Mozambique with their particular form of European culture: the peasant settler is to be the leaven that leaveneth the whole African lump. To quote from the preamble to the second overseas development plan. published in 1958:

> The state of peace in the Portuguese territories... is in itself important contribution towards the solidity of the defence of the values we have sustained for centuries our indestructible belief in the equality of the human species and... a conception of human democracy wholly alien to the idea of conflict, to the feeling of racial superiority or inferiority.[14]

The Portuguese settler is carrying out a national mission that transcends the national sell-interest, and this historic mission must be justified; the development plan for Angola in particular must be judged exclusively by its effects on white settlement.

This criterion [the preamble goes on] will not the understood by one who seeks to transform the African native into an abstract type of civilised man... For us... Africa is also our motherland and we wish to make the natives into Portuguese and not simply *civilizados*. We must therefore people Africa with Europeans who can assure the stability of our sovereignty and promote the 'portuguesation' of the native population.[15]

These views are seriously meant, for all that they represent only an uncontradicted minority (though perhaps a majority among the politically conscious) in Portugal itself; the African majority in the overseas territories is naturally not consulted. Leaving aside the possibility that Africans might not co-operate in being made into Portuguese, the question arises whether enough Portuguese settlers can ever be found to do the job. It is not enough to point to the vertiginous increase in the European population of Angola, which quadrupled between 1940 and 1960 and may now (1972) he more than a quarter of a million, compared with perhaps live million Africans, the European population of Mozambique likewise quadrupled between 1940 and 1960, hut was still under 100,000 at the latter dale, compared with an African population of nearly six and a half million. However, the Europeans in both provinces are predominantly town dwellers, remote from the rural African: more than one-third of the European population of each province lives in the respective capitals, Luanda and Lourenco Marques, and some towns, such as Sa da Bandeira and Mocamedes in Angola, have more white and *mestico* inhabitants than Africans.

There are, it is true, a handful of rural settlements for whiles, most of them heavily financed by government, that are pointed to with pride as offering op-portunities for the settlers and Africans to work side by side. However, the best known of these, Cela in Angola, was designed to the cnlirely while, settlers being forbidden to employ African labour. This decision is traceable, as was noted earlier, to the influence of Vicente Ferreira, who shared his great predecessors' views on the undesirability of miscegenation views nowadays so out of fashion that attempts are made to deny that they were ever held. Later settlements both in Angola and Mocambique have specifically provided for both immigrant Portuguese and Africans to serve as part-time labour on European lands. The Cela project, moreover, now admits *mesticos;* and the original plan of 1952 for as many as two thousand subsistence (50-acre) holdings has been modified to allow for some holdings as big as 250 acres, employing hired labour recruited in Portugal.[16]

It is too early to say whether these schemes will turn out to be permanent successes, although they embody a determination and a care in planning that were conspicuously absent from earlier proposals of the kind. In any case, their extent has been too limited to have serious impact on the problem that the government sees itself lacing in Africa, and the prospect of enlarging their scale significantly appears to be dim. Already there have been complaints of bad choice of colonists for the schemes, including some who cannot read and write; the colonising power, it is pointed out, loses face when the black man has to write the while man's letters for him.[17]

Insistence on farming as a principal employment for settlers from Portugal goes strongly against the grain for the majority of those wishing to emigrate, who, on reaching Brazil and Africa alike have traditionally chosen to work otherwise than on the land. Nearly a century ago a district governor of Mocamedes scornfully noted the propensity for petty trade: 'Trading is here a vice; the aim of the majority is to fill up time without working, neglecting the advantages offered by tillage.' A modern official echoes him: 'The prime objective of every *civilizado* [in the district of Huila] is to obtain a nest-egg and a connection, so as to devote himself to storekeeping, cither as an employee or on his own account. Not because this business always brings evident profits, but because sometimes it is highly lucrative, and principally because it allows a life without physical effort.' The principal commodity sold to the African is said to be wine, which is in accordance with longstanding tradition.[18]

It seems out of the question that peasant agricultural settlement in Angola, lei alone in Mocambique where climatic conditions are less favourable to while men, could ever be on a scale that would do much more than demonstrate its feasibility. It is true that emigrants are available in Portugal; as many as 100.000 have been leaving each year for the last decade (1961-70), nearly half of them for France. But, the proportion going to the overseas provinces has been diminishing, even though Brazil has, temporarily al any rate, ceased to be a major recipient of Portuguese immigrants; and of the 12,000 or so who have been going to Angola and Mocamhique annually, the majority slay in the towns. In many areas of the interior, 'the only props of the colonising power's culture and civilisation are the district officer and the missionary'.[19] It is hard to see how this situation can alter in the foreseeable future.

This docs not mean that very considerable economic development has not taken place in both Angola and Mocambique since the Second World War. It does mean that a great number of Africans remain peripheral to the modern money economy, something that can he said, for that matter, of a substantial number of country people in Portugal itself. In neither instance is self-sufficiency absolute: there is always something that has to be obtained from out-side the local community and some surplus commodity, or service, to be exchanged for it. The subsistence economy differs in degree, not in kind, from the exchange economy. But, in extent of dependence on the exchange economy, the peasant in Portugal and the tribesman in Portuguese Africa are comparable, each being fur removed from the Portuguese governing class.

Portuguese critics have sometimes remarked of the official Overseas Development Plans, of which the first covered the years 1951-8 and the second the years 1959 64, that they overemphasised additions to economic infrastructure and did not invest enough in social development or in improvements to the native economy. It is hard to say how much there is in these criticisms. The plans did not cover the total of public expenditures, and in many instances they set maxima for expenditure that proved impossible of fulfilment. The first plan, for instance, allocated 235 million escudos for the extension of the northern Mocainbique railroad towards Lake Nyasa; but by September 1957 nothing had been spent. By the same date, only one-eighth out of a I-million-escudo allocation for land drainage and reclamation in Sao Tome-Principe had been spent. There has, in fact, been a chronic tendency—as so often in Portugal itself—for colonial public-works projects to fall behind schedule. In a way, this offers an insurance against over-sanguine budgeting, or against the tendency—which Portuguese critics have also pointed out—to ignore the possibility that changes in economic circumstances (for example, in the terms of trade) might prevent development plans from being accomplished.

In fact, however, it seems that though budgeted improvements in infrastructure have not always been carried out on time, they have been carried out eventually. The northern railroad from Nacala, for instance, has now (1972) reached the border of Malawi, so providing that country with an alternative outport to Beira, which has frequently been congested in recent years. The resulting transit traffic may make the line profitable for tile first time.

Another important rail link, completed in 1955, is the Limpopo branch of the Lourenco Marques system, which joins the Rhodesian railways at Malvernia, so providing another alternative to the Beira railway, particularly for Zambian copper. The Beira railway was itself bought from its British owners by the Portuguese government in 1949; in 1951 a convention between Great Britain and Portugal guaranteed the line's transit traffic in return for a Portuguese undertaking to make improvements in the port of Beira. In Angola the most significant railway development in recent years has been the extension of the

Mocamedes railway to Serpa Pinto, nearly 500 miles inland, and the construction of a branch line from it to serve the newly exploited haematité iron-ore workings at Cassinga, 400 miles from Mocamedes. Yearly shipments of iron ore through that port, which was very substantially improved in the 1950S, are expected to reach more than 5 million tons; as late is 1966 the line carried less than 300.000 tons. Another huge iron-ore deposit is about to be exploited near Nacala, in northern Mozambique, by building a special railway line and export quay.

Apart from improvements in ports and railways, the most striking developments of infrastructure have been in hydro-electric the power. Five hydro-electric plants have been completed in Angola since the Second World War; the largest of them is at Cambambe, on the Cuanza river at the head of navigation, near the market town of Dondo. It supplies electricity to the city of Luanda. A much larger scheme is planned to grow out of the existing Matala project on the middle Cunene, near the holder with South-West Africa; this plant will ultimately have a capacity of 300.000 kilowatts, and the dams will irrigate over a million acres. These plans are being concerted with those of the government of South-West Africa.

Similar international co-operation lies behind the huge Cabora Bassa scheme on the Zambezi in Mozambique, situated, incidentally, in an area handed over to Portugal by the British in 1891 to compensate Portugal for the seizure of the (supposedly gold-rich) plaleau of Manica by agents of Cecil Rhodes's Chartered Company. Proponents look forward to the ultimate generation 50.000 million kilowall-hours a year, to the irrigation of over 3-5 million acres, and to making the Zambezi navigable all the year round from Tele to the Indian Ocean, about 400 miles. These prospects have been made possible because the Republic of South Africa will he the principal buyer of Cabora Bassa power, Hydro-electric and irrigation projects have already been built on the Revue and Limpopo rivers in Mocanihique; the Limpopo Dam serves also as a bridge for the new rail link to Rhodesia. and irrigates the lands of the Limpopo agricultural settlement scheme.[20]

The most important new industrial developments to occur so far in Angola are the iron-ore mines of Cassinga and the discovery of petroleum, both on shore and off-shore. On-shore, substantial oil reserves have been found near Luanda, and a refinery with a capacity of million Ions a year has been built. Even more important is the off-shore field of the tiny enclave of Cahinda, which by itself will produce twice Portugal's current oil needs. Oil and iron ore already rival coffee and diamonds as sources of export income, which now appears to be large enough to contribute substantially towards a favourable balance of payments—an achievement that has eluded Angola through most of its existence—and to relieve the dependence on coffee exports that has characterised the economy of the province since the Second World War. The chief agent, indeed, in the post-war economic transformation, and a wholly fortuitous one so far as Angola was concerned, was the development of the 'instant coffee' industry in the United Stales, which provided a huge new market for the hitherto cheap and despised *robusta* coffee in which the province specialises.

By the 1960s, coffee had far outstripped diamonds as the most valuable single export, accounting for close to half the total. For the first time in its history. Angola appealed to have found a means of paying for the imported capital goods it needed for development; in only four of the fifteen years 1952-66 did the official accounts not show a favourable balance of external trade. The balance-of-payments situation is somewhat less favourable when 'invisibles' are taken into account, which explains why the Angolan escudo—formerly called the angolar—still stands at a varying but substantial discount from the metropolitan escudo on the free currency market.[21]

The currency situation in Mocambique remains similar—if anything rather worse—inasmuch as no money-making physical export comparable with coffee or iron ore has so far been found, and 'invisibles', mainly transit trade, earnings of migrant labour and tourist expenditures, continue to bulk large on the credit side of the provincial balance of payments. The Mozambique escudo likewise stands at a considerable discount from tin' metropolitan escudo on the flee market, and various administrative devices have not. apparently. been able to solve the problem of currency transfer to continental Portugal. The declared ideal of a common currency for tile whole 'escudo area' appears to the as far from effective realisation as ever: it is maintained in principle only by rationing the supplies of metropolitan currency available to the provinces, and by imposing many months' delay on the settlement of their accounts.

These changes have had widely differing effects for the economies of Angola and Mozambique, viewed as wholes. The development of Angolan exports of coffee, about one-third of which is grown by Africans, and of cotton exports from Mozambique, virtually all of which are grown by Africans, has brought substantial numbers of country people into the exchange economy. The same is line of the export from Mozambique of cashew nuts, which are mostly gathered by Africans from trees growing wild, but are now being grown on European-owned plantations. The oil and iron die enterprises on the other hand, are essentially European enclaves employing little African labour. It seems likely that the variety of comparatively minor industrial enterprises that has grown up, more particularly around Luanda, and the growth of 'service' industries that has gone along with it, have had more direct effect on the African population. Half a million people, or one tenth of the total population of Angola, are now said to live in Luanda and its environs; Europeans account for rather less than one-third of these. Such an increase in urban living, much of it in hastily erected slums, is, of course, common to many African cities in the last quarter of a century. It means that Luanda is outdistancing Oporto as the second city of Greater Portugal. It means also that the capital city not the peasant settlement, is likely to be the chief agent of Portuguesation among Africans. Lourenco Marques, by reason of its eccentric situation on the extreme southern border of Mozambique, is less well placed to perform this task, and it is anyhow growing far less fast than Luanda.

The influx of Africans into Luanda and other cities may suggest that traditional tribal links in Angola are beginning to break down. They have, of course, never existed in the Cape Verde Islands or in Sao Tome-Principe. It seems possible also that within the past twenty years or so the exchange economy has at long last been able to recruit enough African labour more or less freely, so that the long-standing device of a compulsory labour contract for male Africans, reinforced by a hut tax, can be dispensed with. Compulsory labour has, of course, long been a target for missionary and oilier critics of Portuguese colonial administration. Criticism has tended to be levelled not so much at compulsion for public purposes (such as road-making) but at that for the benefit of planters and oilier private employers. 'I 'his used to he common (and not only in Portuguese territories), but it was explicitly forbidden in the new Native Labour Code that was introduced in 1928; what many critics have doubted is whether the new Code was strictly, or at all, enforced. Obviously it is never easy for an unlettered African to insist on his rights against a European administrator, or for sympathisers to get a hearing for complaints against the administration under a dictatorship that censors the press. Even before Salazar, moreover, it was common ground among foreign critics that the letter of the law and its enforcement were two different things.

In 1960, the Portuguese government ratified the 1957 ILO. Convention for the Abolition of Forced Labour. an act that was immediately followed by a complaint by Ghana, supported by the United Arab Republic, that Portugal continued to rely on forced labour as the pivot of its native policy, and that the ratification was only a subterfuge. The visiting commission, comprising experts from Switzerland. Uruguay and Senegal, that was appointed by the ILO to investigate the complaint, unanimously rejected the charge of bad faith: the changes in policy were. it declared, real. The commission made one comment, however, that points up. more clearly than most of the writing on the subject, the difficulty about establishing firm conclusions about the quality of administration in a primitive country: that in some cases, notably that of the Cassequel sugar plantations near Lobito. 'the bulk of the working force is at so backward a stage of development that the question whether the labour exacted from them is forced labour becomes virtually meaningless'. The lives of such people (the commission went on) 'are a series of conditioned relieves which are less than human... An order is an order: a suggestion is indistinguishable from an order: and the inertia of ages maintains a social pattern in which people do what they are (old to do because they have always done so.'[22]

Much the same, however, might he said of the masses in Portugal itself; they have always been separated from the government and the ruling class by a gulf of poverty and illiteracy. This was just as true under the liberal monarchy and the democratic republic as it was under Salazar; in 1915. for instance, the number of persons who might legally vole was less than half a million, one tenth the population. The earlier regimes allowed more freedom than did that of Salazar to the minority interested in politics; full the vast majority of the nation has always been completely outside political activity. Moreover, the absence until recently of industrial development in Portugal would have prevented the rise of strong trade unions, even had not the unions been deprived of political significance under the Salazar regime.[23]

The close analogies between the social structures of continental Portugal and Portuguese Africa seem to have escaped most foreign critics. In neither has there ever existed any force capable of defending the rights of the majority of pool citizens. while or black, against abuse or neglect by government. In these circumstances, the effectiveness of laws. however, wise and good they may appear to be in principle, cannot hill the decidedly limited. This, presumably, is what the ILO commission meant to imply by its comment on the Cassequel sugar workers. There is no lack of enlightenment on paper, any more than there was in earlier colonial labour legislation that equally came under foreign criticism for insincerity. There is no necessary lack of good intentions on the part of government. But, there is no external check on the conduct of bureaucrats in the field, no freely elected legislature dial can question their behaviour, no independent judiciary. no uncensored press that can expose scandals and no interested and sizeable public opinion to which appeal can be made. There is not even, for what it might be worth, a single political party with a mass following, as there was in fascist Italy and Nazi Germany, and as there is in the Soviet Union.

Of course, this situation is the normal one of' mankind through the ages; the Portuguese government and bureaucracy, regarded historically, are not exceptionally inhumane or irresponsive. Rather do they represent a survival that to many outside the Portuguese dominions appears an intolerable anachronism. Mutual want of sympathy is so great is to make mutual understanding out of the question; the Portuguese government and its critics are not talking the same language.

It is against this background that, one has to consider what at first sight might appeal to be a revolutionary economic and social change: the abolition, in September 1961, of the special status of non-assimilated Africans in the territories, the *indigenato.* This removed at a stroke the legal obligation to be contracted for labour service, formerly imposed on non-assimilated male Africans who could not show themselves to he already at work either on their own or another's account, (It has never been deal how. in the absence of an independent appeal tribunal, this demonstration could the made good.) What was not removed was the chief sanction behind the legal obligation—namely, the head (ax on African males, which in February 1962 was extended to all male inhabitants between eighteen and sixty, along with females employed by the government. Moreover, the contract labour system was continued on a voluntary basis, in accordance with a new and (on paper) enlightened rural labour code. What is difficult, as the ILO inquiry of 1962 found, is to discover how much practical difference these legal changes have made.

It is likewise difficult to know what the real effect of the Angolan 'revolt' of 1961 and the corresponding movements in Mocambique and Portuguese Guinea, has been. Those events postdate the period of history with which this volume is concerned, and the time has not yet come which a full account 'if them can be written. Nevertheless, some comment on them by way of conclusion is possible.

The movements were made feasible by the fact that the frontiers between all three Portuguese territories and their neighbours did not correspond to ethnic boundaries between African tribes and were not physically closed. It was thefe-fore possible for dissidents, unobserved by Portuguese authorities, to use neighbouring slates as their bases of operations. The government in Luanda, for instance, was taken completely by surprise by the events of early 1961; the Salazar secret police (PIDE) had recently, for the first time, established an office there, but this had been done to watch for individual opponents of the regime, European, *mestico* or African, not to forestall an organised African movement directed from without.

None of the various opposition groups has ever commanded a mass inter tribal following. The Portuguese have, as they have for centuries, been able to recruit Africans to fight alongside the European garrisons. The failure of the majority of African tribes in the territories to make common cause with such in surgent tribes as the Bakongo in Angola or the Makonde and Nyanja in Mocambique has been patent. Even in Portuguese Guinea, the largest single tribe the Fula, has sided with the administration.

NOTES AND REFERENCES

1. Eric Axelson, Portugal and the Scramble for Africa, Johannesburg University Press, 1967, pp. 232ff
2. Sybil E. Crowe, The Berlin West African Conference, 1884-1885, London, 1942.
3. Villiers Lister, quoted in Richard J. Hammond, Portugal and Africa, 1815-1910: A study in uneconomic imperialism, Stanford Univ. Press, 1966, p. 61.
4. *Poutugal and Africa*, pp. 313-25.
5. Jaime Walter, *Honorio Pereira Barreto*, Hammond, *Poutugal and Africa*, pp. 46-50.
6. Afredo Freire de Andrade, Relatorios de Mocambique, Loureco Marques, 1909, 1,103; translation in Hammond, *Poutugal and Africa*, pp. 294-95.
7. The Act is 9 Edw. 7, c.9. See Hammond, *Poutugal and Africa*, pp. 326-32.
8. William Roger Louis, Ruanda-Urundi, 1881-1919, Oxford, Clarendon Press, 1963, pp. 233-55.
9. Sena Sugar Estates, Ltd., *Moçambique e o problema acucareiro*, Lisbon, 1945.
10. J.C.B. Stathan, *Angola: a coming colony*, Edinburgh, 1922.
11. Sir Cecil H. Kisch, *The Portuguese bank-note case*, London, 1932; Murry Teigh Bloom, *The man who stole Portugal, New York, 1966.*
12. Roberto S. de Medeiros Fernandes, 'Portugal and its overseas territories: economic structure and policies, 1950-1957', Ph.D. diss., Harvard University, 1960.
13. Manuel Domingos da Cruz, *A Crise de Angola, Lisbon 1928, p. 60; Francisco Pinto da Cunha Leal, Subsidios para o estudo do problema do credito em Angola, Lisbon, 1930.*

14. S. van Dongen's in David M. Abshire and Michael A. Samuels, eds. Portuguese Africa: a handbook, London and New York, 1969, p. 270.

15. Translation from Portugal, Presidencia do Conselho, *Relatorio final preparatorio do II plano do forento (IX) Ultramar*, Lisbon, 1958, p. 32.

16. Irene S. van Dongen in Abshire and Samuels, eds., *Poutuguese Africa*, pp. 280-84.

17. Jose Maria Gaspar, 'A colonizacao branca em Angola e Mocambique', in Junta das Investigacoes do Ultramar, *Coloquios de politica ultramarina internacionalmente relevante,* Lisbon, 1958, pp. 42-53.

18. Afonso Mendes, *A Huila e Mocamedes: consideracoes sobre o trabalho indigena,* Lisbon, 1958, pp. 34-35.

19. Gaspar, 'A colonizacao branca', pp. 42-53.

20. David M. Abshire in Abshire and Samuels, eds., *Portuguese Africa,* pp. 301-3 and 311-13.

21. Frank Brandenburg in Abshire and Samuels, eds., *Portuguese Africa,* pp. 238-52.

22. International Labour Office, *Report of the Commission appointed... to examine the complaint field by the Government of Ghana concerning the observance by the Government of Purtugal of the Abolition of Forced Labour Convention, 1957 (No. 105),* March 1962, p. 378.

23. Frank E. Huggett, *South of Lisbon,* London, 1960.

4

Portuguese Colonial Policy in Angola

Portugal's Compulsion to Move Towards Angola

After the much lamented 'loss' of Brazil to independence in 1822, Angola replaced the South American giant at the centre of affections of the idealists of Portuguese grandeur. This very large, under-populated territory in south-west Africa held the aspirations of those who still believed in the possibility of a return to past greatness that, since the seventeenth century, had become more and more elusive for Portugal. The wealth and potential of Brazil had been lost, but, by the mid-die of the nineteenth century onwards, it was being sought in Angola.

Actual pursuit of wealth in Angola during the nineteenth century, however, fell far short of the achievements claimed by successive regimes in Portugal anxious to impress their more powerful European neighbours. Attempts to conceal the reality of what was going on in Portugal's somewhat disproportionate share of African territory did not simply reflect grandiose delusions of a declining colonial empire, but were an intrinsic part of an astute diplomatic policy aimed at defending Portugal's diminished role in a world of rapacious politics. The workings of the complex

European alliances of the end of the nineteenth century often threatened to dismember the Portuguese territories in Africa and distribute the pieces among the major powers. Despite singularly humiliating incidents,[1] this diplomacy was largely successful. By acting as a buffer between Britain, France and Germany in Africa, Portugal managed to retain control of Angola and the other overseas territories into the twentieth century.[2]

Berlin Conference and Partition of Africa

When the Berlin conference of 1884-85 sought to determine European spheres of influence in Africa, it also established the new rules of imperialism. No longer was colonial rule to be defined simply by historical right. The General Act of the conference, that claimed to define a 'new colonial public law',[3] determined that only effective occupation constituted colonial sovereignty. The Act was clearly unfavourable to a small and poor colonizer such as Portugal and placed Lisbon under pressure to extend its hitherto largely coastal administration of colonies to the hinterland. Effective occupation had to be established or Portugal risked losing its colonies altogether. Lacking the necessary funds and the manpower to achieve this objective, the government in Lisbon nevertheless organised a number of expeditions between 1885 and 1890 in an attempt to 'pacify' the colonies and meet the conditions set by the 'imperial club'.[4]

'Pacification' (the enforcement of both military and economic control of a territory through the establishment of an administrative unit) had not previously been characteristic of Portuguese colonial policy. The greater part of Portuguese dealings with the territories they claimed control over was made up of commercial trade. In Angola, this was secured by the numerous traders based in the coastal ports of Luanda and Benguela. Through intermediaries, they would barter with the African kingdoms of the interior. After the Berlin Conference, the commercial nature of Portuguese interaction in Africa, once informal, became increasingly inserted into a framework of colonial control and administration. Despite centuries of presence in Africa, Portugal only began to establish a colonial state in Angola and other territories towards the end of the nineteenth century, and then only as a result of pressure from the Great Powers which threatened to push the Portuguese off the continent altogether.

Colonial Policy of Portugal under the Republic

In Portugal, the pressure to establish full control of its overseas territories and develop colonial state structures, therefore, became part of the political programmes of the day. Even before the overthrow of the monarchy in 1910, colonial reformers were already campaigning for the development of autonomous colonies with a large degree of administrative and financial independence from the metropolis.[5] However, such a sophisticated stage of colonial development could not be reached without the establishment of military control over the entire expanse of the colonies' territories. This task of imperial proportions implied enormous expense and the dispatch of large military forces to Africa. Already on shaky ground at home, the monarchy could ill afford this, either financially or politically.

With the overthrow of the monarchy in 1910, that reform agenda, in an expanded form, was taken on by the new governments of the republic. In keeping with its modernist and progressive ideology, they called for the rational, colonial exploitation of Portugal's territories. In their view, the potential of the colonies was to be harnessed and developed for Portugal's benefit. This republican model of colonialism envisaged a number of measures that would bring the territories under control. The colonies were to be taxed and viable produce cultivated. The practice of enforced labour was established and legislation on the status of the colonial population was implemented, separating the 'civilised' Europeans from the African 'natives'.[6] While merely a version of the 'civilising mission' of other European colonizers, the republican ideal of colonialism also recognised the role the colonies could play in the development of Portugal itself.

Colonial policy under the republic, during the period between 1910 and 1925, can only be described, however, as over-ambitious. Much of the grand legislature that aimed at developing the overseas Portuguese empire remained on paper. Increasingly decentralised rule in the colonies themselves resulted from difficulties in stabilising the metropolitan economic and political environments. Acute budget crises and political instability crippled governments in Lisbon, and colonial administrations were given wide powers to administrate their territories almost independently of the metropolis.

In Angola, the periods of Norton de Matos's administration characterised the high level of authority increasingly delegated to each colony.[7] As the highest government official in the territory, Norton de Matos ruled by decree and could even solicit international loans independently of Lisbon. Supported only by deficit financing, he launched frenetic development projects aimed at setting down hitherto non-existent infrastructures. These projects included the establishment of transportation networks in the country, seeking to attract a settler society that the republicans dreamed would thickly populate their overseas empire. Although, the colonies were, during this time, thrown open to foreign investment, the Portuguese Republic was considered a risk liability in an unsympathetic Europe. Consequently, there was precious little incoming investment capital. Levels of colonial trade actually fell during the republican period although this could also be attributed to the crackdown on slavery and the profitable alcohol trade, as well as to the stagnant pace of economic development in Portugal itself.[8]

But, despite political instability in the metropolis and meagre economic development, republican colonial policy and Norton de Matos's projects established the basic pillars on which the

Angolan economy later emerged: a significant road and railway network, the encouragement of cash crop production and the contracting of (wage-earning) labour. Furthermore, the minor, but nevertheless increased, levels of capital investment did help to attract a higher number of metropolitan immigrants.

The first republican era in Portugal was, however, short-lived. The financial chaos of the country was crippling government after government, and conservative forces had been waiting since the overthrow of the monarchy for an opportunity to strike back at the republicans. In a climate of political instability,[9] bombings, strikes, high inflation and corruption, the republic was an easy prey for the concerted revenge of the dispossessed Catholic Church, landowners fearing the reform of the feudal system they relied upon, monarchists and industrialists alarmed at the radicalisation of the working classes. The constant disruptive activity of anarchists and left-wing extremists helped to send the worried urban middle classes (hitherto the backbone of the republican experiment) and the frustrated armed forces into the waiting arms of the right wing. A military coup destroyed the republic on 28 May 1926.

The new administration of General Oscar Carmona ran into trouble almost immediately. In the throes of a financial crisis, the government invited a popular right-wing academic, Antonio de Oliveira Salazar, to solve the mounting problem of the budget deficits that gripped Portugal and its colonies. Lisbon feared that its near bankruptcy would lead to, among other things, the loss of the colonies.[10] Balancing the books was a priority for the new regime and it handed Salazar, the new finance minister, the absolute powers over public spending he demanded as a condition for entering government. Once he had obtained the power of veto over the budgets of every single government department, Salazar implemented his long-standing doctrine of balancing the budget and clearing the deficit. This policy was also applied to the colonies, including Angola where the colonial government had built up chronic deficits.[11] His immediate success (the 1928-29 domestic budget showed a surplus, the first for 15 years),[12] brought Salazar wide support and allowed him to extend his claim to intervene in other aspects of government beyond the financial sphere.

Formation of New State in Portugal

This was the beginning of Salazar's process of regime-building which culminated in what was called the New State *(Estado Novo)*.[13] While the military coup of 1926 had been supported by a number of right-wing factions, monarchist groups and the Church, only the latter saw any significant satisfaction of its desiderata. Salazar managed to allay, yet not meet, the demands for either the restoration of the monarchy or a more dynamic commitment to fascism. The Church, however, saw its role in society restored to that of the pre-republican era. In fact, the Catholic Church became intimately involved with Salazar's regime, playing the role of its spiritual partner in this and the other world. This was partly the result of Salazar's own devout faith which brought him great popularity throughout the country. But, there was also another more practical consideration.

The Church had been the only effectively organised political opposition to the republicans, and Salazar owed his own rise to power to his prominence within this circle. When the armed forces moved in to wrench power from the republicans, the choice of Salazar resulted as much from his dominant position as a political actor for the Catholic Church as from his academic prowess and financial acumen. Nevertheless, he stopped short of returning the bishops to direct political power, allowing them instead to dominate social life.

The New State regime has been described as an organic socio-political state that directly implemented Salazar's economic directives. The principal pillars of Salazar's authority were the bureaucracy, which ran all the state bodies, and the armed forces, which had established the conditions that brought him to power in the first place. The security of these two groups guaranteed, and were themselves guaranteed by, the survival of the New State. Salazar's authoritarian regime relied on taking over each and every body. Public institutions and government departments, manned by a loyal bureaucracy which imposed mounds of paperwork on the Portuguese, probably did more to suffocate resistance to the regime than the use of outright repressive force. Without a doubt, the security of the regime ultimately lay in the control and repression of dissent, on the mainland as well as in the colonies, through the use of a powerful police force known as the PIDE.[14] But, the successful control of all information, a steady flow of propaganda and the establishment of state control of any institution in the public domain, even in the economic sphere, played an important part in perpetuating the survival of the regime for nearly fifty years.

In the larger sectors of industry, shipping and banking, a few corporations had acquired what amounted to monopoly control. These were the domain of the social and political class that provided much of Salazar's immediate support. The economic power of the country was centralised in the hands of a small number of families and groups that dominated their respective economic sectors. After the Depression, a large amount of bankruptcies led to the additional concentration of capital in an even smaller number of hands, further reinforcing the old system of oligarchic control of the economy which had prevailed under the monarchy. This control in the metropolis, more often than not, resulted in the corresponding supremacy of the respective financial and industrial groups in the colonies as well. Furthermore, the top governmental positions were often held by members of these extended families.

Salazar was careful never to challenge the security of these families and corporate groups that dominated Portugal's industrial and financial sectors. Associations for employers *(Grémios)* and syndicates for workers were created in most sectors of private and public enterprise as well as in agricultural production. The resulting effect was the imposition of a centralised economic order. The institutionalisation of all sectors of society in this manner under the direct control of Salazar's government ensured authority and stability for the regime. This hold was complemented by governmental economic intervention according to a logic defined centrally. The near total control of the economy by the New State regime was achieved through the use of price controls and production quotas to regulate private enterprise, and by nationalisation wherever necessary.

In this context, Salazar did not establish a new state as much as he institutionalised socio-economic power relationships that had their roots in Portugal's nineteenth-century political order. The New State seems merely to have re-established the traditional political and economic forces previously dominant under the monarchy and temporarily displaced by the republican experiment.[15] Thus, the originality (and, perhaps, durability) of Salazar's New State lay in the systematic process of institutionalising these social, political and economic relationships.

The regime was undoubtedly authoritarian but Portugal under Salazar cannot be considered to have been a fascist state.[16] Despite the creation of a one-party political environment—the National Union *(Uniao Nacional)*—the activity of a paramilitary organisation—the Portuguese Legion *(Legiao Portuguesa)*—and even a nationwide youth movement—the Portuguese Youth *(Mocidade Portuguesa)*—there was little in the way of the creation of a wider fascist movement. Like Mussolini's evocation of the Roman Empire, Salazar did promote a mythology of the Portuguese nation as a timeless colonial empire with global reach. But, the order over which Salazar presided was fundamentally a conservative one, both in political and social terms. The Catholic and nationalist bases of the regime's ideology were not compatible with the ideas of national socialism that were being promulgated by other dictatorships in Europe at the time.[17]

It could be argued that by taking on certain trappings of the totalitarian regimes in Italy and later Germany and Spain, Salazar was trying to ride the wave of authoritarian change that spread through Europe in the inter-war period. This change was welcome to Salazar as, in his view, it warded off liberalism which he believed to be a dangerous precursor to socialism and too weak to defend itself effectively from the greater evil of communism. To Salazar, however, fascism as a total doctrine was far too progressive, too dynamic.[18] His political discourse and personal ethos yearned for a return to a pre-industrial revolution era in both social as well as economic terms. Helped by the Catholic Church, the regime promoted a paternalist ideology of God and nation which sought to hold the mass of the populace to the semi-feudal economic order that Salazar had institutionalised. In this ideology of the New State, the colonies and the images of empire played a central role.

Salazar's priority with regard to the colonial territories was to reaffirm Portugal's ability to run an empire. He held a mistrust of Great Power intentions, a mistrust that may have fed his isolationism and overwhelmingly nationalistic developmental policies for both Portugal and its colonies. According to Salazar's early policies, all colonial territories were to be primarily developed by Portuguese capital. Tight exchange controls were placed on commercial trading, echoing the mercantilism of the monarchy. At the same time, access by foreign capital to Portuguese markets in general was greatly limited, with the exception of those industries such as diamonds and other mining activity in Angola where foreign technological know-how was essential. This development policy was based on strict budgetary controls and sought to utilize, as much as possible, internally generated resources. Within this developmental strategy, Portugal's own economy was not seen in a separate light from that of the colonies. On the contrary, under Salazar's centrally planned economy, all the so-called regions of Portugal (a term which included the colonies) were to be fused into '... an integrated Lusitanian world economy',[19] the central priority of which was, however, to provide for the requirements of Portugal itself.

Thus, in Salazar's economic strategy, the colonies, and Angola in particular, played a subsidiary role to the planned semi-autarchic development of Portugal during the inter-world-war years. But, as well as playing this economic role, the colonies also represented what Duffy has called 'a living link with the past'.[20] Already in the early 1930s, Salazar was expounding his myth of empire, based solidly on the exploits and adventures of the navigators and discoverers of a far-off age.

Despite never having personally visited any of the Portuguese colonies throughout his years in power, Salazar gave paramount importance to the notion of empire in the political structure of his regime. According to this concept, the Portuguese 'nation' was indivisible and consisted of both continental Portugal as well as all its overseas territories. This contrasted sharply with, for example, the constitutional detachment of Britain from its own colonial empire. A link was established, therefore, between Portugal's overseas possessions and Salazar's domestic political power, a connection that was cast at the level of historical myth-making. It was woven into the retelling of the very origins of Portuguese independence, characterised heroically by the maritime discoveries of the fifteenth and sixteenth centuries. This adventurous and worldly image of Portugal was paradoxically espoused by the isolationist New State, contrasting with its nationalist economic and foreign policies. In political discourse, the Portuguese colonies were held to be an integral part of the nation, and tied to the very structure of Salazar's regime. For Salazar and others, the remaining colonial territories, a historical legacy of those seafaring times, were hard evidence that their nation was still great:

> We must always keep alive in the Portuguese people the dream of the beyond-the-seas *[Ultramar]* and the consciousness and pride of empire. Africa is more than a land to be exploited... Africa is

> for us a moral justification and a 'raison d'etre' as a power. Without it we would be a small nation; with it we are a great country.[21]

In this way, waxed the editorial of *O Mundo Portugues* in 1935, on the occasion of the first of a number of cruises to Angola and the islands of Cape Verde and Sao Tome and Principe designed to inculcate a sense of duty in the young Portuguese students they carried. The organizer of those cruises was Marcello Caetano, later to succeed Salazar and inherit his state.

What played a part in attempts to aggrandise the country's importance on the world stage also underlay the legitimacy of the regime at home. The territories became central to an intensely nationalistic ideology of society based on a spiritual sense of civilising duty. When confronted with a changing world in which the early grandeur of the country was recalled when reciting at school the epic poem, *Os Lusiadas,* the New State ideologues clung to the colonial world as an extension of the regime, as its legitimisation when proclaiming the existence of a Lusitanian world. This sense of organic nation, in which the 'country' of Portugal is treated in abstract to include the widespread colonial territories under its rule, was a central theme of colonial policy under the New State. This ultranationalism became even more emphatic, and perhaps necessary, when the regime came under fire from international public opinion in the post-war world of anti-colonialism. But, it had its roots and political justification in the ideology of nation developed by Salazar for his state.

The New State's colonial policy had a number of distinct formulations throughout its lifetime but really only two separate tendencies. The first period, lasting from the late 1920s to the late 1950s, was characterised by a reversal of the republican drive for decentralised autonomy and the firm establishment of the colonies in Lisbon's administrative orbit.

Emanating from the central hub of the capital, the needs of the new regime were placed above all else, and the surrounding periphery, the colonies as well as the less-developed mainland regions, were placed at the economic disposal of the centre. The Ministry of the Colonies in Lisbon was given full financial and political authority. The once powerful position of governor was reduced to a role of formal representation stripped of any opportunity for local initiative. Under Salazar, the colonial budgets were to be balanced directly from Lisbon, and any loans were to be procured only by the ministry in Portugal.

Impact of Colonial Policy on Metropolis Portugal

Colonial policy, like economic policy as a whole, reflected the progress of the regime in the metropolis. With its consolidation of power in overlapping circles of institutionalised public life, colonial policies sought also to achieve the collusion of the colonial state to the metropolitan one, the two becoming one. The legislation and implementation of policy in the colonies thus became centralised in the metropolitan state.

The structure of authority in the colonies was clear and simple. In the mid-1950s, the chain of command ran directly from Salazar to the African population;[22] all the intermediary positions were no more than the bureaucratic administration for the implementation of the directives of the governor-general, who, in turn, had little room for manoeuvre outside that which was approved by the colonial ministry in Lisbon. In the colonial minister lay all powers of legislation, loan procurement and appointments, after final approval by Salazar, of course. Should the governor have exceeded the expenditure authorised by the minister he would have been liable for prosecution. A legislative council in Angola (which included members chosen by an electoral college) had little power beyond passing minor legislation, serving more as a safety-valve for local issues that arose among the European population. In this way, the colonial state as an administrative unit was linked directly to the source of government in the metropolis, with budgetary control, economic policy and practically all legislative authority determined in Lisbon.

This structure of state authority was rooted in the legislative promulgations of the government, issued through the powerless National Assembly. In 1930, with an already firm grip over the emerging regime, Salazar legislated a bill for the colonies, which was later appended to the Constitution of 1933, where the particularities of the first period of colonial policy are evident: the proclamation of the abstract Portuguese nation including its colonial empire, the primacy of Portuguese over foreign capital and the use of forced labour.[23] This bill was sufficient to sustain colonial policy until after the end of the Second World War.

Portugal's economic position after the war improved significantly. During the conflict, Lisbon had profited from its neutrality by trading with both the Allies and the Axis powers; but the post-war boom in commodity prices, for a country that had good access to colonial raw materials, was an even greater windfall. This relative commercial success also made Portuguese capital available for colonial investment and, in a rare display of foresight, the early 1950s saw a legislative accommodation to those changing economic times.

During the early 1960s, the emergence of pro-decolonisation forces in international fora, particularly in the United Nations, questioned Portugal's legitimacy to maintain colonial possessions. Despite such opposition, however, the government in Lisbon refused to deny Portugal's 'right' to hold onto a colonial empire. While Britain and other European colonial powers were shedding, albeit under pressure, the economic and political justifications for keeping their own far-flung possessions, the Portuguese closed ranks and claimed their colonial empire was actually one single nation that had many territories spread out around the world. From 1951, the colonies ceased to exist in the public lexicon and the 'empire' was replaced by one Portuguese nation made up of both continental and overseas *(ultramar)* provinces.[24]

In the 1960s, a more fundamental shift in the New State's colonial policy became evident. By the beginning of 1962, a radically different colonial policy, involving a greater role for foreign capital, full-scale development plans, the foment of colonial-specific production and a large increase in the settler population, had begun to be implemented. This shift has been explained away as 'late colonialism', the reaction of a dying regime to the internal anti-colonial challenge, attempting, in vain, to postpone the inevitable. Because greater development of the colonies began in the 1960s, this has been attributed to the events of February and March 1961 when the anti-colonial war in Angola is considered to have begun. In other words, the colonial development policies were part of a strategy by the Portuguese regime to appeal to the 'hearts and minds' of the population and crush the anti-colonial challenge. However, there are both economic and political reasons to claim that this cannot explain fully that late period of active colonial development in Angola.

Paradigm Shift in Portuguese Economic Policy

As Newitt has shown, the shifts in economic policy had already taken place by the mid-1950s.[25] These new directions were a reaction to the enhanced performance of the Portuguese economy itself which had begun to take off, and could not, therefore, have emerged as a reaction to the anti-colonial challenge of the early 1960s. Newitt argues that Portugal was entering a modern economic phase, with high industrial annual growth rates of 9 per cent in the mid-1960s and expanding international economic relations with Europe, the times were demanding a different approach to the economy, distinct from the self-sufficiency of the first Salazarist period. It was the needs of the expanding Portuguese economy, therefore, that spurred plans for a limited industrialisation of the colonies. The anti-colonial challenge in Angola later emphasised the need for change and reinforced this underlying tendency.

On the other hand, the New State was already under strong domestic political pressure to change before the Angolan uprising in 1961. Opposition forces in Portugal, effectively quelled during most of Salazar's rule, began to exploit the limited relaxation of authority surrounding the 1958 presidential campaign, expressing both their number and passion. Running against Salazar's candidate was General Humberto Delgado, himself a product of the regime, but who had collected around him a circle of broad support which cut across the political spectrum, from communists to monarchists. Inevitably, Delgado was not elected but his bid for power demonstrated to Salazar that the regime was not unassailable.

Increasingly, the call for political modernisation was heard. At the end of January 196), the hijacking of the ocean liner *Santa Maria* by an anti-Salazarist, Captain Henrique Galvao, attracted world attention and turned the spotlight not only on the authoritarian regime in Lisbon but also on Portuguese colonialism in Africa.[26] Also in that year, Salazar was threatened from within the regime when senior military figures, allegedly with support from the elite and the US Embassy in Lisbon, attempted to have him removed.[27] While unsuccessful, these incidents reveal the extent of both internal and external pressure to which the New State was increasingly submitted.

Implications of Angola Revolt on Portuguese Establishment

The anti-colonial revolt in Angola intensified the challenge to Salazar's authority. But, Newitt argues, it may also have, paradoxically, given the regime a reprieve. The February 1961 attacks in Luanda, followed by the March violence in the Northern coffee-growing areas, marked the start of the war for independence in Angola.[28] These incidents, followed as they were by a military clamp-down and a long period of eclipse for the movements, may actually have prolonged the life of the regime for another 13 years. They allowed the New State, 'with the perverseness with which cause and effect sometimes appear to operate',[29] to overcome the political threats from within Portugal itself.

The wars of independence in the colonies (beginning in Guinea-Bissau and Mozambique in 1963 and 1964 respectively) became a crusade for Salazar that may have salvaged his tottering regime and led the Portuguese to rally around a nationalistic cause. A jingoistic campaign to defend the colonies may have come at the right time to help postpone the downfall of the regime, announced at the end of the 1950s. Beyond performing an important ideological function in the definition of nation for the regime, the colonies may also have played a significant political role in maintaining the authority and control of the state in the metropolis.

Of course, there is little evidence that Salazar's early withdrawal from power would have necessarily led to the democratic (and anti-colonial) reform of the New State. In fact, as the ailing of Salazar in 1968 showed, the perpetuation of the regime was in-built, and when Marcel to Caetano took the reins of government, no change to the colonial status of Angola and the other territories was envisaged.

So, while the underlying economic shifts should be recognised as well as the political pressures within Portuguese society, it is impossible to avoid attributing a major part of the responsibility for the increased pace of colonial development in the 1960s to the nationalist revolts of 1961 in Angola. As Heimer has put it, the period of 'late colonialism' in Angola:

> ... was originally economic in nature, but became predominantly political within the framework of a colonial 'counter-insurgency strategy'.[30]

The New State found itself increasingly under international pressure. During the 1960s, the intransigent Portuguese colonial empire stuck out in a pro-decolonisation international environment. Despite this notoriety, at no time did the Portuguese regime ever publicly consider or assume the future possibility of decolonisation. Even when faced with *faites accomplis,* Lisbon was unwilling to accept any changes to this world-view. When it became clear that Portugal would not voluntarily renounce its colonial concerns, some newly independent states began to take matters into their own hands.

In 1960, Dahomey demanded that Lisbon give up its sovereignty over the fort on the former's coastline at Sao Joao de Ajuda. It was clear that Portugal could not maintain effective control there, and yet the Portuguese government ignored all calls for a formal hand-over. The Portuguese governor did finally, if reluctantly, return to Portugal but only after having spitefully set fire to the fort.

In India, Portugal had the administration of Goa and two enclaves.[31] On 18 December 1961, and after a tense diplomatic confrontation with Portugal, Nehru sent 45,000 troops and 26,000 reservists into Goa against 4,000 poorly-armed Portuguese forces. Twenty-four hours later, and despite Salazar's appeal for martyrdom from the defending forces,[32] the conflict was over. However, he never accepted the loss of Goa, always considering it temporarily occupied. A so-called representative for that territory continued to sit in the National Assembly in Lisbon long after it was seized by India.

Colonial policy under Salazar and his successor, Caetano, consisted, in its most basic characterisation, of maintaining the integrity of Portugal's overseas possessions, while all around them others were losing their own. This apparently anachronistic stance was determined by the importance that Angola, in particular, and the Portuguese empire, in general, played in supporting the authoritarian regime established by Salazar. Whereas other colonial powers were, in general, able to withdraw from their dominions without suffering major internal costs, the Salazarist regime, as a result of its political and economic dependence on the colonies, could not have decolonised on the one hand and survived in Portugal on the other. For this regime then, basic colonial policy was always the defence of sovereignty, if necessary to the very end. The loss of the colonies would have signified the end of the New State.

This intransigence and inability to accept change must be emphasised as it reflects the structural relationship that existed between the Portuguese regime and its colonial possessions. Salazar believed, perhaps with good reason, that once the principle of decolonisation was accepted by Portugal anywhere, for example in the case of Goa, the consequences for the other colonies, as well as for the authority of the New State at home, would have been overwhelming. The regime was built partly on the economic and political pillars of colonial rule and its very authority based on a mythical idea of empire. It was, therefore, inevitable that it would reject the nationalist urge for change and self-determination in Angola and the other colonies. When faced with this intransigent colonial state, the Angolan nationalists could only consider and eventually adopt a violent expression of anti-colonialism. And as will be shown later, this limitation of political choices to guerrilla warfare had a profound radicalising effect on the organisation and nature of the nationalist movements.

Economy of Colonial Angola

Colonial Angola played an important economic role for Salazar's regime. The economic relationship between Portugal and Angola was, in many ways, central to the New States' own economy. This was especially the case during the early period of Salazarist rule that preceded the onset of what has been called 'late colonialism'. During this time, the Angolan economy functioned mainly as, on the one hand, an exporter of agricultural and mineral raw materials[33] and, on the other, a market for Portuguese products.

Angolan importers were actively encouraged to purchase manufactured goods from Portugal, while exporters were enticed into selling to the- metropolis by prices that were fixed by the government generally above the average on the world market, as well as by other incentives such as tax rebates (50 to 60 per cent) on sales to Portugal. Colonial exchange funds were created to support Angolan purchases of metropolitan goods. The foreign exchange revenue of local exporters was sunk into this fund and emerged as Portuguese escudos, good only for purchases in the metropolis.

This commercial relationship, somewhat typical of that between colonies and their metropolitan rulers (i.e. characterised by the unequal exchange of raw materials for manufactured goods), had as a priority the specific needs of Portugal's domestic economy. The regime used exchange fund restrictions and fixed pricing, as well as obligatory production and purchase quotas to orchestrate this system in accordance with domestic needs, accommodating wherever necessary Portuguese metropolitan industrial and other economic interests.[34]

While providing a captive market for Portuguese products, Angola supplied raw materials at beneficial prices to a number of industries, which helped to spur growth in the metropolitan economy. These industries would then offer their finished products for sale to the colonies. A case in point was the post-war revival of the metropolitan textile manufacturers. Using cheap raw cotton imported from their African possessions, Portuguese textile firms would spin fabrics and clothing which would then be resold back to the colonies.[35] As with other exchanges involving raw materials on the one hand and manufactured products on the other, this trade did not distribute benefits equally among the producers of the primary products and the manufacturers.

The comparative profit levels of Angolan cotton producers and Portuguese textile manufacturers can be seen in the following figures for the period between 1939 and 1949: profits of colonial raw cotton purchased by the metropolis rose by 61 per cent; profits of metropolitan cotton textiles sold in the colonies rose by 224 per cent.[36]

Even more dependent on sales to the colonies were the wine producers in Portugal. As commercial activity with Brazil was replaced by trade with Portugal's African possessions, the revenue of wine sales to Brazil also fell drastically, threatening to bankrupt the Portuguese viniculturalists. With the help of the government, however, they managed to establish the colonies as exclusive markets for Portuguese wines, inviolable even to local wine producers. The result was a very sizeable export market which helped to support domestic wine production. In 1960, Angola took 53 per cent of all Portugal's exports of wine.[37]

According to one source, the export of primary commodities in 1957 accounted for 71.1 per cent of Angola's total exports.[38] This ratio can be seen in the official figures given in Table 1.

Table 1 shows that nearly two-thirds of Angolan exports were of an agricultural or vegetable origin, making the economy significantly dependent on the fluctuations of world commodity prices. In 1966, the primacy of raw materials in Angolan exports was still maintained as Table 2 shows in greater detail.

Although, the sale of these goods to Portugal was an important part of the latter's supplies of raw materials, it was only a proportion of total Angolan exports. During the early 1960s, only around 20 per cent of Angolan exports were to Portugal.[39] However, regardless of their final destination, the sale of Angolan exports was a major revenue earner for Portugal. In 1957, according to one source, Angolan exports accounted for nearly 40 per cent of Portugal's total foreign sales.[40]

During this period of the New State's colonial rule, local industry in Angola had little opportunity to get off the ground. Attempts to establish a cotton mill in Angola were bitterly resisted by metropolitan competitors until 1943.[41] Only those industries that had dominant positions in domestic Portuguese markets would venture into colonial manufacturing. When domestic capital was unavailable (or insufficient), or where technology was inadequate, the largest investments were held by foreign interests, despite a legal stipulation that half an enterprise's capital be of

Portuguese origin. The Benguela Railway and Diamang, the diamond extraction giant, were the largest examples of this period.

TABLE 1

Value of total Angolan exports by origin, 1961 and 1962 (million escudos)

	1961		1962	
Product Sector	Value	%	Value	
Agricultural or vegetable origin	2,285	59	2,802	65.7
Industrial products of agricultural origin	243	6.3	223	5.2
Mineral extraction	882	22.8	761	17.9
Fishery products	289	7.4	235	5.5
Animal husbandry	57	1.5	51	1.2
Various	117	3.0	192	4.5

Source: *Situacao Economica de Angola no am de 1962* [1963], p. 12. Number of Esc$ to US$ between 1950 and 1970, roughly 29 (G. Clarence-Smith, *The Third Portuguese Empire: Study in Economic Imperialism,* Manchester University Press, 1985, Annex 2, p. 228).

TABLE 2

Main Angolan export commodities, 1966 (million US$)

Product	Value	Percentage of total
Coffee	107.2	48.1
Diamonds	39.4	17.6
Fish products	14.1	5.8
Sisal	10.5	4.7
Iron ore	4.7	2.0
Timber	4.3	2.0
Maize	4.1	2.0
Cotton fibre	3.7	1.7
Other	34.8	16.1
Total	222.8	100

Source: F. Brandenburg, 'Development, Finance and Trade', in D.M. Abshire and M.A. Samuels (eds), *Portuguese Africa: A Handbook* (London: Pall Mall Press, 1969) p. 241.

Despite strict controls on the entry of foreign capital, and Salazar's seemingly personal aversion to its promotion, the regime made sure, however, that these and other large enterprises remained happy in the colonies, allowing the repatriation of their profits without too much bother. Furthermore, these and other major ventures were exempt from contributions to the colonial exchange fund.

To sum up, the early period of Salazarist colonial rule of the Angolan economy had the following characteristics: Angolan production and export of raw materials was primarily subjugated to metropolitan industrial and consumer needs; at the same time, Angola also provided a significant proportion of Portugal's foreign exchange earnings.

Portuguese colonial rule had vast formative effects on the economic structure of Angola. During almost fifty years of the New State, Portugal imposed, extended and developed a network of economic relationships which went to great extremes in restructuring the economic, and consequently social, character of indigenous Angolan societies.

In very general terms, the effects of colonialism on Angolan society were instrumental in establishing certain economic production regimes which were inherently distinct from those of traditional societies. The introduction of wage-earning and of cash-crop production radically changed the rural subsistence lifestyle of the great majority of the population. From very early on, certain indigenous groups in Angola had established economic relationships with the Portuguese through trading, especially in slaves. By the twentieth century, however, economic interaction between the Portuguese and indigenous societies had surpassed its early commercial nature.

The cultivation of cotton was an example of the radical change colonialism brought to the rural hinterland. An exploitative system of contract farming was imposed wherein the growth of anything but cotton was prohibited, and the sale of all produce dictated and determined by the Portuguese dealers. This cotton growing system was in force in the Baixa do Cassanje area where a violent anti-colonial disturbance erupted in 1960. The cotton revolt did not appear to be organised nor politically motivated, seeming instead to be a reaction to the extreme conditions of poverty resulting from the effects of that cash-crop economy. In March 1961, similar sentiments of revolt were expressed during widespread violence against settlers in the north. The imposition of contract labour on the indigenous population for the cultivation of cash crops, changed the basic economic structures of many areas. Independent African farmers were cultivating crops beyond subsistence levels in order to sell the extra harvest to the Portuguese, while others were contracted, forcibly or otherwise, as wage labour.

These characteristics of the Angolan economy remained in place until after the end of the Second World War. After this, the Angolan economy exploded into growth, partly as a result of the increased cultivation of one single commodity: coffee. According to Paige:

> ... the modern economic history of Angola did not begin until the rise of the coffee economy in the 1950s... [that] radically changed the internal economy of Angola, altered its relationship with the metropolitan and world economies... [and] converted the colony into a mono-cultural export economy.[42]

The dominant role played by coffee in Angolan exports by 1966 can be seen in Table 2, accounting for nearly half of the total value of sales abroad. Between the early 1950s and the early 1960s, Angola experienced a coffee boom, the effects of which laid down the new bases for economic and social development experienced under the period of late colonialism.

The neutrality maintained by Portugal throughout the Second World War was a profitable one. With its production and distribution capabilities undisturbed, Portugal continued to supply the world market with raw materials from its colonies at the far higher prices which prevailed during the war. The global shortages of raw materials çontinued into the period of the Korean War, which helped to sustain a period of generally high commodity prices. Consequently, the value of Angolan sales of coffee, one of the most important commodities in world trade after crude petroleum and grains, multiplied dramatically. Increased revenues from coffee plantations soon attracted metropolitan cultivators wanting to make their fortune, while existing African and European production was vastly expanded with the increased profits. The result was a rocketing of production, quadrupling harvests in the space of 15 years, making Angola by 1967 the third or fourth largest supplier of coffee in the world.[43] Table 3 shows the expansion of Angolan coffee exports between 1948 and 1970. The steep rise in price between 1948 and 1952 more than doubled the value of the coffee sold abroad, despite the fact that less was sold during that period. The high prices continued until about the end of decade, when they collapsed worldwide. But, the effect of a decade of high prices led to an increase in Angolan coffee production which eventually became noticeable in the increased export tonnages of the 1960s.

According to van Dongen, coffee production in Angola jumped from under 50,000 tonnes in 1948 to over 200,000 tonnes a year by 1965.[44] This increased production of coffee brought a dramatic change to Angola, especially in its northern regions. Taking the province of Uige as an example, Paige calculated that over 75 per cent of the indigenous male working population in 1958 was involved in the production of coffee.[45] The cultivation of coffee is highly labour-intensive, and the boom brought even more of the population into the cash-crop and wage-earning agricultural economy of the colony.

In 1941, African producers accounted for nearly 40 per cent of all coffee producers. By 1958, the expansion of massive European estates, the largest of which employed over 11,000 workers, had reduced the proportion of indigenous producers to 26 per cent.[46]

TABLE 3

Coffee exports from Angola, 1948-70

Year	Value (million Esc$)	Weight (000 tonnes)	Price (Esc$ per kiln)	Percentage of agric. exports	Percentage of total exports
1948	459.8	53.4	8.6	39.6	30.9
1952	1,137.6	47.7	23.8	52.3	41.3
1955	1,275.6	60.1	21.2	62.8	45.5
1958	1,539.4	79.6	19.3	67.5	41.7
1961	1,398.5	118.1	11.8	57.5	36.1
1964	2,859.1	138.7	20.6	71.8	48.7
1967	3,546.8	196.5	18.0	88.3	51.9
1970	3,880.0	180.6	21.5	61.0	31.9

Source: J. Paige, *Agrarian Revolution* (New York: Free Press), p. 227.

One of the effects of this new production regime was to bring undue stress to ethnic divisions among the indigenous population. The high demand for labour to work in the coffee estates was often met by contracting Ovimbundu workers from the south and centre of the country. However, there was a history of intercommunal friction between the northern peoples, of a Bakongo or Mbundu background, and the Ovimbundu. In March 1961, during the outbreak of anti-colonial violence in the north, a number of sources have noted that, as well as European settlers, Ovimbundu contract workers were also victimised by the Bakongo who revolted. The latter considered that the Ovimbundu profited from and defended colonialism.[47] The rival anti-colonial movements that competed for power in Angola emerged from these ethnic groups. While it is difficult to identify fully the nature of the inter-ethnic facet of the anti-colonial violence of March 1961, it can be claimed, however, that the new coffee production regime resulting from the boom of the 1950s and 1960s artificially intensified the economic and social relationship between those different ethnic groups.

At the same time, as Angola was experiencing a coffee-led boom, Portugal itself was beginning to take a relatively faster track towards industrial development. The war profits, expanded colonial trade and more dynamic development plans had all led to a certain amount of growth by the end of the 1950s. But, it was the burgeoning trade with Europe that provided the basis for this economic drive. The increased economic dynamism provided, in turn, large amounts of investment capital that began to look for opportunities in Africa, and Angola in particular. It was at this time, during the mid-1950s, that the regime began to alter its policies and usher in a new direction in colonial development.

Large conglomerates of Portuguese capital were in a position to provide investment capital to finance such a change in economic direction. In the long term, the colonial economy was to move from primary production to industrial development based on import substitution. Theoretically, this transformation was to be achieved by financial support from mainly Portuguese capital sources. State and private capital began to pour into Angola, framed by the ever-present hand of the regime in the form of two five-year plans which ran between 1953-58 and 1959-64. These were the beginnings of the final period of colonial rule under the New State.

During late colonialism, a basic reversal of the regime's previous colonial policies occurred. Angola became less and less a subsidiary of the metropolitan economy. From there on, the separate industrial development of the Angolan economy, eventually more widely penetrated by foreign capital,[48] was pursued. The Angolan economy was no longer determined primarily by Portugal's necessities but seemed to be following its own path of development, in both the public and the private sectors. The State financed the development of infrastructures such as roads,[49] port facilities[50] and hydroelectric projects to supply cheap energy.[51]

Public investment was complemented by the larger corporate conglomerates in Portugal. The opportunities in diversifying, vertical integration, relocation and in supporting this new process of industrialisation were looked upon kindly by leading industrialists. With a view to encouraging the major financial-industrial groups to invest in Angola, the State allowed certain firms to hold privileged, and many times monopolistic, positions in both the colonial and metropolitan economies.

In general terms, the period of late colonialism from the late 1950s to the early 1970s witnessed a very significant increase in the economic activity of Angola as it attracted greater and greater levels of investment. At the same time, however, Angola was in economic terms becoming less important to Portugal. Increased trade with Europe and the ever-burgeoning remittances of Portuguese emigrants abroad relegated colonial trade to a relatively less important role in the Portuguese balance of payments. On the one hand, a significant strategy of colonial development, comparable to those of other colonial powers,[52] was being implemented in Angola, markedly transforming production regimes and their social frameworks, and linking the Angolan economy more emphatically with diverse markets. But, on the other hand, the colonies themselves became, while more profitable, actually less economically necessary for Portugal and its own expanding economy.

Colonial Society

The proclaimed basis for Portugal's civilising mission of creating a multi-racial society in Africa was broadly similar to French attempts at assimilation in their own territories. Rather than placing a time limit on colonial tutelage as the British did eventually, this stance envisaged an infinite imperial existence for mainland Portugal and its overseas provinces. In 1933, the Portuguese colonial minister stated:

> We don't believe that a rapid passage from their African superstitions to our civilisation is possible. For us to have arrived where we are presently, hundreds of generations before us fought, suffered and learned, minute by minute, the most intimate secrets in the fountain of life. It is impossible for them to traverse this distance of centuries in a single jump.[53]

Officially, the Portuguese 'nation' was made up of all peoples under its sovereignty. However, the colonial policy behind this multi-cultural fantasy may have had the unintended effect of creating some of the very conditions under which Portuguese sovereignty could subsequently be challenged. Despite its ethnically divisive nature, Portugal's colonial policy in Angola produced an indigenous class that came to both accept and expect the economic and social rewards of joining the central society at the heart of the colonial regime.[54]

Furthermore, this class also began the process of defining a collective idea of a wider Angolan national identity beyond that of their own ethnic origin. Finally, this process of assimilation contributed to the creation of an intellectual class that was able to interpret and express this latent nationalism and eventually direct it against colonial rule.

The process of assimilation as envisaged by the Portuguese regime was fundamentally aimed at the 'lusofication' of the indigenous population, that is, 'making' them Portuguese. According to the official ideology of the regime, the empire (or, as it had become, Portugal and its overseas provinces) was to be inhabited by a Portuguese population that was defined culturally rather than racially. This policy had a political rationale: to ensure the survival of the New State by defending the possession of overseas territories. By declaring the colonies to be an organic part of the 'nation', the regime believed they were inseparable from the mainland metropolis.

To the heroic image of the timeless Portuguese voyager as the modern colonizer and the definition of Portuguese nationality as not being that of race or territory but as existing on a spiritual plane somewhere between the ends of the earth and heaven itself, another illusion was added and perpetuated by the New State and its apologists. An even more ephemeral quality, that of non-racism, was attributed to the Portuguese. This alleged characteristic of the Portuguese people was based on the development of a fanciful theory called lusotropicalism, wherein a historically unique absence of racism in the Portuguese was declared:[55]

> ... if one day the Lusotropicology here suggested is developed into a science, one of its main objects of study will be this process of the surpassing of the ethnic condition by the cultural, by virtue of which the blackest of blacks of tropical Africa is considered Portuguese without having to renounce any of his dearest habits of an ecologically tropical man.[56]

Portugal's Policy of Assimilation

In 1954, a statute was adopted defining the rights of indigenous colonial populations based on the pursuit of a cultural assimilation policy. In Angola, offspring of mixed African and European parentage, *mesticos,* could expect citizenry immediately, but the remainder of the indigenous population had to prove themselves deserving of the status. The basic requirements were the ability to read and write, to have paid employment and no criminal record. Even if these conditions were met by any prospective candidate, *civilizado* status was ultimately only endowed if the vaguely defined qualities of Portuguese civilisation were present, making the process of assimilation in Angola largely arbitrary.[57]

Furthermore, the prerequisites to obtaining full rights before the law were absurd when considering the social reality of Portugal where the official rate of illiteracy in 1950 was 40 per cent of the population. Demanding that an African read and write, have the means to support himself and his family and sport an impeccable civil record before he could even be considered for 'civilised' status was farcical when illiterate and unemployed Portuguese with criminal records could move freely about the colony. Even leaving this stark contradiction aside for the moment, this process of assimilation in Angola fell far short of the regime's vision of a multi-cultural society.

The colonial ideologues of the New State sought to utilise the policy of assimilation to further justify the unique character of Portuguese colonialism which they felt should have been considered in a different light than that of its European counterparts. Through this policy, the Portuguese regime affirmed their view of colonial society, not officially defined in racial terms but in equally discriminating cultural ones.

TABLE 4

Angolan population by race and 'civilised' status, 1950

Race	Total Population	Total 'civilised'	Per cent 'civilised'	Per cent 'civilised' in 1940
African	4,036,689	30,089	0.7	0.7
'Mestico'	29,648	26,335	88.8	82.9
White	78,826	78,826	100	100

Source. G. Bender, *Angola under the Portuguese: The Myth and the Reality* (London: Heinemann, 1978c) p. 151.

Despite the attractions of holding Portuguese citizenship, however, not many ventured forth to apply for such a privileged status. In 1950, out of a total number of over 4 million Africans, only 30,089 (including dependents) were registered as *civilizados.* One reason for this low number may have been the desire to avoid taxation, one of the perquisites gained by the newly civilised.[58]

In 1961, Portuguese law was changed and this paternalistic policy of assimilation was dropped in favour of a blanket declaration of citizenship. It is difficult, therefore, to assess the overall impact of this process. However, the very low percentage

TABLE 5

Racial composition of Angolan population, 1777-1970

Year	White		Mestico		Black		Total	
	No.	%	No.	%	No.	%	N0.	%
1777	1,581	–	4,043	–	–	–	–	–
1845	1,832	0.03	5,770	0.10	5,378,923	99.9	5,386,525	100
1900	9,198	0.20	3,112	0.06	4,777.636	99.7	4,789,946	100
1920	20,700	0.48	7,500	0.18	4,250,000	99.3	4,278,000	100
1940	44,083	1.20	28,035	0.75	3,665,829	98.1	3,737,947	100
1950	78,826	1.90	29,648	0.72	4,036,687	97.4	4,145,161	100
1960	172,529	3.60	53,392	1.10	4,604,362	95.3	4,830,283	100
1970	290,000	5.10	–	–	–	–	5,673,046	100

Source: G. Bender, Angola under the Portuguese: The Myth and the Reality (London: Heinemann, 1978c) p. 20.

of 'civilised' African population in 1940, which remained the same in 1950 (Table 4), indicates that Angolan society was not exactly on the way to becoming the multi-racial ideal dreamed up by the apologists of lusotropicalism. For the great majority of the Angolan indigenous population, the privileges of colonialism were unknown.

Within the *mestico* population, however, a sense of participation in and belonging to central colonial society, however limited, did develop. The figures in Table 4 show that the regime's policy of assimilation, contrary to its multi-racial aims, led to a divided colonial population by driving a discriminatory wedge between traditional African communities and those who were allowed to join central society.

One of the characteristics of the rivalry that emerged between the two main Angolan anti-colonial movements, the MPLA and the FNLA, was a hostility between, on the one hand, *mesticos* and *assimilados*[59] and, on the other, Africans who had not been co-opted by colonial society. Privileged status also brought access to education which divided Angolans even further. This is how the FNLA saw the MPLA in 1962:

> [The MPLA]... especially recruited their members from the Angolan population classed as 'civilised' by the colonial regime; i.e. the half-castes and the *assimilados*... But, they never got very far in [the regions outside urban centres]. Their lack of support was principally due to the privileged position granted to the half-castes and the *assimilados* by the colonialists (education, exemption from forced labour, official recognition of property ownership and of liberal professions, existing civil rights, and a standard of living far superior to that of the exploited peasant mass). This ordinance [granting these privileges] dug a social and psychological trench between them and the oppressed peasant mass.[60]

Critical references to the cultural background of the MPLA's leaders seem to betray a sense of inferiority on the part of the FNLA. Portuguese colonial policy, therefore, served to divide a small elite of Angolans from the majority, a schism that subsequently emerged in Angolan politics and, in particular, in the rivalry between the MPLA and the FNLA. The leader of the third major Angolan anti-colonial movement, Jonas Savimbi, also revealed the importance of this racial issue when he referred to the domination of the MPLA by *mesticos:*

> It may sound like racialism, and it is certainly not the way we feel today because we have learned a lot. But, it is a fact that it was very difficult at that time for blacks to understand why *mesticos* should be leading a liberation movement to fight the Portuguese. It was not clear to us that *mesticos* were suffering in Angola; they were privileged people.[61]

The racial composition of the population of Angola did not alter significantly until the last two decades of colonial domination. As Table 4 shows, no more than a negligible percentage of the African population ever achieved the *assimilado* status and gained access to central colonial society. This signifies, if we consider the figures for 1960 in Table 5, that before the period of late colonialism, no more than 5 per cent of the Angolan population was ever able to obtain direct access to the privileges of colonialism. Until the early 1960s, over 95 per cent of the Angolan population remained outside the hub of colonial life.

In the period of 'late colonialism', however, Angola experienced an explosion of economic development and social reform, such as the abolition of different racial statutes and the extensive development of health and educational services available to African populations. This altered the picture shown above. The growth of the Angolan economy had transformed its requirements. The new industries now needed a semi-skilled, semi-urban mobile workforce. Initially, this new labour force was drawn from the African population, and education, social services and benefits, training, etc., became available to a number of a growing African bourgeoisie. According to a survey carried out by Heimer in 1970, 74 per cent of Luanda slum children aged 6 to 12 were attending or had attended school.[62]

These centripetal economic forces drew more and more Africans into urban colonial society and began to create a semi-industrial class where a traditional tribal identity was supplemented with a wider sense of community. The 1950s had seen the nationalist challenge grow in the British and French colonies. The emergence of forces of self-determination in neighbouring colonies was not lost on an increasingly aware Angolan bourgeoisie. As the economy provided more benefits and a place in urban colonial life, a sense of Angolan nationality began to emerge without, however, the total dissolution of tribal and racial identification. According to Heimer:

> ... it is not much of an exaggeration to say that only by the beginning of the seventies had one all-encompassing, though still very loose and highly heterogeneous, Angolan social formation been brought into existence. One of the ideological consequences was that, for the first time, important numbers of Africans in the central society (and not just small segments) had begun to think of themselves as Angolans instead of, or, more frequently, as well as, members of a given ethnic group... And even in an increasing number of tribu-tary societies, a kind of a 'secondary identification' with Angola as a whole had begun to take place.[63]

The consolidation of a national identity was, therefore, partly rooted in the formative influence of colonial society as well as in the nationalist anti-colonial challenge. But, 'late colonialism' did not prevent the challenge to the colonial regime. By the time the Angolan movements had been organised in the early 1960s, they and their leaders already had a basic political character of anti-colonial resistance which had been formed in the 1940s and 1950s. The final period of colonial development came too late to alter this response.

The post-war coffee boom in Angola and the growth of the economy did introduce a new factor to this period. While the need for more labour was initially met by the African population, the New State's industrialisation programme for Angola included plans to significantly increase white immigration to the colony. To the ideologues of the regime, the settlers represented a second wave of discoverers and navigators, who braved the unfriendly seas (in this case the international tide against colonialism) to live and work in the tropics, once more emphasising the unique Portuguese way in the world. To the industrialists they represented a workforce, much needed as the Angolan economy expanded. To the colonial developers they represented a settler class ready to spread out over Angola, to continue the unfinished job of 'pacification'. Despite considerable expense,[64] Lisbon considered the immigration a success, at least quantitatively (see Table 6).

The effects of this increased immigration, however, did not live up to expectations. The great majority of this immigrant population had a very low level of education and training. In the period between 1965 and 1972, over 55 per cent of Portuguese emigrants to Angola over the age of 7 had zero years of education.[65] Furthermore, only a few chose to settle in rural areas and attempted agricultural activities. Most had wanted to escape that same life in Portugal and chose instead to settle in the cities and towns. The result was the flooding of the lower end of the urban job market by a workforce with little or no skills. However, the market was racially weighted in their favour.

Despite claims of impartiality, it was difficult to see an employer picking an African over a European for most jobs. Despite the availability of opportunities for trained Africans, the predominance of uneducated whites at the lower end of the market began to threaten the newly promised lifestyle opportunities of the African urban population.

From 1961, there were also increased attempts at establishing multiracial settlements in Angola by directing emigrants from Portugal and Cape Verde, usually of mixed extraction, into the rural hinterland. Bender has concluded that this policy was a failure:[66] from 1961 to 1968, the directed settlement programme cost over US$ 100 million and, out of the original number of settlers less than half remained at the end of this period. Those settlers who abandoned attempts to populate rural Angola, did not, however, leave the country. They moved to the cities and towns and, while basically unskilled and uneducated, added to the already crowded 'lower strata' competing with Africans for jobs and living space.

TABLE 6

White population in Angola, 1940-73

Year	Total
1940	44,083
1950	78,826
1960	172,529
1970	290,000
1973	335,000

Source: M. Newitt, Portugal in Africa: The Last Hundred Years (London: C. Hurst, 1981) p. 164.

According to Heimer, this process had a far-reaching effect as the denial or displacement of privileges anticipated under 'late colonialism' may well have proved to be a fertile ground for gathering support for the emerging anti-colonial challenge:

> The petty bourgeoisie was primarily motivated [to protest] by its frustration over a *manque a gagner* - an economic 'upward mobility' and an equality of social treatment it aspired to, but which it was denied by a racial barrier reinforced by the ongoing immigration of 'poor whites'.[67]

Furthermore, the majority of poor whites, perhaps as a result of the competitive job market, tended to wield their racial power to ensure that African challenges to the colonial regime were put down. This was the case in 1961, and on subsequent occasions, when reactionary groups of white vigilantes would carry out terror raids of the slums in Luanda, or when groups of farmers carried out revenge attacks in the north after the March attacks by the FNLA. With a few exceptions, most white sympathizers of Angolan self-determination tended to be of an educated background. But, over 83 per cent of white immigration to Angola in the period between 1965 and 1972 had had less than four years of education.[68] This source of anti-African nationalism emerged again and again in the capital, Luanda, even after the New State had been toppled in 1974. In July of that year, over a hundred people were allegedly killed in white-black violence.

The Angolan experience of the colonial policy of assimilation seems to have had two major aspects related to the emergence of the political conflict between the anti-colonial movements that led to the civil war in 1975. First, the process of 'civilisation' created a tiered society in which the privileged centre was separated from and resented by those who remained outside. This segregation of privilege tended to be identified in racial terms. *Mesticos* and educated Angolans were the object of scorn on the part of other Africans. This division was a facet of the MPLA-FNLA rivalry. Second, the assimilation policy helped to create in the privileged centre not only an acute sense of national identity, as will be shown later, but also the enhanced expectation of material and political benefits. The frustration of those expectations by the white society and by an intransigent regime in Lisbon helped to feed an already growing sense of nationalism and anti-colonialism in Angola.

NOTES AND REFERENCES

1. The British issued an ultimatum to Portugal in January 1890, which forced Lisbon to desist from its dreams of establishing a trans-African empire, linking Angola to Mozambique, one that would have conflicted with Rhodes' own dream of 'British dominion from the Cape to Cairo'.
2. The Great Powers were deftly played off each other. For example, Portugal managed to fight off Bismarck Germany's claims on its territories by enlisting the support of the French, who in turn

sought to contain German expansion. Similarly, the British could be counted on in disputes with either the French or the Germans. By appealing to British interests, Lisbon also managed to ward off Boer designs on the Louren9o Marques (now Maputo) port. This small-state diplomacy was no easy task for the Portuguese governments, which faced at all times the threat of financial collapse. A default on international payments would have delivered the colonies to the Great Powers on a platter.

3. A.H. de Oliveira Marques, *History of Portugal Volume 11: From Empire to Corporate State* (New York and London: Columbia University Press, 1972) p. 111.
4. A.H. de Oliveira Marques, *ibid.*
5. Colonial reformers such as Mouzinho de Albuquerque and Ant6nio Enes emphasised that colonial policy should focus on decentralisation, development and autonomy. M. Newitt, *Portugal in Africa: The Last Hundred Years* (London: C. Hurst, 1981) p. 177.
6. G. Clarence-Smith, *The Third Portuguese Empire 1825-1975: Study in Economic Imperialism* (Manchester: Manchester University Press, 1985) p. 12.
7. Norton de Matos was twice the highest ranking Portuguese governing official in Angola: in 1912-15 as Governor and in 1921-23 as High Commissioner.
8. G. Clarence-Smith, *op. cit.* (1985), p. 116 and p. 120.
9. Between 1920 and 1928 there were 29 inaugurated heads of government, 15 of which were in a 12-month period between 1920 and 1921. See A.H. de Oliveira Marques, *Historia de Portugal, Vol. Ill: Das Revolucoes Liberals aos Nossos Dias* (Lisbon: Palas Editores, 1981) pp. 611-12.
10. The government investigated the possibility of securing a loan from the League of Nations. The conditions demanded by the League were that Portugal be submitted to international financial controls, implying that Portuguese Africa would be transferred to international control. See David M. Abshire, 'From the Scramble for Africa to the "New State"', in D.M. Abshire and M.A. Samuels

(eds), *Portuguese Africa: A Handbook* (London: Pall Mall Press, 1969) p. 85.

11. By 1931, Angola's accumulated debts amounted to Esc$ 300,000,000, the servicing of which consumed half of the territory's income. M. Newitt, *op. cit.* (1981), p. 178.
12. A.H. Oliveira Marques, *op. cit.* (1981), p. 371.
13. The *Estado Novo* was the name given to the regime established by Salazar in Portugal where it was in power between 1928 and 1974.
14. International Police for the Defence of the State *(Policia Internacional e de Defesa de Estado).* It was later transformed into the Security Directorate *(Direccao-Geral de Seguranca)* before the collapse of the Salazarist regime.
15. It is important to dispel any idea of the republican period of 1910-26 as an attempt to establish democracy. It too was a period of one-party rule: the Portuguese Republican Party, and later the Democratic Party. At one point, the latter was even considered by the armed forces as a potential ally in the dictatorship they were planning. The republicans systematically enforced their 'revolution' quashing any organised opposition, including by socialists and syndicalists, and unleashed a period of arbitrary state terror. See Vasco Pulido Valente, *O Poder e o Povo: A Revolucao de 1910* (Lisbon: Publicacoes Dom Quixote, 1974).
16. It is difficult to come up with a definition of fascism as a single doctrine but if we consider the Fascist state of Italy under Mussolini, there were certain similarities with the New State in Portugal. However, the extent of popular dissemination of the fascist movement in Italy was not replicated in Portugal. In a sense, there was instead a superficial engagement with certain aspects of fascist politics.
17. Freitas do Amaral argues that the New State was closer to the absolutism of the seventeenth or eighteenth centuries than the totalitarianism of the twentieth century; and Salazar, by his own admission, wanting to be the Prime Minister of an absolutist King. D. Freitas do Amaral, *O Antigo Regime e a Revolucao:*

Memorial Politicas (1941-1975) (Venda Nova: Bertrand/Nomen, 1995) p. 57.

18. According to Oliveira Marques, Salazar spoke against totalitarian regimes and criticised both the Italian Fascists and the German Nazis. In 1931, Salazar defined the goals of his regime as the establishment of a 'well-understood political, economic and social nationalism, controlled by the unquestionable sovereignty of the strong state'. A.H. de Oliveira Marques, *op. cit.,* (1972), p. 181.
19. M. Newitt, *op. cit.* (1981), p. 121.
20. J. Duffy, *Portuguese Africa* (Cambridge, Mass.: Harvard University Press, 1959) p. 269.
21. *O Mundo Portugues,* II (1935), p. 218, quoted in J. Duffy, *ibid.*, p. 276.
22. For the description of the colonial structure of authority in the 1950s J. Duffy, *op. cit.*, pp. 283-8.
23. A.H. de Oliveira Marques, *op. cit.* (1981), pp. 521-2.
24. The regime believed that this constitutional reform helped Portugal bypass its obligations under Article 73 of the UN Charter which required administering powers to submit information on their respective non-self-governing territories. By defining its territories as provinces, Lisbon considered that this article did not apply to Portugal and its colonies. At the end of 1956, Salazar replied to the Secretary-General of the United Nations that "Portugal did not administer territories which could be included in the category indicated in article 73.' J. Freire Antunes, *Kennedy e Salawr: O Leao e a Raposa* (Lisbon: Difusao Cultural, 1991), p. 39.
25. M. Newitt, *op. cit.* (1981), pp. 220-1.
26. The flamboyant Captain Galvao and a small force took control of the *Santa Maria* in the Caribbean and were lost at sea for a number of days. The liner was finally located by the US Air Force. Under the glare of the world press, Galvao declared the political status of his act and intimated that the ship might set sail for Angola. From there, he claimed, an anti-Salazarist challenge would be based. He said nothing about decolonisation, however.

The incident finally ended in surrender in Brazil and the *Santa Maria* was returned to Portugal.

27. The pro-American Defence Minister, General Botelho Moniz, planned a palace coup but was outmanoeuvred by Salazar. J. Freire Antunes, *op. cit.* (1991), p. 198.

28. *Ibid.*

29. M. Newitt, *op. cit.* (1981), p. 220.

30. F.W. Heimer, *The Decolonisation Conflict in Angola 1974-1976: An Essay in Political Sociology* (Geneva: Institute Universitaire de Hautes Etudes Internationales, 1979) p. 12.

31. Diu and Damao.

32. On 14 December 1961, Salazar sent the following cable to General Vassalo e Silva, commanding officer of the Portuguese forces in Goa: 'It is terrible to think that this may mean a total sacrifice, but yet I recommend and expect such a sacrifice as the only way to live up to our traditions and to best serve the future of the Nation. I see no possibility of truces nor of Portuguese prisoners, as there will be no surrendered ships since I feel that there can only be victorious or dead soldiers and sailors.' My translation. Quoted in J. Freire Antunes, *op. cit.* (1991), pp. 311-12.

33. Coffee, cotton, sisal, sugar, timber and maize; diamonds, iron, manganese, copper and ferro-mangancse.

34. For example, when sales of Angolan maize threatened to undercut metropolitan producers, the authorities enforced a strict sales quota and fixed a low price, hitting the Angolan producers hard. Consequently, sales of Angolan maize to Portugal, unlike other agricultural exports, fell dramatically. G. Clarence-Smith, *op. cit.* (1985), p. 148.

35. By 1960, over 90 per cent of cotton goods imported by Angola, Guinea-Bissau, Cape Verde and Sao Tome were of metropolitan origin. However, this represented only 30 per cent of manufactured cotton sales. G. Clarence-Smith, *ibid.*, p. 159.

36. *Ibid.*, p. 160.

37. *Ibid.*, p. 162.

38. A. Castro, *O Sistema Colonial Portugues em Africa* (Lisbon: Editorial Caminho, 1980) p. 164.

39. In 1962, the major proportion of Angolan sales were to the US (25.2 per cent) and to Europe (24.7 per cent to the EEC and 16.5 per cent to EFTA). *Situacao Economica de Angola no ano de 1962* (1963), p. 14.

40. In 1957, Portugal's exports totalled Esc$ 8,253,000,000 of which Esc$ 3,328,000,000 were of Angolan origin. A. Castro, *op. cit.* (1980), p. 165.

41. *Ibid.*, p. 164.

42. J. Paige, *Agrarian Revolution* (New York: Free Press, 1975) pp. 212, 226, 227.

43. I.S. van Dongen, 'Agriculture and other primary production', in D.M. Abshire and M.A. Samuels, *op. cit.* (1969), p. 255. Van Dongen placed Angolan coffee's share of the world market in 1967 at 6.1 per cent, just behind the Ivory Coast which, at 8.1 per cent, was the largest African producer.

44. I.S. van Dongen, *op. cit.* (1969), p. 255.

45. J. Paige, *op. cit.* (1975), p. 247.

46. *Ibid.*, pp. 228, 230.

47. D.L. Wheeler and R. Pelissier, *Angola* (London: Pall Mall Press, 1971) pp. 178, 182; J. Paige, *op. cit.* (1975), pp. 249-50.

48. Restrictions on foreign capital were lifted in 1965.

49. Paved roads increased from 250 miles in 1960 to 2,200 miles in 1967. P. Brandenburg, 'Transport systems and their external ramifications', in D.M. Abshire and M.A. Samuels, *op. cit.* (1969), p. 326.

50. The natural facilities and increased capacities at the ports of Lobito, Luanda and Mocamedes coped with increased international traffic, including minerals from the Katanga copper region of Zaire and Zambia. See F. Brandenburg, *ibid.*, pp. 321-2.

51. In 1965, the Portuguese and the South African governments reached an agreement on the expansion of the Cunene River project which sought to establish an Angolan-Southwest African power grid. D.M. Abshire, "Minerals, manufacturing, power and communications', in D.M. Abshire and M.A. Samuels, *op. cit.* (1969), p. 303.

52. Amounts apportioned to Mozambique were broadly comparable to those spent by other colonial powers during the same period:

	1953-58 £m	1959-64 £m
Mozambique	20	41
Uganda	16	30
Tanganyika	17	18

Source: M. Newitt, *op. cit.* (1981), p. 196.

53. Armindo Monteiro quoted in G. Bender, *Angola under the Portuguese: The Myth and the Reality* (London: Heinemann, 1978) p. 150.

54. This view of Angolan society has been usefully developed by F.W. Heimer. *op. cit.* (1979). Heimer calls the core European society *central.* This supported the colonial state and economy. Access to central society was limited and required the acceptance of colonial norms. Outside central society were the ethnically centralised *tributary* societies. Centred around traditional political and social hierarchies, these represented the 'uncivilised' legacy which Africans had to renounce to be considered Portuguese. Central society was fundamentally coastal, urban and industrially based, while tributary societies remained confined to the rural hinterland. Overlapping occurred when labour was sought or when cash crops were grown for sale to central society.

55. Lusotropicalism was derived from the socio-anthropological work undertaken in Brazil during the 1930s on miscegenation. For a critical view of lusotropicalism see Chapter One of G. Bender, *op. cit.* (1978c).

56. Gilberto Freyre, a Brazilian sociologist whose work was prominent in both Portugal and Brazil. Reproduced in R.H. Chilcote,

Emerging Nationalism in Portuguese Africa: Documents (Stanford, California: Hoover Institution Press, 1972), p. 19.

57. All inhabitants of Cape Verde, Macao and Goa had full Portuguese citizenry.

58. According to A.H. Oliveira Marques, thousands avoided *civilizado* status for this reason. See *op. cit.* (1981), p. 525.

59. Assimilated individuals declared citizens.

60. 'Glimpses of the Angolan Nationalist Organisations'. GRAE (FNLA) Press Release (Leopoldville, 11 December 1962). Reproduced in R.H. Chilcote, *op. cit.* (197-2), pp. 150-1.

61. F. Bridgland, *Jonas Savimbi: A Key to Africa* (London: Hodder & Stoughton, 1986) pp. 45-6.

62. F.W. Heimer, *op. cit.* (1979), p. 13.

63. *Ibid.*, p. 14.

64. The cost of transplanting a family from a village community in Portugal to Angola was placed at US$ 100,000. G. Clarence-Smith, *op. cit.* (1985), p. 177.

65. G. Bender, *op. cit.* (1978c), p. 230.

66. G. Bender, *ibid.*, pp. 107-31.

67. F.W. Heimer, *op. cit.* (1979), p. 20.

68. G. Bender, *op. cit.* (1978c), p. 230.

5

Genesis of Anti-Colonialism in Angola

It is important to recognise that the liberation movements are forming rather than expressing a national consciousness.[1] The Portuguese colonial regime in Angola went far and deep to determine the parameters within which modern Angolan politics have been carried out. The very concept of an Angolan nation-state land the imposition of economic and authority structures are a legacy of colonialism which shaped domestic political and social forces and set up conflicts between them. Yet, modern Angolan nationalism was riot a creation of colonialism. It emerged from the political choices made by different groups of people, in different parts of the country, for various reasons but with one single goal: to end Portuguese rule in Angola.

The intransigence of the Portuguese colonial regime in denying political expression and representation in Angola was partly behind the choices made by the three main movements, the MPLA, the FNLA and UNITA. The authoritarian nature of the New State! precluded the development of nationalist political parties along the lines of those that emerged elsewhere in Africa, Under such circumstances, the resort to clandestinity and, subsequently, guerrilla warfare as the form of challenging

Portuguese rule was inevitable. The repression of Angolan nationalism by colonial authorities, therefore, narrowed the options available to anti-colonialists for political expression.

In fact, colonial repression in Angola may have helped to define the radical political character of the anti-colonial movements. The ideological outlook of a nationalist movement may be influenced by the willingness of the colonial regime to accommodate the former's political agenda. To the British, it was apparent that intransigence to nationalist demands would result in a more radical anti-colonial challenge; Sir Andrew Cohen believed that successful co-operation with nationalism would be the best bulwark against communism in Africa. This dynamic was apparent when Algerian nationalists radicalised and resorted to an armed challenge after France showed itself unwilling to consider independence for that territory Conversely, nationalists in other parts of French Africa achieved independence organised in non-violent political parties.

In the case of Angola, the extreme option of resorting to armed force by the anti-colonial movements in the early 1960s may have had long-lasting effects to the point of determining the form of conflict taken in 1975 when civil war broke out among them. Had those movements been able to develop as non-violent political parties of mass appeal, the events of 1975 might well have been altogether different.

The Origins of Angolan Nationalism

Colonial authority in Angola emanated from a coastal administration that had been extended inland, mostly during the early twentieth century. The so-called 'pacification' of the colonies sought to secure and, therefore, claim their territorial integrity and Portuguese sovereignty, thereby meeting the 'standards' of imperialism established at the Congress of Berlin. As elsewhere, however, colonial boundaries cut across and included within them numerous ethno-linguistic groups and indigenous political communities which would otherwise not have considered themselves one single entity. Despite this fact, however, a current of Angolan nationalism did emerge out of these heterogeneous ethnic societies, upholding a common political goal of self-determination for Angola and its people as a whole.

While formed by the colonial experience, the national integrity of the Angolan state, both in territorial and demographic terms, was eventually accepted and promoted by all three anti-colonial movements. An MPLA programme, published in the early 1960s, stated that the '... sovereignty of the Angolan state will belong entirely and solely to the Angolan people, without distinction as to the ethnic origin, class, sex, age, political leanings, religious beliefs or philosophical convictions.'[2] The FNLA emerged from the Union of the Peoples of Angola (UPA),[3] whose motto was: 'For the national, territorial and social liberation of Angola'.[4] Finally, UNITA too framed its political identity and goals in a national idea of Angola. According to a later UNITA publication:

> The peculiar social situation of Angola calls for harmonious co-existence of all ethnic groups and races that are the components of the Angolan nation.[5]

Despite this almost universal[6] acceptance of one Angolan nation and state, the origins of these three movements are set in that 'peculiar social situation of Angola' referred to in the UNITA document. The origins of the MPLA, the FNLA and UNITA emerge not only from the political consequences of challenging colonialism but also from specific ethnic and social circumstances.

The main thrust of Portuguese colonial subjugation destroyed beyond recognition the Ndongo kingdom, the principal pre-colonial Mbundu political organisation. The Mbundu people, numbering about 700,000 in the 1960s,[7] were generally located around the Kuanza river, in an area that runs inland from Luanda to the Cassanje highlands in the north-east.[8] The Mbundu had had the longest contact with the Portuguese, as the area they occupied was the most geographically propitious corridor linking the interior to the coast. This made it principally, but not exclusively, the main trading route for slaves.

To the north of the Mbundu area is the Bakongo homeland which extends ethnically over the border into Zaire, and to the Cabinda enclave, which is separated from Angola by Zairean territory.[9] This was the area of the ancient Kongo kingdom which, unlike the Ndongo kingdom, retained some of its structures of authority throughout Portuguese colonial rule. A Kongo king, Pedro VIII, was enthroned in 1962. These institutions were, of course, strictly controlled by the Portuguese but remained, nevertheless, a focus for Bakongo political life. In the 1960s, the Bakongo population numbered approximately half a million.[10]

The Ovimbundu, numbering over 1,700,000 at the time, are the largest ethno-linguistic group in Angola, and occupy mainly the plateau highlands south of Luanda. In the north-eastern and central parts of Angola, are the Lunda-Chokwe who, like the Ovimbundu, are primarily migratory peoples.

These major ethno-linguistic groups in Angola are generally seen to be the main streams from which emerged the nationalist movements. Marcum's important work on the Angolan movements constructed their political constituency and historical significance from their ethno-linguistic origins.[11] Under this approach, the MPLA is seen as primarily a Luanda-based Mbundu movement which established links with historical Mbundu resistance against colonialism. Similarly, UPA, and its later incarnation, the FNLA, established itself around the modern embodiment of the Kongo kingdom. Lastly, UNITA was seen as representing the interests of the Ovimbundu and the Lunda-Chokwe.

While they are undoubtedly crucial to tracing the origins of each movement, their ethno-linguistic foundations should not be seen as a primary determinant in the political conflict that emerged. This is to say that while the movements do have different ethnic origins, the civil war between them did not break out because of these differences. Certainly in other Portuguese colonies, in Mozambique for instance, one unified nationalist pan-tribal movement managed to emerge despite the country's stratification along different ethnic lines.

Furthermore, there was political travelling between the Angolan movements by major figures, casting further doubt over a solely ethnic explanation to the civil war. The leader of UNITA himself, Jonas Savimbi, of Ovimbundu origin, was a leading member of the UPA and the FNLA before reluming to the south of Angola and establishing UNITA. Similarly, Daniel Chipenda, an Ovimbundu, was a prominent military leader in the MPLA before defecting to the FNLA in 1975. Both of these examples of many such cases support the argument against an overwhelming reliance on the ethnic factor as a determinant in Angolan politics. While undoubtedly present in the Angolan conflict, especially in pinpointing the identity of the rival constituencies and when used to draw upon loyalty, ethnicity does not seem to be able to completely explain the origins of the conflict. That is to say, Angolan ethnicity may have been exploited by movements and personalities in their political conflicts but the latter do not emerge solely from the differences between the ethnic groups.

The concurrent development of Angolan anti-colonialism and nationalism within two separate social and political communities, the Bakongo and the Mbundu, gave rise to two well-rooted movements, the FNLA and the MPLA. But, the conflict between them cannot be seen to have emerged solely or even mainly from their ethnic differences. Other equally important influences such as race, education, personality clashes and basic political choices must be looked at to understand the roots of the civil war.

The origins of modern Angolan nationalism are set in two interrelated streams of protest, one pre-colonial, the other colonial.

The history of pre-colonial Angola and especially of resistance to Portuguese military conquest played an important symbolic role in the anti-colonial war. For example, the resistance of Queen Jinga in the seventeenth century and of the warriors of the Dembos became part of the military and political ethos of the MPLA guerrilla groups of that area. This historical link between modern anti-colonialists and African resistance to the Portuguese was referred to by the leader of the MPLA, Agostinho Neto, who set the two different eras, past and present, within the same continuous framework of resistance to colonialism:

> For Angolans, clandestine action means the resumption of a long battle against Portuguese domination. From the time of Portuguese penetration, our history has been marked by great feats of resistance.[12]

Similarly, the restoration of the glory days of the Kongo kingdom played an important historical role for the political constitution and military ethos of the PNLA. But, such an image initially implied a separatist aim since only northern Angola was included in the territory of the old Kongo kingdom. During the mid to late 1950s, the restoration of the Kongo kingdom was clearly the focus of Bakongo politics in which the Union of the Peoples of Northern Angola (UPNA),[13] a precursor to the FNLA, was heavily involved.

As well as drawing upon references to historical resistance against Portuguese rule, the anti-colonial movements were also able to mine a more recent body of protest that had emerged in Angola during what Wheeler has called the 'stirrings' phase of Angolan nationalism.[14] During this time, an active political life developed that was a direct precursor to the anti-colonial movements of the 1960s. This political activity coincided with an era of relatively free press from the 1880s to the end of the republic in 1926, and was expressed most emphatically by the *assimilado* and *mestiço* sectors within colonial society, particularly in the urban port areas of Luanda and Benguela.

These two urban and commercial centres were the focus of colonial trade for most of the period of Portuguese presence in Angola. Despite the low number of white settlers in the colony as a whole, Luanda and Benguela were bustling cities where trade was centred. Before the early twentieth century, a low level of white female immigration to Angola had helped to create a *mestico* class, one that generally tended to fill the economic space between the Portuguese and the Africans. Accorded a higher status in colonial society, this *mestico* class was often educated and helped to man some of the levels of colonial administration and the trading structure with the interior, often acting as intermediaries. Trading success and the benefits of colonial-society gave *mesticos,* along with established *assimilado* African families, a relatively significant social and economic niche in the coastal societies of Luanda and Benguela.

By the late nineteenth and early twentieth centuries, this urban *mestico* and assimilated class had developed a modest, if moderate, level of political expression, most accentuated during the republican interregnum, between 1910 and 1925. Associations, such as the Angolan League (1912)[15] among perhaps a dozen,[16] and a free press environment permitted a brief flourish of political expression during this period. According to Wheeler, the goals of the Angolan League were:

> (i) to fight for the general interests of Angola; (ii) to further African education; (iii) to defend the interests of their members and protect their rights; and (iv) to establish physical education classes.[17]

Although, some members were more radical than others, their general approach was not anti-colonial but co-operative and even supportive of the republican cause in Portugal. The League mainly sought to advance the lot of the *assimilado* within colonial society. Access to white collar jobs by *mesticos* and *assimilados* was being challenged by increased white immigration, and this early twentieth-century political protest in the form of such associations and publishing focused on the increasing frustration felt by the *mesticos* and *assimilados* in being pushed away from the promised rewards of colonial society.[18] Despite this sectional interest, however, it should be noted that the first goal of the League, 'to fight for the general interests of Angola', reflects the presence of a concept of the Angolan nation in this early political activism.

African political activity also emerged at this time in Lisbon, predating the anti-colonialists of the 1940s and 1950s who met, organised and developed their challenges to colonial rule from within the heart of the regime. The African League,[19] established in 1919, and the African National Party (PNA),[20] in 1921, were self-proclaimed non-violent lobbying groups with an *assimilado* membership which sought to represent '... the progress, rights and interests of the masses of Africans...'[21] in the Portuguese colonies as a whole. These groups become linked to the wider streams of pan-Africanism and pan-Negroism that were emerging at the time. W.E.B. Du Bois held the second session of the Third Pan-African Congress in Lisbon in 1923.[22]

This *assimilado* political activity in both Angola and Portugal was generally non-confrontational[23] and survived throughout the republican period. However, once the New State began to emerge after the coup in 1926, the official life of these associations was rapidly snuffed out. Nevertheless, these associations, and their more sterile successors under the New State, such as the Angolan National League (LNA),[24] played an important role in the development of Angolan nationalism and anti-colonialism. They provided a forum for an exchange of views and an expression of dissatisfaction with colonial society and the Portuguese regime. They were built on and helped to develop a form of protest, which took as its subject and victim the African Angolan. For example, the issue of race and its exploitation was brought to the fore during the last decades of the nineteenth century in the protest writings of Jose de Fontes Pereira and in a collection of

Luandan press articles titled 'The voice of Angola crying out in the desert.[25] This issue subsequently became central to the political expression of the anti-colonialists in the late 1940s and 1950s. Both these protest writings and the political activism of the associations further reinforced the idea of an Angolan nation which remained firmly planted in the field of Angolan nationalism.

In this context, it is worth mentioning the existence of European opposition in Angola to mainland regimes. On the one hand, there was a reactionary class of settlers and traders that had developed in the coastal towns which lived mainly off the commercial links established directly with Brazil. Their political complexion was often anti-metropolitan, and autonomy for Angola a common goal. But, they were, of course, very much against African self-determination. A number of these groups even threatened to secede from Portugal, but were never sufficiently organised to bring this about. This stream of Angolan settler nationalism was somewhat reinforced throughout the twentieth century especially as a result of increased poor white immigration. In 1961, and later in 1974, it emerged violently against the anti-colonial movements and the African population in general.

At the same time, there developed within European colonial society a radical body of opposition to the colonial regime, especially among the white, liberal, professional and semi-professional classes. After the end of the Second World War, literature on fascism and Marxism was brought into Angola, especially from Brazil, and was particularly prevalent in white anti-Salazarist circles which were active in the main urban areas of Luanda and Benguela. By the end of the 1940s, there was a significant level of political interaction between these white opponents of the regime and the *assimilado* and *mestico* activists who were becoming increasingly radical.

Urban Radicalism and The MPLA

By the late 1940s, small clandestine groups of opposition to colonialism had begun to form in the urban centres of Luanda and Benguela. The composition of these groups was mainly of *mestico* and *assimilado* origin: educated Angolans with a place in colonial society. The issues focused on by their political criticism were long-standing ones within Angolan nationalism: race, exploitation and colonialism. But, mere reform was no longer the main political goal. Increasingly, a radical anti-colonial programme was developed, one that was couched in the political language of Marxism, and which sought the end of Portuguese rule, by force if necessary. This more radical political framework set these groups apart from previous generations of Angolan nationalists that had mainly sought to develop a non-violent dialogue with the Portuguese on those questions. The new generation of Angolan nationalists did not differ from previous generations in their social and racial background.

In fact, many urban radicals came from families whose previous generations had also been active politically. They continued, furthermore, the development of an Angolan African national identity, attempting to break out of the Portuguese rationalisation of colonial assimilation policies. But, by the early 1960s their anti-colonial challenge, as expressed in the programme and policies of the MPLA, had become violent in method and revolutionary in intent.

The intellectual starting point of this new radicalism was the idea of Angola and the Angolan. The clandestine protest literature assumed and continued to stimulate a national identity. In 1948, a group of Luandans linked to an authorised association, the Regional Association of the Angolan-born (ANANGOLA) published a literary review called *Mensagem,* with the motto 'Let US Discover Angola'. In its poetry and prose, young *assimilados* and *mesticos* expressed outrage and bitterness at the submissive status of the colonised. They focused on bringing to the fore a sense of the 'African ness' of Angolans. As in other colonies on the continent at the time, their literature sought to assert an identity, one that was both African in race and Angolan in nationality. Despite the fact that only two issues of *Mensagem* were published (it was banned by the authorities in 1950), it is seen, particularly by the MPLA, as a formative stage in the development of modern Angolan anti-colonialism. Its editor was Viriato da Cruz, a young *mestico* intellectual who played a crucial role in the development of a Marxist tendency within the MPLA. According to Marcum:

> They featured poetry that not only invoked Angola's African heritage but called upon Angolan poets to create an "Angolan language'... [Viriato da Cruz's] work reflected what a leading commentator on Portuguese Negro poetry, Alfredo Margarido, has termed a 'new awareness of the motives behind the exclusion of the Negro from colonial society'. Such poetry produced a new internal freedom that was, Margarido predicted [in 1962], 'bound to be externalised eventually by means of revolt against the established order'.

Between the late 1940s and the mid-1950s, a flurry of clandestine political activity was experienced in main urban centres. Small groups of intellectuals and students met secretly and discussed colonialism and its violent demise. They exchanged smuggled radical literature, produced their own, named and renamed their discussion groups, but little else was done. According to Van Dunem:

> They believed that to fight against Portuguese colonialism all that was needed was a conspiracy on the part of intellectuals. They believed that all people needed to do was get together in somebody's house one day, and, the next day, colonialism would collapse.

The most pervasive political influence during this time was undoubtedly Marxism, and, despite the claims of Viriato da Cruz that 'the Communist Party of Portugal... had no appreciable influence in either the preparation or the launching of the Angolan revolutionary movement', it seems very likely that Portuguese communists were an important element in establishing its prominence among Luandan anti-colonialists.

The Portuguese Communist Party (PCP) was the only anti-Salazarist opposition that was active throughout the period of the New State. According to Pelissier, the PCP succeeded in infiltrating authorised colonial associations, the Angolan National League (LNA) and the ANANGOLA. In 1961, a prominent MPLA leader, Mario de Andrade, in an article published in *Pravda,* seemed to confirm this penetration by Portuguese communists when he referred to the 'revolutionary character' of the LNA, the ANANGOLA and a third group, the African Association of Southern Angola (AASA). One of the first overtly Marxist groups to be constituted was the Angolan Committee of the Portuguese Communist Party, established sometime in 1948. The links between the PCP and the MPLA are clearly long-standing. Indeed, some of the current members of the PCP are originally from that group of anti-Salazarist whites in Angola.

From this group of Angolan nationalists and people linked to the Portuguese Communist Party, the Angolan Communist Party (PCA) emerged in 1954. According to Van Dunem, the party was formed by '... four or five people...', among whom was Ilidio Machado, '... the thinker in the PCA'. Ilidio Machado is considered to be one of the founding members of the MPLA. Yet, according to Van Dunem, Machado himself denied this. Even if this was the case, his influence on Viriato da Cruz and others who subsequently became members of the MPLA makes it possible to consider the PCA a precursor to that movement. Subsequent MPLA historiography, however, omits any reference to the PCA, probably in the interests of appearing to be a broader political movement and thereby appealing to a wider range of internal and external support.

It is important to point out that the *mestico* and assimilated semi-middle classes were not universally developing a Marxist challenge to Portuguese colonialism. On the contrary, the young intellectuals espousing Marxism must certainly have been a thorn in the side of the more conservative elements, many times within their own families, who had achieved a significant position of social and economic importance within Luandan and Benguelan societies and, consequently, were not particularly receptive to an ideology that called for an end to private property, even if it did promise the demise of colonialism.

In parallel to the clandestine activity in Luanda, Angolan nationalists were also organising in Lisbon, the destination for those Angolans who wanted to obtain university degrees. A small number of *mestico* and *assimilados* went to Portugal to study. There, they came into contact with underground political opposition, mostly led by the PCP, as well as with students from other Portuguese African colonies. Among those Angolans studying in Lisbon and Coimbra during the mid-1950s were Mario Pinto de Andrade (the founder of the MPLA), Agostinho Neto (the leader of the MPLA and first Angolan president), Lucio Lara (the MPLA ideologue) and Jonas Savimbi (the leader of UNITA). From Mozambique, there was Marcelino dos Santos (FRELIMO) and from Guinea-Bissau, Amilcar Cabral (PAIGC). Later, these latter contacts would prove to be very useful to the MPLA leaders when deep in their conflict with the FNLA. Through interterritorial organisations such as the Conference of the Nationalist Organisations of the Portuguese Colonies (CONCP), the MPLA benefited internationally from its links to the PAIGC and FRELIMO, whose own positions were unassailable.

While each pursued their own studies, the nationalists congregated in places such as the Home for Students from the Empire, an official hall of residence for colonial students. While Mario Pinto de Andrade and Lucio Lara tended to concentrate more on the intellectual facet of the anti-colonial challenge, Agostinho Neto was more active. He was a member of MUD

Juvenil (the youth section of a movement very close to the PCP), and was arrested a few times. Neto established close links with an association of Angolan sailors as well as with other students. The regular voyages of Angolan sailors on merchant ships back and forth between Portugal and Angola provided a makeshift transmission belt that informed Angolans in Lisbon and in Luanda of what the others were doing. According to Van Dunem:

> The axis was, therefore: Mario Pinto de Andrade (students in Lisbon), Agostinho Neto (sailors), Ilidio Machado and Viriato da Cruz (Luanda).

This axis was not so much a formal structure of organisation as a network of exchange that carried news and ideas about anti-colonial stirrings. Yet, it was also the skeleton of what later became the MPLA.

The clear increase in nationalist activity, even if limited and clandestine, was rapidly picked up on by the colonial authorities. In 1957, a section of the regime's political police, the PIDE, was established in Angola. To all accounts, the PIDE set up a good underground network of informants that managed to penetrate many of the Luandan groups. However, it was done, the results were spectacular. A wave of arrests in 1959 decimated the clandestine nationalist network, depleting it of its most prominent leaders either by imprisonment or by pushing them underground or into exile. By 1960, Ilidio Machado and Agostinho Neto, among many others, were in prison. Mario Pinto de Andrade and Lucio Lara had left Lisbon and were in Paris. The regime made it perfectly clear that it would not tolerate nationalist political activity. During this time, the military presence of the colonial power was significantly stepped up. In March 1959, the air force transferred a district base to Angola, marking their arrival with a bombastic air drop of paratroopers over Luanda. A few weeks later, an additional 2,000 infantrymen reinforced the already 20,000-strong army stationed in Angola. A year later, in April 1960, the navy positioned warships off the Angolan coast.

The clamp-down by colonial authorities on the nationalists was as much a reaction to the increase in opposition locally as it was a reflection of the New State's preoccupation with the changing map of Africa. To some extent, it was influenced by the events in the neighbouring Belgian Congo where anti-colonial agitation had broken out in January 1959. Rioting in the capital, Leopoldville, led quickly to a decision by Belgium to grant independence in June 1960. Notwithstanding, Belgium attempted to maintain a strong military and administrative presence but rapidly lost control of the situation and the newly independent Congo descended into civil war.

Boiling Point of African Nationalism

The 1950s had been a period of relatively secure European colonial control, but nationalist politics in Africa were about to reach boiling point. Before 1960, only ten African countries were independent and only two (not including South Africa) of these were below the Sahara. It was at the turn of the decade that the full force of the decolonisation process was delivered. In 1960, alone, 17 countries in sub-Saharan Africa became independent. The effect of this process in general, and of events in the Belgian Congo in particular, on the Portuguese authorities was to deepen fears of a nationalist challenge to their own colonial rule.

It was clear that Portugal was alarmed by the possibility of an anti-colonial challenge, particularly in Angola where they believed it would come from across its borders. In 1960, official Portuguese documents, smuggled out of the country and leaked to the *New York Times,* described the putting down of an armed rebellion in Angola. Those documents were, in all probability, 'instructional wargames' as claimed by the colonial authorities. However, such training materials revealed that the Portuguese did fear a nationalist uprising and indicated that the regime expected a nationalist threat to come from across Angola's borders and not from within. In fact, the Portuguese government insisted that no separatist movements existed in their territories except those that were fomented from the outside. In particular, to the Portuguese, the ethnic commonality that linked the Bakongo people across the Angola-Congo border made it dangerously permeable.

Following the wave of repression at the end of the 1950s, most of the urban nationalists were either in prison or abroad in exile. The intransigence and efficiency of the colonial authorities had made staying in Angola an impossible option. Harassed by the PIDE, Viriato da Cruz had left Angola and joined Mario de Andrade and Lucio Lara abroad. These three Angolan intellectuals (the first two were *mesticos* and Lucio Lara is white) worked from Paris, from where they attempted to further the cause of anti-colonialism. Working under a general denomination, the Anti-Colonial Movement (MAC), they, and other leading nationalists from Portuguese colonies such as Amilcar Cabral and Marcelino dos Santos, were active in left-wing political and literary circles of Western Europe. From them emerged the MPLA.

The creation of the MPLA is a subject of controversy. At the heart of the dispute lies the question of the historical legitimacy of the movement, an issue that played an important role in the subsequent inter-nationalisation of the Angolan conflict. Here, the two competing versions will be summarised.

The 'official' version, which has been written into much of the material relating to the MPLA, contends that the MPLA was founded on 10 December 1956 by Ilidio Machado (PCA), Viriato da Cruz *(Mensagem)*, Matias Migueis, Higino Aires and Andre Franco de Sousa. In 1990, this version was vigorously reaffirmed in an open letter by the single surviving member of this group, Andre Franco de Sousa. According to Franco de Sousa, the founding members met in Luanda at Ilidio Machado's house where a manifesto of political action was drawn up and the Popular Movement for the Liberation of Angola *(Movimento Popular para a Libertacao de Angola)* was born. From here, the MPLA expanded inside the country only to run afoul of the colonial backlash at the end of the 1950s. Still, according to this version, the MPLA then moved abroad, first to Guinea and later to Leopoldville in the newly independent Congo. Then, on 4 February 1961, the remaining activists who were neither in prison nor in exile, mounted an attack on the gaols of Luanda, that, although unsuccessful, is considered to mark the beginning of the MPLA's anti-colonial war against the Portuguese.

But, this account of the foundation of the MPLA is now openly challenged by a number of people, including Joaquim Pinto de Andrade, the brother of Mario Pinto de Andrade and an early honorary president of the MPLA. According to him there was no movement known as the MPLA as such at that time. He told *Expresso* that 'before 1960 there was no document that referred to the MPLA'. Joaquim Pinto de Andrade claims that in 1956 he had read a manifesto drawn up by Viriato da Cruz but stresses that it had only been a declaration of intent to form a movement and not the actual foundation itself. During that period, he claims that:

> ... there were countless groups of 3-4 people [in Luanda] that would emit pamphlets abroad, to seem like many. There was the PLUA, MIA, MINA, MNA... But, these were all acronyms without programmes, without founders.

But, those who stick to the original version maintain that the MPLA was not known nor referred to at this time because it was secret. According to Andre Franco de Sousa, after the foundation of the MPLA, it was decided that this acronym would be kept secret and reserved for later use. In the meantime, they would call themselves the Movement for the Independence of Angola (MIA). Joaquim Pinto de Andrade rejects this outright:

> '... at the time, the MPLA did not exist, even secretly'. 'If it had existed', he went on, 'he would have known of it, since he was active in MIA, the very same cell in which Andre Franco de Sousa *was*'.

The revised history of the foundation of the MPLA, as claimed by Joaquim Pinto de Andrade, an unnamed source in the *Expresso* article and others, can be summarised in the following manner. Having left Luanda under pressure, Viriato da Cruz joined Mario Pinto de Andrade and Lucio Lara in Paris in 1957. In Angola, small cells remained which were active but dispersed. The exiles in Paris discussed the need for one broad movement to unify anti-colonial efforts in Angola, and, according to one source, it was only at the end of 1958 at the All-African Conference held in Accra that this core in exile decided to create the MPLA. Subsequently, Viriato da Cruz drew up the statutes and programme of the movement allegedly based on those of the Vietnamese National Liberation Front. The movement was to be named according to a phrase with which Viriato da Cruz had ended his 1956 document calling for 'the creation of a broad popular movement for the liberation of Angola'.

Establishing themselves in Conakry, sometime in 1959 or 1960, the MPLA had yet to act but now had at least a structure of leadership. The Directing Committee was made up of Mario Pinto de Andrade (President), Viriato da Cruz (Secretary-General), Lucio Lara, Azevedo Junior, Matias Migueis, Eduardo dos Santos and Hugo de Menezes. This revisionist version claims that far from being conspired by the MPLA, the attack on 4 February 1961 was, in fact, a spontaneous, somewhat suicidal, action carried out by anti-colonial elements at the time unconnected to the MPLA. However, after that spontaneous attack took place, the newly constituted MPLA in exile claimed it for themselves. According to the words of Mario de Andrade, conveyed by his brother:

> I arrived at the MPLA office and I come across Liicio Lara, who was permanently listening for news, and he told me that there had been an uprising in Luanda. I was amazed; I considered it for a while and then I turned to Viriato Cruz and told him: 'Viriato. Write. We have to claim that act.' And so he wrote: 'On the morning of 4 February, the Angolan patriots, led by the MPLA...'

According to Lima:

> ... when the attack on the prisons takes place, the exiles have to admit that the people are moving faster than they are. We were intellectuals, students, moving in environments outside the country, while inside the country, people felt the necessity to turn to action. In order not to be left behind, it was necessary to transform that spontaneous movement and give it a voice, and a direction.

Subsequently, the movement backdated its origins in order to situate its birth earlier, in 1956, and inside the country. This was done in order to legitimise its constitution and shore up its credibility. They feared that any movement led by *mesticos* in exile, and only hurriedly exposed after a suicidal attack on Luandan gaols which had left many dead, would not have been accepted, either externally or, more importantly, internally as a legitimate representative of Angolan anti-colonialism.

If this new version is indeed accurate, then the establishment of the MPLA took place outside Angola and not inside, and three, perhaps four, years later than it has hitherto been claimed. In fact, a press report of statements made in July 1962 by Jonas Savimbi in London while still in the UPA seem to support this revised version of the MPLA's origins: 'The MPLA are a party of students and intellectuals in exile: their movement was started in Paris.'

This revision of its origins challenges the legitimacy of the MPLA's claim to have launched the anti-colonial war, and makes the 4 February incident a spontaneous act carried out by desperate people. According to Mendes de Carvalho, who was one of the prisoners the revolters sought to release, the men who attacked the prison knew nothing of the MPLA and were shouting the name of another, rival movement, 'UPA... UPA!' At the time, and as will be seen below, the UPA was the most prominent Angolan movement and the precursor to the FNLA.

What this reveals is that already at the birth of the MPLA, the competitive pressures of legitimisation wielded an overwhelming influence. These pressures to endow the movement with an internal and external validity are also the driving force behind subsequent alliances made by the movement, not only to help it fight colonialism, but also to legitimise its identity *vis-a-vis* its rivals.

Although, this controversy has emerged, and it becomes important to document the origins of the MPLA as accurately as possible, the fact is that by claiming the act of 4 February for itself and by giving it the symbolic value it has hitherto maintained, the MPLA has, in effect, assumed the responsibility of the act to itself even if, in reality, it had nothing to do with it. It signified that Neto could claim in 1964 that:

> Incontestably, that date marked the first phase of armed fighting against Portuguese colonialism.

An attempt to pinpoint the ideological influences on the MPLA leads indisputably to two main currents: nationalism and Marxism. The general aspects of Angolan nationalism have already been outlined above, and the idea of Angolan nationality was undoubtedly part of the literature and political lexicon of the MPLA. On the other hand, Marxism in the MPLA takes on a similar hue as it does in other anti-colonial situations where revolutionary Marxism is allied with anti-colonial nationalism. Marcum believes that it may have been a natural consequence of their *mestico* origins that a political prism such as Marxism was favoured by the leaders of the MPLA, as it was an ideology that focused on class rather than racial conflict. The Ottaways support this conclusion:

> [The racial] characteristics of the MPLA help explain why Marxism held a special appeal for its leaders. By stressing class conflict over all others, it provided the urban *mesticos* and *assimilados* with an ideology that transcended race and allowed co-operation between them and the black workers and lumpenproletariat of the *musseques.*

Such a conclusion would apply equally to the case of assimilated Africans who were also caught, socially and culturally, between two worlds. It is not orthodox Marxism, as a theory of class struggle, that forms the ideological backdrop for the MPLA before 1975 but the wider doctrine and practice known as national liberation.

Angolian Anti-colonialism after the Second World War

After the end of the Second World War, anti-colonialism began to emerge as the dominant political goal in the developing world. The politics of the end of colonial rule and self-determination swept through the European overseas dominions for a number of reasons that actually derived from the course of that war. The same colonial powers that claimed the war was a struggle against authoritarianism and for freedom could not very well argue that those ideals did not also apply to their colonial subjects. Furthermore, the early defeat in Asia of the European powers at the hands of the Japanese helped to crack the myth of the invincibility of the white man.

Finally, the post-war international scene saw the emergence, at opposing poles, of two superpowers both of which defended anti-colonial positions, albeit from different perspectives. These factors, among others, brought anti-colonialism to the forefront of political discourse throughout the developing world, including Africa.

While influenced by events and thinking from abroad, self-determination as a goal emerges principally from the reaction of the colonised to the experience of domination. According to an MPLA leader:

'We are humiliated as individuals and as a people.' The desire for independence became a common goal of anti-colonial movements throughout the continent although some new governments did defend a more radical approach than merely striving for sovereignty. This was the 'first wave' of decolonisation.

The goal of independence was merely the starting point for the doctrine of national liberation which emerged in the anti-colonial conflicts of the 1960s and 1970s. Among those anti-colonial movements which took up this doctrine is the MPLA. In ideological terms, national liberation is where Marxism, as an interpretive and political instrument, enters the anti-colonial stream, leading to a far broader definition of colonial domination. In particular, the experience of the Chinese communists was an influential factor on the development of revolutionary anti-colonialism.

Aspects of Maoism, ironically developed in a non-colonial context, are at the core of the ideology of national liberation. By advocating revolutionary transformation anywhere and not just in industrial societies, Maoism seemed to be more applicable to the experience of the developing world. To self-determination as a goal of anti-colonialism, Marxist doctrine added economic independence. No longer was the end of colonial authority a sufficient objective; the economic structure established by it also had to be overturned, or else colonial control would not be terminated. What had to be confronted, the Maoists claimed, was 'the double-edged sword of imperialism'. In its declarations the MPLA clearly saw themselves through a similar prism:

> The MPLA is a revolutionary movement. The MPLA plan aims at the complete destruction of the colonial machinery and of all forms of domination.

Thus, in the Third World, Marxism as an ideology had been further altered and "... had... march[ed] from a theory of the self emancipation of the industrial working class to a voluntaristic recipe for rural insurrection followed by state planning and capital accumulation.' Therefore, liberation movements, in adopting revolutionary socialism as a model of anti-colonial conflict and economic development, ignored the supposed succession of historical stages determined by orthodox Marxism. According to White, national liberation became 'a vehicle for radical nationalism in non-industrial societies'.

National liberation was more than a modified Marxist doctrine for anti-colonial conflict and development in the Third World. The experience of those movements that adhered to it created a world-wide stream of revolutionary anti-colonialism, to which the MPLA, like other movements, turned and felt part of:

> We know that victory in the righteous struggle of our people is not far off now... Guaranteeing this is the unswerving desire of the Angolan people for freedom, the powerful national liberation movement (and) the support of all progressive humanity.

In its anti-colonial war in Angola, the MPLA turned to the experience of like-minded movements in other so-called national liberation wars, such as those in Algeria and Vietnam which were held up as examples to emulate. According to Lucio Lara, the principal ideologue of the MPLA:

> The Vietnamese armed struggle was very human, a blend of political and military action which became our model. In drawing up our MPLA programme, we were strongly influenced by the Vietnamese experience. Obviously we also studied their military tactics, their concepts of people's war.

The ideological complexion of the MPLA placed it firmly in the socialist camp, a conditioning factor of undeniable importance which determined the external links the movement would establish throughout its conflict against Portuguese colonialism and its struggle for power in Angola.

The FNLA, Holden Roberto And Bakongo Nationalism

A particular feature of modern Angolan politics was the role played by nationalists based in the neighbouring Congo (Leopoldville). Out of the Bakongo ethnic group that straddles the border between the two countries there developed a strand of Angolan nationalism which produced one of the major anti-colonial movements in Angola, the FNLA. Precisely because of its strong tribal base, the FNLA has often been subjected to criticism which cast doubt on its claim to represent Angola and not just one part of it. But, throughout the anti-colonial war it was the MPLA's strongest rival and, after the collapse of Portuguese rule in 1974, the FNLA was determined to contest power in Angola.

After the Congo became independent of Belgium in 1960, there were as many as 58 Angolan nationalist organisations working out of Leopoldville. Among the Angolan expatriate population, these groups jockeyed for position while manoeuvring for official Congolese backing and independent African support. One of those groups, the Union of the Peoples of Angola (UPA), formed the core of what was to become the FNLA. As we have seen, the UPA was the most prominent Angolan anti-colonial movement at the beginning of the conflict with the Portuguese in 1961. For a while, the UPA, representing the Kikongo-speaking peoples, and its leader, Holden Roberta, were the best-known face of Angolan nationalism.

Despite the fact that he was born in Angola, Holden Roberto was raised in Leopoldville and was, according to all accounts, very much at home in that city's political scene. His rise to prominence within the UPA occurred under the protective wing of his uncle, Barros Necaca. Originally, the group was known as the Union of the Peoples of Northern Angola (UPNA), and Barros Necaca was its president. Their political constituency was the Baxikongo tribe, whose leaders were Baptists and Kongo royalists. The UPNA organised around their professed aim of restoring the ancient kingdom of the Kongo to full independence. The constitution of a separate Bakongo state would have changed Angola's borders. On 20 May 1956, Roberto was one of the young Baxikongo who co-signed a letter to a visiting US State Department official emphasising the separate nature of the Kongo and calling for an end to Portuguese rule in that kingdom. A year later, the restoration of the independent Kongo kingdom was invoked in a letter to the UN Secretary-General.

As he ascended within UPNA, Roberto was chosen to represent the group at the first All-African conference that was held in Accra, Ghana, in December of 1958. At that conference, where there was, according to Marcum, an 'exuberant pan-African spirit'. Roberto established contacts with other African nationalists such as Franz Fanon, Kenneth Kaunda, Patrice Lumumba, Kwame Nkrumah, George Padmore and Sekou Toure. It was in the light of exchanges with those major anti-colonial figures that Roberto is said to have decided that the separatist nature of the UPNA should be cast aside in favour of a total Angolan identity. In Accra, Roberto became convinced that the organisation should be modernised and drop the 'tribal anachronism' of its restorational aims. The name of the group was changed to UPA, and the reference to 'northern' peoples dropped in order to impart a broader appeal. A manifesto in the name of UPA calling for the liberation of all Angola made its first appearance at the Accra conference in 1958.

During the following two years, Roberto toured international circles and published damning articles on Portuguese colonialism, steadily increasing the profile of his own movement. He visited Accra, Conakry, Brazzaville, Tunis, Monrovia and New York. In August of 1959, he attended a foreign minister's Conference of Independent African States held in Monrovia. In September 1959, attached to the Guinean Mission to the United Nations, Roberto argued that Portugal's African territories should be assigned to UN tutelage. While in New York, he established a wide range of American contacts with the help of the American Committee on Africa (ACOA). Further reinforcing his prominence among African nationalists, Roberto took part as an observer in the second Conference of Independent African States which was held in Addis Ababa in June 1960. By the beginning of the 1960s, while the leadership of what would become the MPLA was dispersed and barely organised, Roberto was a well-known figure in the international African political arena and had already established good links in the US.

While this active international canvassing by Roberto was good strategy, it mainly resulted from the fact that the Belgian colonial authorities had clamped down hard on Angolan nationalists following the Bakongo-led riots in Leopoldville of January 1959. Taking advantage of the belief that Angolan emigres had participated in the rioting, the Portuguese pressured the Belgian police to arrest several hundred Angolans suspected of anti-colonial activity. The arrests led to the repatriation of those alleged nationalists to Angola. Unwittingly, this may have had a negative effect from the perspective of the Portuguese colonial regime. The reintegration of ex-emigres who, on the one hand, brought with them nationalist ideas and, on the other hand, talked of higher wages over the border was not what the Portuguese wanted during such a volatile time. The UPA later claimed that these extraditions enabled them to infiltrate the colony with 'cells' which were credited with preparing the groundwork for the uprising of 15 March 1961.

In July 1960, after the Congo became independent, Roberto returned to Leopoldville, where he was warmly received. His international prestige had helped to make this a period of expansion in the fortunes of the UPA. It was also a time during which Roberto consolidated his own dominance of the movement. In the heady summer months of Lumumba's rule, Roberto disseminated the cause of the UPA and challenged Portuguese colonial administration through writings and broadcasts. He was already working with those who would form his very personalised structure of command. Most prominent among these were Jose Manuel Peterson and Johnny Edouard, son of Eduardo Pinock, a veteran of the Protestant challenge to the Kongo succession.

Roberto's rising star was momentarily eclipsed, however, by the dismissal of Patrice Lumumba by President Kasavubu, in September 1960. His past association with Lumumba allowed his political opponents in the Congo to accuse him of being a communist. Roberto fled to Ghana (where he was spurned by Nkrumah's government and accused of being 'in the pay of

America'), and from there to New York where he attended the 15th session of the UN General Assembly. While in New York, a situation developed which might have marked an end to Roberto's rise to power within the UPA and, consequently, changed the course of Angolan politics.

While Roberto was in the United States, the UPA Steering Committee had committed the movement to a loose coalition of Angolan parties, known as the Common Front of the Political Parties of Angola. The other parties involved were the following: an MPLA group led by a Bakongo, Antonio Josias; ALIAZO, an association representing the Bazombo tribes; and a Cabindan group, the AREC. The figures in the UPA that had committed the group to the Front also planned to hold elections for the leadership in November while Roberto was away from Leopoldville.

Roberto hastened back from New York to see the challenge off. The ensuing power struggle resulted in a major split within the UPA: 17 out of the 20 members of the UPA Steering Committee resigned, including Roberto's uncle and initial patron, Barros Necaca. From this point onwards, Holden Roberto became the uncontested leader of the UPA. His first act was to withdraw the UPA from the Front, and the latter subsequently collapsed.

This challenge to Roberto's leadership has been written off as a conservative reaction to his tendency to move increasingly away from non-violence towards direct action against colonialism. On the other hand, it may also have represented the first of what were to be many dissensions from Roberto's allegedly autocratic style of leadership. What was later revealed through the many abandonments of the FNLA was that Roberto was unwilling to dilute his own power at the head of the movement. Other Angolan nationalist groups, unless dissolved within his structure of authority, represented an unacceptable threat to Roberto. According to the US State Department, Roberto was 'inflexible, resolute, anti-communist and incapable of delegating authority'.

By the beginning of 1961, Roberto was very much in control of the UPA. He had firmly established himself at the centre of power and placed members of his own tribe and family in the most important executive posts. Under Roberto, the UPA's internal and external profile became pronounced, and was, at the time, the best known Angolan nationalist group.

In early 1960, the second All-African People's Conference was held in Tunis, and marks a watershed in the paths chosen by the Angolan nationalist movements in the anti-colonial challenge. Until that time, self-determination was considered an objective to be negotiated with the Portuguese:

> ... the UPA, aware of the responsibilities it is assuming toward the Angolan people, toward Africa and toward history, makes a solemn appeal to the Portuguese government and people to agree to negotiate as soon as possible on ending the colonial regime and recognising national Angolan sovereignty.

Meanwhile, the MPLA nucleus in exile had been busy making contacts and putting across the case against colonialism in Angola. But, this movement too, saw the end of colonialism as coming from a negotiated process. At that time, only a war of communiques and newspaper replies marked the confrontation with the Portuguese colonial authorities. Peaceful self-determination, however, was increasingly put in doubt as the determination of the Salazar regime to refuse even to address the issue of self-government became patently clear. In reply, the nationalists began to warn of the responsibility the Portuguese government would bear for the 'bloody conflict' that would ensue from that intransigence. But, even as late as 1960, the resort to armed action did not seem inevitable. According to the first military leader of the MPLA:

> ... Mario de Andrade himself hesitated considerably before taking the option of armed struggle. When this was talked about in terms of political speculation, I remember Mario de Andrade until 1960.... was very hesitant.

According to Marcum, this perspective began to change at the All-African meeting in Tunis, where both the MPLA and the UPA were present. With the Algerian war of independence in full flow, Franz Fanon cast an authoritative shadow over the workings of the conference. Among others, he called for the peaceful option to be cast aside in favour of direct action. In Tunis, the call for an Angolan war of independence was being heard by the UPA. But, this vision was challenged by Mario de Andrade who held that war was not necessarily essential for the anti-colonial process. This resistance by the MPLA to Fanon's calls for a war may explain the support that was subsequently given to Holden Roberto's UPA by the Algerian National Liberation Front (FLN).

By 1961, the MPLA and the UPA seemed to be going in opposite directions. The latter, internally cohesive under Roberta's leadership, was considering launching direct military action against Portuguese colonialism. The former was still attempting to consolidate its organisation. But, then early that year, an event of paramount importance changed this situation. The 4 February attack on the Luanda gaols brought the MPLA out of relative obscurity and established it as a major force of anti-colonialism in Angola. While the movement's direction of the attack has been placed in doubt, the effect of that action, after the MPLA claimed it for itself, was overwhelming. The attack forced the movement's hand in opting for a military strategy. But, by claiming to have played a part in the beginning of armed conflict against the Portuguese, the MPLA placed itself at the forefront of the nationalist conflict against the Portuguese, a role it shared with the UPA, especially after the latter unleashed the violent attacks in northern Angola on 15 March 1961.

The combined impact of the February and March anti-colonial viol-ence propelled Angolan nationalism towards a significantly increased level of international attention. The sheer violence of the UPA attacks and of the far more vicious colonial backlash marked a new phase in nationalist anti-colonialism. Reprisals by the Portuguese during the eight month long uprising resulted in thousands of deaths, the final total being placed variously by sources at 8,000, 25,000 and 50,000. Furthermore, the attacks coincided with a UN Security Council debate on Portuguese colonialism. News that a revolt had begun in Angola sharpened the debate and helped to push the tide against the Portuguese. During the course of 1961, both the desperate bid for self-determination in Angola and the intransigent nature of the Portuguese colonial regime were revealed to the watching world.

At first, Roberto denied that the UPA had been involved in the attacks. Subsequently, however, they claimed responsibility for them, and the attacks entered the historiography of the UPA/PNLA, and even of Angolan nationalism as a whole, as the beginning of the end of Portuguese colonialism. Roberto believed that an Angolan uprising would isolate Portuguese colonialism internationally: 'Portugal will have no support, for its colonial system is known for being one of the most retrograde. According to claims, the attacks were aimed at creating a situation of extreme terror and violence in Angola which would bring negative international attention to Portuguese colonialism. Under pressure from the international community, Lisbon would renounce sovereignty while the violence would impel the European settler population to give up and leave Angola. This scenario seems to have been modelled closely on what occurred in the Belgian Congo. A witness to the rapid demise of Belgian colonialism, Roberto seems to have believed that the experience could be repeated in Angola. However, the nature of Portuguese colonialism produced an entirely different result.

Lisbon's Response to the Angolan Revolt

The 1961 anti-colonial actions did not drive Portuguese colonialism out. Instead, the regime in Lisbon sent more troops into Angola, while reaffirming its determination to hold on to its colonies. Even diplomatic isolation did not seem to bother the Portuguese regime. When the Kennedy administration reversed the US policy of not supporting anti-Portuguese positions at the United Nations and approved a Security Council resolution condemning the repression of nationalist action in Angola, the United States embassy in Lisbon was stoned. This seemed merely to reinforce the regime's resolve to resist change. The Portuguese representative at the UN accused the US of courting the Third World vote, and Salazar told the National Assembly:

> The United States is pursuing in Africa, although with other intentions, a policy which is parallel to that of Russia... [one that is] incompatible with what she is trying to achieve through the North Atlantic Treaty.

By this time, the effects of 'late colonialism' were beginning to emerge, and colonial development policies designed to bring Angola and Portugal even closer were implemented. After the actions by nationalists in 1961, particularly those of the UPA in the north of the country, Portuguese colonial resolve became even more deeply entrenched.

Shortly following the March action, Roberto and the UPA's privileged position in Leopoldville became momentarily threatened. Congolese fears of Portuguese retaliation led President Kasavubu to consider expelling Roberto and his movement from Leopoldville. Kasavubu was a leader of the Congolese Abako party which shared the UPA's political constituency among the Bakongo and was thus in direct competition with Roberto's movement. By putting pressure on Roberto to please the Portuguese, the Congolese president was killing two birds with one stone.

By that summer, and despite the rivalry with Abako and outright antipathy from Kasavubu in the presidency, the Congolese political climate changed once again, this time significantly in favour of Roberto. In July 1961, his old friend and fellow footballer, Cyrille Adoula, was appointed Prime Minister, an appointment which gave the UPA a very secure political footing in Leopoldville. The Adoula-Roberto link provided the UPA (and later the FNLA) with a secure base across the border from Angola. Furthermore, Adoula favoured the UPA in its bids to gain the allegiance of the Angolan emigres of Leopoldville, the numbers of which had swollen considerably as people fled the 1961 violence in Angola.

After the March attacks, the UPA attempted to throw off further its tribal identity and expand into an all-encompassing Angolan nationalist force. During that year, the UPA expanded beyond its Bakongo base with the appointment of Jonas Savimbi as Secretary-General of the union. The appointment of Savimbi, an Ovimbundu, was an influential factor particularly in leading other Angolan students in Europe to join the UPA. The inclusion of Rosario Neto, a Luanda-Mbundu, in the UPA leadership was a further attempt to transcend the Bakongo image of the party. The political legitimacy gained by launching an armed conflict against a colonial power allowed the UPA to grow. The prestige of military action and the broadening of the ethnic make-up of the UPA leadership established the strength of the party and, consequently, that of Roberto at its core.

In early 1962, the UPA was a founding member of a front that in effect replaced it as the vehicle for Holden Roberto's political power. On 27 March 1962, the National Front of the Liberation of Angola (FNLA) was formally established. Although, the movement was based on a political union between the UPA and another large Kikongo-speaking movement, the ALIAZO, the FNLA's political structure was completely dominated by Roberto's own personal power network. The ALIAZO was little more than a tribal association to further the interests of the Bazombo. It had protest roots in the Simao Toco sect, an anti-colonial but somewhat obscurantist group active in 1949-50. But, like UPNA before it, ALIAZO broadened its political horizons and renamed itself the Democratic Party of Angola (PDA). Within the FNLA decision-making structure, the PDA retained the right of veto. This was, however, meaningless, as Roberto avoided using due processes and wielded almost absolute power within the FNLA.

The FNLA was created to fulfil a very clear objective. While Roberto believed he could maintain his group's predominance within the Bakongo ethnic constituency, the creation of a front, uniting more than just a single movement or party, allowed him to claim that the FNLA represented an attempt to unite anti-colonial Angolans. The following are the first two decisions of the FNLA:

1) To unite our forces in one national liberation front to hasten the independence of the country.

2) To group in an Angolan national liberation front, all organisations truly representative of the Angolan people who accept the general policies of the front.

On 5 April 1962, after barely a week in existence, the FNLA formed a so-called Angolan revolutionary government-in-exile (GRAB). Undoubtedly taking inspiration from the success of the Algerian FLN's experience with its own government-in-exile, the establishment of the GRAB was a useful strategy for bringing attention to the conflict against Portuguese colonialism. But, it also served another purpose, in that it helped the FNLA gain ascendancy within Angolan nationalism. The Algerian government-in-exile had bestowed authority and legitimacy on the FLN, and the FNLA sought the same effect with the creation of the GRAB.

The ideological orientation of Holden Roberto and the FNLA seems patently obvious. In the early stages of the anti-colonial war, the predominant political currents in this movement were anti-communism and African nationalism. Like the MPLA, the FNLA claimed its objective to be the liberation of the Angolan land and people from colonialism. But, unlike the MPLA, it also peppered its public pronouncements with liberal amounts of anti-communism.

> It is common, on the other hand, for some colonists to try to prove to the African people that nationalism and the fight for dignity are identified with Communism. They even went so far as to make this convincing to certain Africans, who thus let themselves be seduced by Marxist and Communist ideology.
>
> In some places, many of those brother Africans say they would prefer this to colonialism. But, the great majority of those who fight for the liberty of their country have no ideology save that of human dignity. It is universally accepted that Africa is imprisoned by its land and its religion, whatever it may be. It knows no other ideology other than patriotism - and it is this which the West calls nationalism.
>
> Let all who want to safeguard their friendship with the peoples of Africa - with the people of Angola - know that we are determined to be not only Africans but also masters of our destinies and lands, and that we will not allow ourselves to be seduced by any foreign propaganda.

While placing itself clearly outside the socialist bloc, the FNLA did attempt to identify itself with the prevailing strain of African anti-colonialism. It referred often to the national liberation struggle, and even ventured to propose a somewhat progressive programme, although suitably vague one. The declaration of the FNLA's constitution claimed that 'agrarian reform' and 'a planned economy' would be established by a 'democratic regime' that would replace colonialism. According to one report in 1963, Roberto affirmed that he envisaged a one-party state for Angola after the rebel war. In the early 1960s, Roberto and the FNLA tried to stand, as much as possible, in the anti-colonial camp without, however, compromising its appeal to anti-communist circles, particularly those in the US.

Like all anti-colonial movements, the survival of the movement itself was the FNLA's primary objective, which led it sometimes to compromise its ideological posture in favour of pragmatism. This resulted, on occasion, in a shift of allegiance. In early 1964, Roberto announced that the GRAB would 'accept aid from Communist China and other Communist countries'. According to Roberto:

> Until now we have kept out of the cold war and within the framework of African politics (but) we are now at a point where a radical change of policy is imperative for us to make headway in our struggle.

In early 1962, Roberto's movement, the FNLA, was acting as a government-in-exile for the Angolan people, and had, for a year, been locked in guerrilla warfare against the Portuguese colonial regime. It had a significant international profile and was the Angolan nationalist movement most favoured by the Leopoldville government. At the time, its prospects looked good.

By the end of 1962, a confident MPLA arrived in Leopoldville ready to begin its first major period of anti-colonial activity. Buoyed, in turn, by the effect of the 4 February attack, the MPLA believed it would be the movement to lead Angolans to independence. It was increasingly clear that a rivalry was emerging in Angolan nationalism, one that would dominate the anti-colonial war and beyond.

NOTES AND REFERENCES

1. M. de Lucena, *A Evolucao do Sistema Corporativo Portugues Vol.* (Lisbon: P. & R., 1976) p. 94.
2. *MPLA Statuts et programme,* Leopold vi lie, 196? Translated and reproduced in R. Chilcote, *Emerging Nationalism in Portuguese Africa: Documents* (Stanford, California: Hoover Institution Press, 1972) p. 229. The date of publication must have been sometime between 1962 and 1963, the period during which the MPLA leadership was based in Leopoldville.
3. *Uniao das Populacaes de Angola.*

4. *Statutes of the UFA*, reproduced in R. Chilcote, *op. cit.* (1972), p. 101.

5. *UNITA* (1984), p. 61.

6. The universal acceptance of national integrity refers to the three main movements that contested power in 1975. Separatism was, however, not absent from Angolan politics. In the Cabindan enclave, a separatist movement, the *Mouvement de Liberation de l'Enclave de Cabinda* (MLEC) sought independence for Cabinda from 1960 onward. In 1963, under the aegis of the Congolese president, Fulbert Youlou, three pro-separatist groups, including MLEC, merged in Brazzaville to form the *Front pour la Liberation de l'Enclave de Cabinda* (FLEC). See J. Marcum, *The Angolan Revolution Volume I: Anatomy of an Explosion 1950-1962* (Cambridge, Mass.: MIT Press, 1969) pp. 172-5, and *The Angolan Revolution Volume II: Exile Politics and Guerrilla Warfare 1962-1976* (Cambridge, Mass.: MIT Press, 1978) pp. 123-5. The FLEC's first resolution, adopted at their August 1963 congress in Brazzaville, begins: 'The people of Cabinda, holding fast to the reaffirmation of their right to self-determination and to total, immediate and unconditional independence...' *FLEC Resolutions*, reproduced in R. Chilcote, *op. cit.* (1972), p. 128.

7. D.L. Wheeler and R. Pelissier, *Angola* (London: Pall Mall Press, 1971), p. 8.

8. The Mbundu are also known as Kimbundu which refers specifically to the language spoken.

9. The Bakongo are also known as the Kikongo which refers to the language spoken by this ethnic group.

10. J. Marcum, *op. cit.* (1969), p. 50.

11. J. Marcum, *ibid.*, and *op. cit.* (1978).

12. A. Neto, 'Angola in historical perspective'. Speech, Leopoldville, April 1963. Reproduced in R. Chilcote, op, cit. (1972), p. 213.

13. Uniao das PopulacSes do Norte de Angola.

14. D.L. Wheeler, 'Origins of African nationalism in Angola: Assimilado Protest Writings, 1859-1929', in R.H. Chilcote, *Protest*

and Resistance in Angola and Brazil: Comparative Studies (Berkeley, California: University of California Press, 1972), p. 69.

15. Liga Angolana.

16. D.L. Wheeler, *op. cit.* (1972), p. 73.

17. D.L. Wheeler and R. Pelissier, *op. cit.* (1971), p. 117.

18. D.L. Wheeler, *op. cit.* (1972), p. 75.

19. Liga Africana.

20. Partido Nacional Africano.

21. D.L. Wheeler and R. Pelissier, *op. cit.* (1971), p. 118.

22. The African League was closer to Du Bois, and was host to his faction in the congress. The PNA apparently leaned more towards Marcus Garvey. D.L. Wheeler and R. Pelissier, *op. cit.* (1971), p. 119.

23. The Angolan League was, however, provocatively called the "association of white killers'. Combined with alleged reports of *assimilado* participation in revolts between 1913 and 1917 and a number of other incidents (the murder of a European clerk and the discovery of an arms cache) this led to a clamp-down by the authorities in the summer of 1917. Dozens of *assimilados* were jailed without a trial. D.L. Wheeler, *op. cit.* (1972), p. 81.

24. Liga Nacional Angolana.

25. Voz d'Angola clamando no deserto.

6

Background of the Angolan Nationalism

In 1483, one of Portugal's venturesome explorer-navigators, Diogo Cao, dropped anchor in the Congo River estuary and inaugurated a prolonged history of Portuguese penetration into, sub-Equatorial Africa. Portugal's King Joao II commissioned Cao to follow up his initial contact with the Kongo kingdom by making a return trip in 1485 to establish permanent relations. Organised within six autonomous provinces and bisected by the great Congo River, the kingdom then contained an estimated two and a half million Kikongo-speaking people residing in an area that covered what is present-day northern Angola and the Bakongo regions of the Congo republics of Kinshasa and Brazzaville.[1]

In response to Cao's mission. King Nzinga a Nkuwu, the kingdom's paramount chief or Mani Kongo, agreed to send a small group of his subjects to Portugal for education, and in 1490 he received in return three ships bringing Portuguese priests and skilled workers to evangelise and instruct in his kingdom. As part of this early day "technical assistance," the Europeans baptized the Mani Kongo and rebuilt in stone his capital situated at Mbanza Kongo (Sao Salvador) in the central province of Mpemba.

Unfortunately, this initially amicable relationship was soon undermined by the multinational slave trade which developed and then continued for some centuries as the principal motive force in Europe's relations with Africa. In the case of the Kongo, slave merchants began operating out of Portugal and the island of Sao Tome. They preyed upon the Mani Kongo's kingdom and short-circuited his pleas to Lisbon for protection, teachers, and priests. After his death in 1506 Nzinga a Nkuwu was succeeded by a son enthroned as Atonso I. The new ruler had been schooled in European culture but had not been taught how to cope with the worldly ravages and intrigues of the likes of the Sao Tome adventurers. Nor was he able to control approximately two hundred Portuguese and mulatto clergy and functionaries who maneuvered for power about his throne. These groups undercut his authority and isolated him from the very people whom he wished to assimilate into the Portuguese culture of his training.[2] The result was the collapse of what might have been a pilot project in acculturation.

Slave Trade

Convulsed by civil strife, Afonso's kingdom began to disintegrate. Conversely, the slave trade flourished and expanded along the coast from the Kongo port of Mpinda southward, and from 1576 on Luanda developed as a major slave port. Moving inland from the Luanda coastal area, Portuguese forces overwhelmed the Mbundu kingdom of Ndongo, a sometime tributary to the Kongo kingdom, and ensconced themselves permanently in a north-central wedge of what was eventually to become known as Angola.

Between 1580 and 1836, when the trade was officially though not yet effectively abolished, some four million Africans were exported to Brazil and elsewhere from the Congo-Angola region, over three million from Angola alone.[3] Whole African communities were decimated. Whereas in 1591 an "enthusiastic official" could assure the Portuguese crown that the densely populated hinterland of Luanda would offer a plentiful supply of slaves "until the end of the world," a century later local authorities "were deploring the serious decline in the population of Angola owing to the internecine wars, excessive forced labour and the ravages of small pox." It reached the point where slave traders "had to travel for three months into the interior before reaching the markets *[pombos]* where slaves were sold."[4]

Only after the long centuries of the slave trade did Portugal gradually occupy the bulk of what constitutes modern-day Angola. Abolition was followed by a program of colonial expansion between 1845 and 1860, which included European colonisation schemes, military ventures, and efforts to plant the Portuguese flag over formerly uncontrolled territory in the interior.[5] Sao Salvador was occupied by Portuguese forces in 1859-60. Disease, distance, and African resistance generally blocked Portuguese efforts to secure authority beyond the coast, however, and a policy of retreat and retrenchment followed from 1861 to 1877. Sao Salvador was abandoned in 1870. Then near the end of the century Portugal joined in the final burst of European colonial expansion in Africa. In an analysis of the motivation behind this new drive, historian Douglas L. Wheeler has concluded that the determining factor was a desire to shore up Portugal's declining prestige and power in Europe. "Imperialism for the Portuguese, therefore, was less an economic drive than a traditional, nationalistic one."[6]

Portugal's ambitions were somewhat thwarted by bigger colonial powers in the partitioning done the Berlin Conference of 1884-85 and by its own inability to move with force and peed into the central African interior. Yet, by the turn of the century, Portugal had gained international recognition for its nominal sovereignty over an African empire—Angola, Mozambique, Guinea—some twenty-two times its own size. The fact remained that effective occupation was limited to the coast and some adjoining plateau areas, and, in spite of more than 300 years of involvement in Angola, Portugal probably controlled less than one tenth of the territory within the colony's official borders. Saved from the territorial appetites of Europe's major colonial powers, whose jealousies largely checkmated their rival designs on diminutive Portugal's claims, Lisbon nevertheless faced serious African resistance to its widening control up to and even after the First World War.

The insecure, even tentative, character of Portugal's authority in Angola as late as the eve of the First World War was confirmed by negotiations between the Portuguese and the Jewish Territorial Organisation of London, which was then looking for a territory within which to establish an "autonomous" Jewish community. Under the auspices of the Lisbon government, the Organisation sent a commission to Angola to investigate the possibility of establishing a Jewish colony on the plateau area inland from Benguela in central Angola. Promoters of the scheme openly conjectured that the Portuguese government would feel compelled to cooperate with the project because it did not effectively occupy Angola, because it faced a threat of German encroachment from South West Africa, and because "a Jewish colony in Angola under the Portuguese flag [might] be the only way of keeping the flag flying there."[7]

Portuguese authorities even initiated contact, with a branch of the Jewish Territorial Organisation in Kiev, and a retired Russian judge and state counselor, Jacob L. Peitel, thereupon visited Lisbon, where he and Jewish leaders from England and Switzerland participated in discussions with government officials and local Jewish circles concerning the Angolan project. It was Peitel's impression that, although Portugal, with at that time only 6.5 million people, was unable to organise massive emigration of its own or to accept settlement by any single non-Portuguese national group, which might produce a conflict of loyalties, it was receptive to promoting settlement in Angola by a multinational Jewish community.[8] By so doing, Portuguese authority might be bolstered at a minimal cost or risk. As a consequence of these initiatives, in June 1912 the Portuguese Chamber of Deputies passed a bill authorising concessions to Jewish settlers. Its provisions for individual settlement, naturalisation, and acculturation did not, however, meet the requirements of the Jewish organisation for collective colonisation, communal autonomy, and an initial grant of 5000 square miles of land. Furthermore, there was apparently some fear in Lisbon that it would be dangerous to enter into a formal contract with such a strong and well-financed London-based organisation. Expression of interest in such an accord from British Foreign Secretary Sir Edward Grey and his ambassador in Lisbon may have contributed to Portuguese suspicion and reticence. In any case, no agreement for the establishment of a Jewish homeland in Angola was reached before the First World War intervened and retocused Jewish attention upon Palestine. (The war, incidentally, also insured Portugal against future German expansion into Angola from the south.)

During Portugal's turbulent life as a democratic republic from 1910 to 1932 European control was secured over all the interior of Angola in spite of violent resistance by Mbundu, Ovimbundu, Cuanhama, and other peoples. The sparsely populated eastern third of the country was the last to come under effective colonial administration—around 1930. The early republican period also saw the continued development of a critical "free press" in Luanda, where in the 1880's a small educated African and *mestico* elite had already begun to use the printed page as a new instrument for asserting indigenous against colonial interests. This promising channel for dialogue and political education was, however, foreclosed by official censorship introduced by the Angolan High Commissioner Norton de Matos in 1922.

With the advent of Dr. Ant6nio Salazar's conservative and ultra-nationalist *Estado Novo* in the 1930's, Portugal's overseas territories assumed increased importance as the *sine qua non* of its claim to a place among the world's major powers. Portugal could bask in the "magnificent certainty" of being "the third colonial power in the world."[9] Within thirty years, of course, it would occupy first place. Moreover, it translated its belief in a self-appointed "civilising mission"—pursued with what was at least a relative freedom from color consciousness—into an official policy of assimilation. In 1951 all of Portugal's overseas possessions were officially incorporated into the Portuguese state. The revised Political Constitution of the Portuguese Republic proclaimed that it was "intrinsic in the Portuguese nation to fulfill its historic mission of colonisation," and "to diffuse among the populations inhabiting [the Overseas Territories] the benefits of [Portuguese] civilisation," since these territories were an "integral part of the Portuguese State."[10] By fiat, then, a small preindustrial state of nine million people with an illiteracy rate of some 40 per cent and a per capita annual income of around 250 dollars, claimed to have done what France, with its much greater resources had, if somewhat half-heartedly, tried and failed to do, i.e., assimilate millions of Africans as black Europeans.

The gap between Portugal's imperial ambitions and its material means was too great. By 1950 at most about 0.75 per cent of the African population of Angola, that is, some 30,000 out of over 4,000,000 Africans, had become *assimilados,* whereas the rest remained "uncivilised" *indigenas* without political or civil rights.[11] Moreover there could be no expectation of a rapid change in this situation, for as late as 1956 only about 1 per cent of the African school-age population was attending school, as compared with a 1958 figure of 11 per cent for neighbouring Northern Rhodesia, where the British were not even trying to assimilate Africans.[12]

Lisbon organised a migration of Portuguese settlers following the Second World War, which pushed the white population of Angola up from 80,000 to approximately 200,000 between 1950 and 1961. Yet even that immigration did little in the short run to further the cause of assimilation. Drawn from "the harsh backlands" and urban slums of Portugal, the settlers were largely illiterate and unprepared for multiracial living. They upset the status quo at African expense, by appropriating farm land and preempting semiskilled jobs such as taxi driving. Feeling insecure and threatened by potential competition from young educated Africans, they were the first to take to antiblack vigilante action and to oppose liberal reforms when Africans rebelled.[13]

The government sought to bar or limit any disruptive foreign influences that might undermine its assimilation policy and was particularly exercised by the "danger" of the Protestant missions that had established themselves in several areas of Angola toward the end of the nineteenth century. The government resented Anglo-Saxon and Swiss missionaries for their allegedly systematic refusal "to educate the native for the Portuguese concept of integration," and for their inherent incapacity to believe that Angolans and Mozambicans were Portuguese. Many Protestant missionaries, it was charged, persisted in "preaching self-determination as the only possible solution for problems and difficulties that foreigners and only foreigners [had] raised in the path so far followed by Portuguese policy."

In order to secure themselves against the unsettling evangelism and heretical schools of these interlopers, the administration responded with a policy of harassment designed to squeeze them out. This policy was sharply intensified after the armed uprising of 1961, and the number of American missionary personnel fell drastically thereafter from 300 to less than 100. During this period, the administration continued to operate under a semi "closed-door" religious provision in the 1951 Constitution (Art. 140) which provided that: "The Portuguese Catholic missions overseas and the establishments for training personnel for their service and for those of the *padroado* [patronage] shall, in conformity with the Concordata and other agreements concluded with the Holy See, enjoy juridical personality and shall be protected and assisted by the State as being institutions of education and assistance and instruments of civilisation."[14]

In addition to factors of national prestige, power, and "mission," the fact that Angola had become a great economic asset by the 1950's had important implications for Portuguese policy. An "estimated half million African *contratados* provided cheap forced labour for Portuguese administrators, traders, and farmers.[15] As of 1959, Angola's annual coffee exports had risen to nearly 50 million dollars and diamonds to over 20 million, and newly discovered petroleum and iron resources, coupled with an influx of West German and other western capital, promised increasing revenue in foreign currency. This Angolan "boom" helped to offset Portugal's own balance-of-payments deficit totaling about 135 million dollars.

Portugal's ability to maintain the colonial status quo, however, weakened in proportion to the growth of African political consciousness and restiveness over the abuses of the conscript labour system. Not only the absence of free ballots, a critical press, or independent courts, but the very permissiveness of article 146 in the Constitution deprived Africans of any protection against systematic exploitation of their labour by local European interests. "The State," said article 146, "may only compel the natives to work on public works of general interest to the community, or tasks of which the finished product will belong to them, in the execution of judicial sentences of a penal character or for the discharge of fiscal liabilities." Accordingly, government administrators needed only to increase local head taxes to produce more laborers through fiscal liability. In addition to rural resentment against conscript labour, the economic modernisation, urbanisation, and education, albeit limited, that came along with European settlement induced social ferment within a growing segment of African society.

On the surface, Angola remained calm and in 1956 such a sensitive observer of African affairs as Oxford's Thomas Hodgkin wrote of "the apparent non-existence of nationalism in Portuguese Africa."[16] Yet, had scholars and journalists been allowed to carry out free inquiry inside Angola, they would surely have come forth with a different assessment. Some literate and literary precursors of modern African nationalism had been protesting as early as the second halt of the nineteenth century, and by the early 1950's, though largely unperceived by the outside world, Angolan poets, prophets, peasants, students, functionaries, and emigres had created a wide assortment of protonationalist movements. Within the decade 1950-1960, Angolan nationalism developed into an important challenge to continued Portuguese rule.

Portugal tried desperately to seal out the wave of political and social change that was sweeping over much of a continent. Yet, five centuries after Diogo Cao's first contact with the Kongo kingdom African nationalists were demanding that Portugal restore the kingdom's sovereignty. More were demanding independence for the whole of Angola. Viewing this state of affairs with his customary coolness, Portugal's Dr. Salazar commented in 1961: "A law recognising citizenship takes minutes to draft and can be made right away; a citizen that is a man fully and consciously integrated into a civilised political society takes centuries to achieve."

The Portuguese premier was unprepared to make concessions to the increasingly impatient demands for political reform. Unlike Britain, France, and Belgium, Portugal seemed unwilling to speed up the pace of social and economic change, or to relinquish political power. If it took centuries to produce Salazar's fully civilised man, however, it took a much shorter time to produce a host of consciously unassimilated and rebellious African nationalists.

Angolan Nationalism Before the Revolution

It is Angola that has loomed largest in the imperial thinking of Portugal's nationalist politicians, commercial investors, and cul-tural evangelists. The temperate climate of its central and southern highlands (Amboim, Bie, and Huila), the homelike qualities of its old-establishment coastal towns (Luanda, Benguela, and Mocamedes), the wealth of its remote diamond fields (replete with company garden town at Dundo), and the remunerative plantation agriculture of its green north (Carmona-Uige)—all these qualities enticed important numbers of Portuguese settlers to Angola, especially after the Second World War. And even more important, these assets excited Portugal's advocates and architects of imperial "mission."

It is also Angola that may claim to have been the first of Portugal's overseas territories to give organised expression to sentiments of modern African nationalism. Political awareness and action developed in a variety of ways and took diverse forms: syncretic religions, movements to restore indigenous kingdoms, ethnic-cultural and mutual-aid societies, and literary, cultural, religious, and youth organisations. All groups suspected of political content were banned. Yet, such suppression was only partly effective, as some groups succeeded for a while in dissimulating their political sentiments, more went underground, and still others directed their activity from adjoining sanctuaries in the Congo or Northern Rhodesia and organised among peoples straddling Angola's frontiers. Within Angola, the demands of secrecy and the exploits of the police and police informers meant that most groups had only short life spans, small memberships, and isolated impact. In the urban matrix of Luanda, for instance, several clandestine groups apparently operated alongside one another for some time without contact or even knowledge of each other's existence.

In time, as police and military repression intensified, many nationalists fled the country. Once outside where they could communicate freely among themselves, they tended to coalesce or to stand apart according to class and communal loyalties. Reflecting the "elite-versus-masses" dichotomy in Portugal's own social class structure, as well as the polarity that was intrinsic in any colonial system, nationalists from the small multiracial class of educated and semieducated town dwellers found themselves competing with rivals more closely identified with the rural, largely uneducated, black peasantry that constituted the bulk of the country's five million people. At the same time, Angolans also clustered together politically on the basis of strictly precolonial ethnic and regional origins. Taken together, the influence of class and ethnicity resulted in a tripolarity, as reflected in what ultimately developed as the major streams of Angolan nationalism: (1) Luanda-Mbundu, with a predominantly urban, elite leadership, and (2) Bakongo and (3) Ovimbundu plus Chokwe, (2) and (3) with rural, peasant orientations.

In addition to producing a number of small particularist organisations, each of these three streams ultimately gave birth to a major nationalist movement, or alliance of movements, with sufficient following outside its own regional base to give it some grounds for a claim to represent an all-inclusive, all-Angolan nationalism. Gradually these same mainstream movements became locked into positions of bitter antagonism as partisan competition, personal ambitions, and cold-war diplomacy reinforced and added to their communal differences. As newcomers from Angola came to the ranks of nationalist movements outside, they found themselves caught up in rough internecine struggles for which their localised experiences inside the country—where the colonial order was more clearly the principal target—had often not prepared them.

Once in exile, idealistic young men who had left their country hoping to participate in a united campaign to liberate it discovered that, not only social and ethnic divisions, but now considerations of party mythology, political ideology, and foreign aid, ranged them against one another.

NOTES AND REFERENCES

1. Roland Oliver and J. D. Fage, *A Short History of Africa* (Baltimore: Penguin Books, 1962), p. 125.

2. James Duffy, *Portugal in Africa* (Cambridge, Mass.: Harvard University Press, 1962), pp. 38-43.
3. *Ibid.*, p. 59.
4. C. R. Boxer, Race Relations in the Portuguese Colonial Empire 1415-1825 (Oxford: Clarendon Press, 1963), p. 28.
5. Douglas L. Wheeler, "Portuguese Expansion in Angola since 1836: A Re-examination" (Salisbury, Rhodesia: Central African Historical Association), Pamphlet No. 20 (1967), pp. 2-5.
6. *Ibid.*, p. 9.
7. Statement by Israel Zangwill in introduction to Report on the Work of the Commission Sent out by the Jewish Territorial Organisation under the Auspices of the Portuguese Government to Examine the Territory Proposed for the Purpose of a Jewish Settlement in Angola (London: ITO Offices, 1913), p. IX.
8. Jacob L. Peitel, *Iz Moei Zhizni* [From My Life], (Paris: Ya Povolotshii and Co., 1925), pp. 215-223.
9. Jorge Ameal as quoted in James Duffy, *Portuguese Africa* (Cambridge, Mass.: Harvard University Press, 1959), p. 270.
10. Amendment Law No. 2048, June 11, 1951.
11. Prof. Gwendolen M. Carter has estimated that even this 1950 figure is swollen by the inclusion of unqualified (less educated) wives of *assimilados,* as well as their children. She concludes that there were "no more than between 8,000 and 10,000 true *assimilados* within Angola" constituting only 0.25 per cent of the African population. Carter, *Independence for Africa* (New York: Frederick A. Praeger, 1960), p. 99.
12. Rev. Thomas Okuma, who spent eight years as a Congregational minister and teacher in southern Angola, has further contrasted the educational programs of the British and Portuguese by noting the following comparison: the Northern Rhodesian government was spending approximately four dollars *per capita* on education in 1959, whereas available data indicated that the equivalent figure of expenditure by the Portuguese government was about six cents. Okuma, *Angola in Ferment* (Boston: Beacon Press, 1962), pp. 45-46.

13. *The New York Times,* March 21, 1961.

14. Portugal, National Office of Information, *Portugal, An Informative Review,* No. 6 (Nov.-Dec. 1961), p. 379.

15. As late as 1961, a British team investigating the situation relating to Angolan refugees in the Congo reported that within Angola men were still being conscripted for periods up to eighteen month?, that women were still being put to work mending roads, and that children from eight years of age and up were known to have been working in the mines and on the coffee plantations. See George Thomas, M.P., and Rev. Eric L. Blakebrough in *Congo-Angola Border Enquiry* (London: Angola Action Group, 1961), p. 12. The British journalist Basil Davidson was among those who had earlier brought international attention to this system. Following a perceptive visit to Angola he wrote an angry article, "Africa's Modern Slavery," *Harper's,* Vol. 209, No. 1250 (July 1954), pp. 56-68.

16. Thomas Hodgkin, *Nationalism in Colonial Africa* (London: Frederick Muller, 1956), pp. 17-18.

17. *The New York Times,* May 31, 1961.

7

Early Phases of the Angolan Nationalism: 1961-1965

In Angola, the colonial period, strictly speaking, was very brief—from 1920 to 1961. Having already achieved military control by 1920, Portugal then proceeded to establish administrative control, promote white colonisation, and build the infrastructure to enable Angola to contribute politically and economically to the metropole. Portugal did not recognise that during this same period anticolonialism was not only keeping pace with colonialism, but was developing into Angolan nationalism.

Formation of African Associations in Lisbon

The republican period in Portugal (1910-1926). which produced a multiplicity of Portuguese political parties, also spawned a variety of African associations. In Lisbon, *assimilados* and mesticos from the various Portuguese African colonies organised "*number* of organisations, each claiming to represent and pro-mote the progress, rights, and interests of the masses in all five Portuguese African colonies and to be strictly constitutional and "legal in all their activities. Among them, the Liga Africana supported the Pan-Africanism of W. E. B. Du Bois, while the Partido Nacional Africano leaned toward the negro nationalism of Marcus Garvey and defended the African personality and character: "We are not simply Portuguese. Before being Portuguese we are Africans. We are Portuguese of the negro [sic] race. We are proud of our double quality. But, we possess, above all, the racial pride... of being negroes [sic]... We must cooperate with the whites."[1]

At the same time, in Luanda, *assimilados* and *mesticos* formed the Liga Angolana, which was not a true political party but an elite lobby of Angolans with a program of improving conditions for the mass of Africans as well as advancing the *assimilados* within the European system. Since the inspiration of these associations was more Pan-African than Angolan, whites did not feel that they really belonged in the Liga Angolana even though a few did join. Hostile whites called it the Associacao de Mata-brancos (The Association of White-killers), even though the Liga was moderate and very loyal to the Republic.

Africans in Luanda had less political freedom than in Lisbon between the two world wars. The Liga Africana in Lisbon had a statutory provision "to revoke all discriminatory legislation in Portuguese Africa," whereas the Liga Angolana in Luanda could not include such a purpose in its statutes. Salazar's New State reorganised these associations both in Lisbon and Luanda to bring them under the direct control of the Portuguese government. In Luanda, the older generation of Liga leaders, who were culturally assimilated Africans, accepted working in strictly legal collaboration with the colonial administration. A younger generation, advocating anticolonialism rather than simply reform of colonialism, urged extension of Liga membership as well as its cultural, social, and political activities to the uneducated masses of Africans.

In 1950, a group of Luanda Africans sent to the United Nations, a document which stopped short of condemning colonialism but criticised Portugal's administration of the colony of Angola:

> because in the course of 469 years of its permanence in Angola it [Portugal] not only has not fulfilled the agreements assumed in International Conferences, but has violated the treaties and demonstrated in-contestably incompetence in administration of the Colony of Angola, practicing acts of slavery, robbery and homicide which are described in this, message... because to colonize is not only to exploit, but to civilize, instruct, educate....

The Angolans closed their exposition by imploring the United Nations to action:

> to order as urgently as possible the end of the Portuguese administration of Angola and Congo, the Government being handed over to the natives who would administer the country under the Protectorate of a nation which would be named by the natives.[2]

This petition to the United Nations was soon passe as Angolans joined Africans across the continent in condemning colonialism itself—not just criticising the particular abuses of each colonial situation. The step from reformism to anti-colonialism took, at the most, a decade—1945 to 1955. The step from anticolonialism to nationalism, however, was more difficult, as it has been in all Africa. It required self-examination and redefinition by peoples whose territory had been defined by European colonial powers until that time. It involved a search in the past for cultural roots, an assessment of the present stale of tradition, and a projection into the future to discover the direction of African history.

In Angola, two movements appeared in the mid-fifties which attempted to mobilise the people into an effective anticolonial force and then to develop Angolan nationalism. The Movimento Popular de Libcrtacao de Angola (MPLA) and the Uniao das Populacoes de Angola (UPA) differed both in the cultural roots with which they sought to identify and in their analysis of the historical significance of the Angolan struggle.

MPLA

The MPLA found its roots in the *assimilado-mestico* community which had formed the various associations in Luanda and Lisbon during the republican period. For its historical analysis of the struggle in which it was involved it drew upon Marxist ideology. By 1948, the Portuguese Communist Party had established a secret cell in Luanda. Two other clandestine groups were also spreading Marxist influence among the city's young intellectuals. The Partido Comunista de Angola (PCA) was formed in 1955, according to Mario de Andrade, the principal historian of the MPLA. Elements from the PCA and other nationalist leaders participated in the formation of the Partido da Luta Unida des Africanos de Angola (PLUA) in early 1956. PLUA then issued a manifesto which invited Angolans to organise themselves clandestinely for a united, armed struggle against Portuguese colonialism. As the urban nationalist movement gathered adherents in Luanda, the Movimento Popular de Libertacao de Angola was formed in December 1956, claiming to be "truly the First party of the masses."

This claim represents more the ideology of the movement than the social reality. Only individuals who had emerged from the masses through their educational and economic opportunities were attracted by the MPLA's intellectual appeal. Such an appeal depended upon the strong, capable leadership that has characterised the MPLA from its beginning. Among the influential leaders were Mario Coelho Pinto de Andrade, Viriato Francisco Clemente da Cruz, and Lucio Lara, but the man who survived all the internal struggles, who conducted international diplomacy to gain foreign support at the crucial times, and who became the first president of the People's Republic of Angola (PRA) is Dr. Antonio Agostinho Neto.

Antonio Agostinho Neto

Dr. Agostinho Neto was elected president of the MPLA at the First National Conference held in Leopoldville in December

1962.[3] He personified in his birth, nurture, education, profession, and political experience the kind of nationalism that MPLA would offer to Angola. Born on September 17, 1922, near Luanda, Neto had roots in the Catete people of the Kimbundu group. The Catetense were closer to the capital than the up-country Ambaquistas but still participated more fully in traditional Kimbundu culture than the urban population of Luanda. His father, a Methodist pastor, the Reverend Agostinho Pedro Neto, shared the common Catetense enthusiasm for education, which was reinforced by the Angolan Protestant conviction that school and church were equally important institutions in the Christian community. A Methodist church report used the colorful simile, "A church without a school is like a couple with-out children." Maria da Silva Neto, his mother, was also a teacher and had a kindergarten in the *musseques*[4] of Luanda.

Neto began his primary education in a village school, then his father was transferred to the church in Luanda, which facilitated his son's high school education. Angola's only two public high schools were located in Luanda and Sa da Bandeira. The few privileged Africans who completed primary school elsewhere in Angola could continue their education only if they could move to one of these cities or pay the high fees of a private *colegio.* Neto went through high school on a government grant for excellence in scholarship and bought books and supplies from the small wage he received as secretary lo the Methodist bishop, Ralph E. Dodge. Dodge reports that

> even as a boy, Neto was quiet, reserved, a bit shy but always correct and businesslike.... Antonio always got good marks in school and progressed from one grade to the next with yearly regularity.... The pattern of the Portuguese was to admit the African students in the same school with the Europeans but thin them out especially in the upper grades. Antonio was one of the few who was able to complete his education in Angola up to the university level.[5]

Neto had set medicine as his goal, but when he completed *liceu* in 1944, Angola had no university or postsecondary courses. So, he worked for three years in the government health services and quietly participated in the formation of a cultural association in Luanda. Since overtly political organisations were forbidden, a cultural association provided the only forum in which social and political issues could be discussed. Poetry was a medium that Neto and his colleagues found useful for rallying the indignation of literate urban Africans against the injustices of Portuguese colonialism and for expressing empathy with the Angolan masses. It is doubtful that his literary attempt to identify with the people was recognised by the rural populations, who lived in an oral culture. Even when the urban, *assimilado-mestico* writers were producing revolutionary poetry, the peasants identified this elite with the Portuguese colonists.

In 1947, the Methodist Board of Missions in New York granted a scholarship to Antonio Agostinho Neto. Before he left Angola to continue his studies in the medical faculty of the University of Coimbra in Portugal, he wrote "Farewell at the Hour of Parting":

> My Mother
> (all black mothers
> whose sons are gone) you taught me to wait and hope as you hoped in difficult hours
> But, life
> killed in me that mystic hope
> I do not wait now
> I am he who is awaited
> It is I my Mother
> hope is us
> your children
> gone for a faith that sustains life... [6]

Neto's passage through the medical course was tortuous, not because of academic problems but because of politics. He had his first taste of prison life in 1951 when he was arrested for collecting signatures for the Stockholm Peace Appeal.[7] After his release from three months in the infamous Caxias Prison near Lisbon, Neto did not avoid political involvement. He became a member of the central committee of an anti-Salazar youth group, the Movimento de Unidade Democratica—Juvenil (MUDJ), and was arrested in 1952 for taking part in a demonstration. His academic education was interrupted, but his political. education and reputation were enhanced as he was arrested again in February 1955 and only released in June 1957. Such international figures as Jean-Paul Sartre, Andre Mauriac, Aragon and Simone de Beauvoir, Nicolas Guillen, and Diego Rivera joined in protesting his imprisonment.[8]

Neto had his textbooks with him in prison, but barely passed his final examination in 1958. In order to practice in Angola, Dr. Neto still had to complete the tropical medicine course, which he did in 1959. Later that year, he and his Portuguese wife, Maria Eugenia, and their baby son returned to Angola. A few months before Neto's arrival the first president of the MPLA, Ilidio Machado, was arrested along with fifty-four other Europeans, *mesticos* and Africans suspected of subversion. Neto had barely begun his medical practice in Luanda when he was again arrested on June 8, 1960, for "subversive activities against the external security of the State."[9] He was one of fifty-two persons seized in this second wave of arrests in a year. Dr. Neto's friends, patients, and supporters planned a demonstration in Catete, the administrative center of his native area, to demand his release. Portuguese officials learned of the plans and when the demonstrators arrived, they were met by soldiers who fired on the peaceful crowd, killing thirty and wounding over 200.

The authorities were particularly apprehensive in June 1960, not only because of the increase in subversive activities within Angola but also because of the imminent independence of the Belgian Congo, set for June 30. In prison, Neto expressed his confidence in the victory of Angolan nationalism:

Here in prison
rage contained in my breast
I patiently wait
for the clouds to gather—
Here in prison
rage contained in my breast
I patiently wait
for the clouds to gather
blown by the wind of history.
No one can stop the rain.[10]

The Portuguese thought they could "stop the rain" by transferring Dr. Neto to Lisbon and then to the Cape Verde Islands, where he continued to practice medicine but under constant police surveillance. By this time, Neto was recognised as one of the principal leaders of the MPLA, having functioned as president of the steering committee for the brief time he was in Angola, and then being named honorary president.[11]

After a year in Cape Verde, Dr. Neto was rearrested and transferred on October 17, 1961, to the Aljube Prison in Lisbon, and another international campaign was launched to free him. This one attracted even more public attention than the first campaign in 1956, as the *Santa Maria* incident and the launching of the war of independence in early 1961 had brought Angola to prominence. A number of leading writers in Britain voiced their protest by writing to the London *Times:*

> We wish to draw urgent attention and that of your readers to the plight of one of Angola's outstanding men, the writer Agostinho Neto, whose life, there is reason to fear, may now be in serious danger. It is not too much to say that the importance of Agostinho Neto in Portuguese-speaking Africa is comparable with that of Leopold Senghor in French-speaking Africa. We believe that every effort must now be made to save this distinguished poet of Portuguese Africa's nationalist awakening.[12]

The Portuguese government was moved, perhaps by international pressure or by internal reasons, to release Neto in

March 1962 and place him under restricted residence. However, the underground railway that had taken scores of African students and other nationalists out of Portugal in 1961-62 now succeeded in carrying Neto, his wife, and two small children across the straits to Morocco.[13]

When Neto and his family arrived in Leopoldville in July 1962, he was the most internationally known Angolan nationalist. Within Angola, Neto was identified with the-Kimbundu-assimilated-mestico-intellectual social class. His ancestry bound him to the Catetense and the wider Kimbundu community. Nine years in secondary school in Luanda (1934-1943) and three more as a government employee in the health department made him at home in the European-mestico-*assimilado* intellectual circles of the capital. Dr. Neto had received not only a medical education during his ten years in Portugal but also a political education through his anti-Salazar and anticolonial activities and his two and a hall years in prison.

Mario Coelho Pinto De Andrade

Six years younger than Agostinho Neto, Mario Pinto de Andrade finished secondary school in Luanda and went to the University cf Lisbon to study philology in 1948. A mestico, born in Golungo Alto on August 21, 1928,[14] he was the younger brother of Father Joaquim Pinto de Andrade, who was the chancellor of the Luanda archdiocese when the war broke out in 1961. Mario de Andrade was in Lisbon until 1954, when he moved to Paris to study social sciences at the Sorbonne. There he joined team of international intellectuals associated with the cultural review *Presence Africaine.* Andrade wrote several articles under the pseudonym Buanga Fele and edited an anthology of African poetry in Portuguese.

More than any other leader, Mario de Andrade contributed to the positive intellectual image of the MPLA in Europe by his writings and international political activities. In 1956 he organised the meeting of nationalist leaders from the Portuguese colonies into an interterritorial Movimento Anti-Colonialista (MAC). Andrade helped guide MAC through various forms until it became the Conferencia das Organizacoes Nacionalistas das Colonias Portuguesas (CONCP), which coordinated the activities of MPLA, PAIGC (Partido Africano de Independencia da Guine e Cabo Verde), and FRELIMO (Frente dc Libertacao de Mocambicque) through the independence struggle. Andrade was the first president of CONCP as well as acting president of MPLA. At the First National Conference in Leopoldville, where Agostinho Neto was elected president, Mario de Andrade became secretary for external affairs of the MPLA executive committee.

Viriato Francisco Clemente Da Cruz

The third of the MPLA founder-leaders, Viriato da Cruz, like his two colleagues Neto and Andrade, was a graduate of the government *liceu* in Luanda. Born March 25, 1928, at Kikuvu, near Porto Amboim, the young mestico was only twenty-one years old when he became editor of the influential and short-lived literary review *Memngem.* He was also a leader in the cultural group which took as its slogan, "Let us discover Angola." Cruz, who made important contributions to Angolan nationalism, analysed this social and literary movement:

> [It] should reassume... the combative spirit of the African writers of the end of the nineteenth century and the beginning of the present century. This movement would combat the exaggerated respect for the cultural values of the West (many of which are already past); inspire the youth to rediscover Angola in all its aspects through collective and organised effort; exhort them to produce results for the people; solicit the study of modern foreign cultural currents, but with the aim of rethinking and nationalising their positive and valid creations; require the expression of the popular interests and authentic African nature, but without making any concessions to the thirst for colonial exoticism. Everything should be based on an esthetic sense, intelligence and on African reason and will.[15]

The urge to "rediscover" Angola was appropriate to Viriato da Cruz and other Angolans who had abandoned or been torn from their mother culture. In his poem "Makezu," da Cruz pictures an African granny-vendor in the *musseques of* Luanda shouting *"makezu"* ("mush") to attract the attention of the servants, washerwomen, and artisans so they would buy her manioc mush as they leave their homes to walk to work in the city. But, this new generation

> ... took to a new custom called civilisation.
> They only eat bread and sausage or take coffee and bread...
> Our roots take their strength from mush.[16]

As poet, politician, and organizer, Viriato da Cruz held the important position of secretary-general of the MPLA from its founding in 1956 until 1962.[17] Da Cruz was on the long list of those to be arrested in 1957 when the political police (Policia Internacional e de Defesa do Estado, PIDE) established headquarters in Angola. However, he managed to flee to Portugal and then to France, where he joined Mario de Andrade and other mestico intellectuals such as Lucio Lara, forming the active nucleus of the MPLA leadership in exile.[18]

Through such leaders as Neto, Mario Pinto de Andrade, Viriato da Cruz, and Lucio Lara, MPLA developed a movement with roots in the urban, assimilado-mestico community and an ideology shaped by Marxism.

UPA

The second nationalist movement, the Uniao das Populacoes do Angola, was led by members of families that belonged to the traditional power structure of the Kongo kingdom and look as its motto, "Land and Liberty." On the death in 1955 of Dom Pedro VII, a king of the Kongo who had remained submissive to the Portuguese authorities during his thirty-two-year reign, Kongo loyalists resident in the Belgian Congo urged the choice of a successor who would better represent African interests. Eduardo

Pinock, who led the self-exiled group, had been bqrn on March 28, 1905 at Sao Salvador, where he attended the local Baptist mission school. Like so many Bakongo, Pinock had found more economic opportunities across the border and for many years held what was then an unusually responsible post for an African, that of railroad stationmaster at the Congolese port of Matadi.[19] In the choice of a new king, Pinock and his associates supported the candidacy of a respected community leader and Protestant, Manucl Kiditu, named for his maternal uncle, Dom Manuel Kiditu, a former king (1912-1915). The Portuguese officials vetoed this choice and crowned Antonio Jose de Gama, described by his critics as "an old handyman and printer at the Catholic mission of Sao Salvador, who suffered from sleeping sickness and had only an elementary education."[20]

Having failed in their attempt to choose their own king, the Protestant reformers then urged that Eduardo Pinock be named first councillor of Dom Antonio III. The Portuguese officials, threatened by this suggestion, not only refused to accept the nomination of Pinock as councillor, but forced the king to prohibit any Sao Salvadorean from returning home from the Belgian Congo after June 30, 1956. Having suffered two political defeats in efforts to use the kingship to achieve political reform, and faced with involuntary exile, the emigres decided that they must organise an underground political movement.

Manuel Barros Nekaka in Leopoldville had been trying to organise Angolans to rally support for the Kingdom of the Kongo since 1942. When the efforts of the Protestant reformers to capture the throne in 1955 failed and the border was closed to the return of the emigres, the Angolans in the Belgian Congo took new initiatives. On May 20, 1956, Nekaka, Pinock, and others, including Holden Roberto, sent a letter to an American State Department official in Leopoldville, asserting that historically and legally the Portuguese Kongo constituted a territory separate from Angola, to which it had been unjustly joined in 1884.[21] In

1956, an anonymous petition was sent from Sao Salvador do Congo to the United Nations by "natives of the territory of the formerly independent kingdom of the Congo," listing their grievances: forced labour, lack of health and education services, economic exploitation, arbitrary arrests, land seizure and expropriation.[22]

In July 1957, Angolans from Leopoldville and Matadi met in Leopoldville to organise the Uniao das Populacoes do Norte de Angola (UPNA).[23] They named Barros Nekaka president and Francisco Borralho Lulendo, of the Matadi group, secretary. Although, the Belgian Congo gave the Angolans more economic opportunity than their own country, the political restrictions were almost as severe. Therefore, UPNA sought to send a representative abroad to lobby for their rights in Africa, in the United States, and at the United Nations. The first opportunity to speak in a larger forum came through an invitation to participate in the All-Africa People's Conference in Accra in 1958. Nekaka was unable to go to Ghana so the assignment was given to his nephew and protégé, Holden Roberto.

Holden Roberto

Born on January 12, 1923, at Sao Salvador, Angola, Roberto was named after a British Baptist missionary, Robert Holden Carson Graham.[24] Two years later, Roberto was taken to the Belgian Congo by an aunt, and his parents soon followed. He was educated at Leopoldville, where he was graduated from a Baptist mission school in 1940 and then sent back to Sao Salvador to "rediscover his roots and perfect his Portuguese." After a year in the Mbanza Kongo, he returned to the Congo where he worked as an accountant in the Belgian administration and then at Nogueira, a Portuguese trading company in Leopoldville. Roberto said that it was during a three-week visit to Angola that he was shocked into political activism by witnessing the brutalisation of a helpless old man by a callous Portuguese *chefe do posto.*[25]

Although, Holden Roberto had no formal postsecondary education, he profited from an intense, practical political education with teachers who were not academicians but African nationalist leaders from the countries which achieved political independence during that period. Roberto had become acquainted with two future ministers of the Congo, meeting Patrice Lumumba at the Cercle des Evolues when they were both Belgian civil servants in Stanleyville, and Cyrille Adoula while playing on the same soccer team in Leopoldville. Accepting the invitation to attend the First All-Africa People's Conference in Accra, Roberto established relations with George Padmore, Kwame Nkrumah, Sekou Toure, Kenneth Kaunda, Taieb Slim, Tom Mboya, and Frantz Fanon. At the second such conference in Tunis the next year, he was elected to the conference steering committee and formed an enduring friendship with Tunisian President Habib Bourguiba. Attached to the Guinean delegation, Roberto also attended the Fourteenth General Assembly of the United Nations.

As soon as Roberto began to meet African leaders with a broader vision, he discovered that the idea of resurrecting the old Kongo kingdom was considered a tribal anachronism. Communicating this criticism to his home organisation, he persuaded them to drop the regional term so that the Union of the Peoples of the North of Angola (UPNA) became the Union of the Peoples of Angola (UPA).[26]

Outbreak of Angolan Revolt

Before 1961, the two main nationalist movements—MPLA and UPA—existed underground or in exile and only surfaced in foreign capitals, at Pan-African meetings, or at the United Nations. At the beginning of 1961, however, two events occurred which forced the Portuguese and the nationalist movements themselves to recognise the seriousness of the Angolan anticolonial sentiment. Before dawn on February 4, 1961, Africans attacked prisons in Luanda. And on March 15, 1961, bands of men began a series of attacks which spread in the next few days to most of the Portuguese trading centers, administrative posts, and coffee plantations in the north of Angola.

In the capital, on February 4, 100 to 200 Africans armed with knives and clubs attacked two prisons and a police station, hoping to free political prisoners who, it was rumored, were to be transferred to Portugal. Reportedly, seven Portuguese police were killed, about forty Africans machine-gunned, and none of the prisoners freed. Agostinho Neto explained the significance of the attacks: "The operation was not, in fact, a success, because the prisoners were not freed, but from that moment the People became conscious of the imperative to fight, and the Portuguese had to face an unexpected situation, a prelude to the difficulties in which they would find themselves in order to maintain their domination."[27]

The violence continued for a week in Luanda. On February 5, armed European civilians leaving funeral services for the seven policemen turned on African bystanders. Five days later a raid on another Luanda prison resulted in seven deaths and seventeen wounded. Portuguese vengeance was awesome. The police helped white civilian vigilantes organise nightly slaughters in the African townships or *musseques.*

International Reaction to the Angolan Revolt

The outburst of violence in Luanda received world press coverage because many foreign journalists had arrived in Luanda at the end of January to report the hijacking of the Portuguese luxury liner *Santa Maria,* supposedly en route to Angola. Captain Henrique Galvao, who had become a critic of Portuguese colonialism through his experience as an administrative official in Angola, organised the seizure of the *Santa Maria* in cooperation with General Humberto Delgado, the opposition candidate for the presidency of Portugal in 1958. The plan had two parts: first, to commandeer the ship after it left Venezuela and take it to

Africa; and second, to overpower the Spanish West African territories of Fernando Po and Rio Muni, which would then be the base for an air attack on Luanda. On January 20, 1961, Galvao, recognising the quixotic nature of the venture, called it Operation Dulcineia. "We were romantics fighting for our lady. Liberty," he said.[28]

The plan was aborted when Captain Galvao decided to slop at Saint Lucia in the Windward Islands to leave a wounded crewman and a sick passenger who needed medical attention. Even so, Galvao considered Operation Dulcineia a success since it called the attention of the world to the plight of the Spanish and Portuguese, and aroused the hopes of the Iberian peoples that the dictatorships of Franco and Salazar could be overthrown. The governor-general of Angola had given credibility to the rumor that Angola was the ship's destination by declaring that he had taken "all possible measure for the defense and security of this Portuguese possession in Africa in view of the approach of the *Santa Maria* commandeered by Henrique Galvao."[29] So the *Santa Maria,* sailing into the harbor of Recife, Brazil, on February 2 after a thirteen-day adventure, focused the attention of the world on Portugal's largest colony, Angola.

This world attention increased the impact of the predawn attacks on the Luanda prisons, but no one knew exactly whom to credit or blame for the incidents. At that time there were two MPL As—one outside Angola, a head without a body, and one inside, a body without a head.[30] MPLA representatives in exile who were able to make public statements claimed only "the participation" of MPLA elements in the February 4 events. As time passed the MPLA assumed full credit for the predawn attacks, and the Angolan national anthem begins: "O Fatherland, never will we forget the heroes of the fourth of February."

Holden Roberto had returned to the Congo after its independence on June 30, 1960 and begun a program of political activity aimed at Angola. UPA couriers were dispatched to Luanda and Nova Lisboa to distribute party tracts among African soldiers in the Portuguese army.[31] UPA also beamed political broadcasts to Angola to exhort Angolans to prepare for action against Portuguese colonialism. The political activity which could now be carried on openly in the Congo by UPA was being done clandestinely in Angola. In fact, when UPA decided to organise the attacks on March 15, it called three organizers from northern Angola to coordinate plans. About February 28, 1961 they were sent back into Angola[32] and, according to the account of one of these emissaries, he instructed the people in the area to burn bridges, crops, houses—to destroy property but not persons.

On March 10, after having sent orders into Angola, Roberto left Leopoldville for the United Nations Security Council meeting in New York. On the day set for the revolt, Roberto gave a press conference without referring to the happenings in Angola but condemning Portuguese colonialism. He maintained that UPA had 40,000 regular members and over a half a million sympathizers.[33]

On March 15 and 16, Angolan mobs, instigated if not actually led by UPA, attacked about thirty small settlements, administrative posts, and coffee plantations in two separate areas of northwest Angola. The first was along the Congo-Angola border near Sao, Salvador, the second the Dembos area reaching to within 75 miles (120 kilometers) of Luanda. For four months the area under attack by Angolans increased until it covered all of northwest Angola from the Atlantic to the Kwango. Only in August did the Portuguese military superiority make itself felt so that the nationalists were pushed back into the two pockets in which the original attacks had occurred in March.

When reports readied New York about the undisciplined nature of the outbreak, Roberto deplored the "extreme violence" of African attacks whose ferocity he described as an "expression of desperation against Portuguese terrorism over the past five hundred years," and added, "We are deeply sorry that women and children have been killed." The Portuguese widely circulated photographs of the corpses—black and white, young and old, men and women—murdered by the mobs who lashed out with their *catanas* (knives).[34]

It is difficult to understand why the poorly organised Angolan nationalists, using only knives and a few muzzle-loading guns, could have been so effective. The lack of preparedness and slow reaction by the Portuguese is even more difficult to explain when we realise they had received warnings of imminent attacks for several months before March 15.

Reasons for the Angolan Rebellion

The official Portuguese explanation of the rebellion in the north was simple—"armed bands coming from the exterior"[35]—but this was refuted in fact by the very traders, officials, and plantation foremen who had escaped. They were taken by surprise precisely because the attackers were their regular customers, clients, or workers. However, it is true that the independence of the Congo on June 30, 1960, gave freedom to Angolan emigrés to organise politically and to extend their in-fluence and activities back into Angola.

The Portuguese also suggested Kongo tribalism and religious rivalry as causes of the rebellion. They attributed the brutal nature of some of the attacks to "atavistic tribal practices" and cited the death of "loyal Bailundos" as proof of the tribal character of the revolt.[36] However, the ethnic hypothesis does not stand up when it is recognised that a majority of the attacks during the first week were in the Dembos, a predominantly Kimbundu rather than Kongo area. The Portuguese official interpretation of the events laid blame also on the Protestants and noted that the Kongo district was the area of Angola with the highest percentage of Protestants. This charge was a corollary of the Catholic criticism that the Protestants were religiously heretical and politically subversive. There is no doubt that the UPA grew out of the

Kongo Protestant community to challenge the dominant political power based on the identification of Catholic Church and Portuguese state.[37]

A more plausible explanation for the 1961 rebellion in the north of Angola is related to coffee, land, and labour.[38] The price of coffee had dropped in 1960 and the African producers suffered more acutely since they could not call on the government or commercial banks to compensate them for their loss of income. The slump of 1960 accentuated the general threat to African farmers presented by the expansion of estate coffee production on European land concessions. The expansion of the plantations also required additional contract labour, which added more inflammatory elements. The correlation between the number and location of violent attacks and the expansion of European-owned coffee plantations seems to substantiate the assertion that this was the inflammable material in which the explosion took place. Was it ignited by spontaneous combustion or set alight by some spark? Holden Roberto, the president of UPA, at different times affirmed both. In a memorandum to the United Nations he explained how the revolt began on a coffee plantation called Primavera near Madimba, some sixty-Five miles from the Congo-Angola border:

On the evening of March 14, the conscript laborers at Primavera gathered before the house of the coffee plantation manager, a Sr. Rcis, and demanded six months' overdue back pay. He allegedly refused to listen and without further ado, took out his gun and fired at the workers, killing several of them. Armed with their catanas (machetes), the farm workers promptly fell upon Reis and killed him and his family. Hearing of the Primavera incident, other Portuguese settlers began shooting Africans on sight. The latter responded by burning crops, pillaging houses and demolishing bridges. The news spread, incidents multiplied—the revolution had begun as a kind of spontaneous combustion.[39]

Roberto contradicted his own description of the revolt as "spontaneous combustion" when he spoke at the Second Anniversary of the Revolution in Leopoldville on March 15, 1963:

"We gave this password [to engage in the fight for independence] on March 15, 1961 and the responsibility is wholly ours."[40] As a matter of fact, the grievances of the Angolans against the Portuguese were so numerous and serious that any one or a combination of incidents could have triggered the revolt: the drop in coffee prices, the loss of land, a violent clash on one plantation, the independence of the Congo, or the encouragement of the United Nations.

The Portuguese Reaction

The question of why the Portuguese were so ill prepared for the rebellion is more difficult to answer, however, especially when it is recognised that personal warnings were given to traders, Portuguese officials, and missionaries by friendly Africans and that a rebellion had started in the Cassange basin east of Malange at the end of 1960.

The peasant revolt in the Cassange basin was never integrated into the nationalist mythologies. As noted before, the Portuguese government forced the population of that area to cultivate cotton and sell it at a fixed price to Cotonang, which held a complete monopoly in its marketing. In a generally deteriorating situation, three factors combined to produce the rebellion, which is sometimes known as Maria's War.[41] First, the independence of the Congo on June 30, 1960 aroused the political hopes of Angolan nationalism, especially in the areas such as the Cassange basin that bordered on the newly independent nation to the north. Second, a sharp drop in the price of cotton reduced the average receipts of producers from forty-eight dollars (U.S.) in 1959 to thirty-four dollars in 1960. Third, a messianic-nationalist movement inflamed the discontent of the peasants against the forced cotton production and the sharp decline in income.

One of the principles of the movement ordered the peasants to kill their animals, which they did in November and December of 1960. Then they abandoned their fields and refused to pay taxes. The people considered this passive resistance, but Cotonang and the Portuguese government did not think it less dangerous for being called "passive." The authorities arrested the ringleaders of the movement, but this did not stop the people's revolt. In January 1961, at planting time, the farmers burned their seed, abandoned their tools, and tore up their identification booklets. To show their enthusiasm, they sang the praises of Lumumba, Pinock, and Maria.

Passive resistance gave way to a more active second phase in which rebels with *catanas* and *canhangulos* (muzzle-loading rifles) attacked rural stores, two administrative posts (Tambo Aluma and Marimba), and a Catholic mission. However the traders, officials, and missionaries were not harmed; they were simply disarmed and allowed to flee. The Portuguese underestimated the strength behind these assaults.

While public attention was focused on the Luanda prison attacks on February 4 and the ensuing funerals and reprisals, the Portuguese sent two companies of infantry *(cacadores especiais)* from Malange to Cassange. Direct combat in the basin began on February 6 near Quela. For the first time the Portuguese air force dropped napalm and fire bombs on Angolan villages. Estimates of the number of victims in Maria's War ranged from a few hundred to 20,000,[42] but the best authority on the period accepts the more modest estimates of "hundreds, perhaps thousands, of African lives."[43]

Both the peasants' war in the Cassange basin in January and the February attacks on Luanda prisons worried the Portuguese, but they still hesitated to use major military power. Perhaps, they did not recognise that the uprising in the northwest was more serious than the rebellion in the Cassange basin. Certainly the Portuguese did not understand the intensity of the resentment of the Africans, nor were they aware of the deep penetration of the UPA. In Luanda and Lisbon, officials could also see the possible negative reactions to massive Portuguese military response. In spite of their rhetoric that the Portuguese would never abandon Angola as the Belgians did the Congo, the experience of their northern neighbour was clearly in mind and the Portuguese did not wish to frighten the Angolan whites into fleeing. The withdrawal of their limited troops from the center, south, and cast to crush resistance in the northwest might have touched off rebellions all over Angola. Finally, Portuguese mobilisation would have supported the argument of the anticolomal nations in the United Nations that Lisbon really was a threat to peace.[44]

The Portuguese in Angola, accepting their own government's propaganda, believed that the whites were in Africa on a civilising mission. Therefore, the assumedly inferior blacks owed respect and gratitude to them as representatives of a superior civilisation even though the individual Portuguese settler might be illiterate. The blacks, too, had been shaped by the colonial pattern so they knew when to say, *"Sim, Senhor!"* and how to keep their hatred hidden, even from themselves. It is not surprising, therefore, that a general disorientation and panic set in when Africans, who had seemingly accepted the assumption that lack of respect for whites was the greatest crime, drew out *catanas* and slaughtered white bosses, foremen, and traders, not even sparing women and children. In spite of the stifling atmosphere which forced all political comments to be made in hushed tones, Angolans shouted "Mate! [kill] *UPA!*" as they assaulted stores, government posts, and coffee plantations. The two words that came to Portuguese stunned minds to express these events which did not fit into the colonial mentality were *acontecimentos* (happenings) and *confusoes* (confusions). The events seemed to admit of no rational explanation.

Military Action

However, the seriousness of the *acontecimentos* of March 15 Finally convinced the Portuguese that they were faced with a challenge which could not be easily crushed with a few bombs, as in the peasants' war in the Cassange basin, nor would civilian reprisals be possible or effective as in Luanda after the February 4 attacks. On March 30, two weeks after the major revolt in northern Angola, Salazar began to act. First he centralised military and political power in each colony in the hands of the governor-general. Within a few days, paratroopers and other special forces arrived in small numbers by air. On April 13, Salazar reshuffled his government and he himself occupied the post of national defense minister, explaining his actions by saying: "The reason is Angola. To act rapidly and with force is the objective which will put to the test our capacity to make decisions."[45]

The steamship *Niassa* arrived at Luanda on May 1 with the first large contingent of troops from Portugal. They paraded down the Avenida Marginal from the port with Dr. Adriano Moreira, the new overseas minister, and Col. Kaulza de Arriaga, the subsecrctary of the air force, in the reviewing stand. On May 13 the newly arrived troops left Luanda for the north to begin the military reoccupation of Angola. The long military column was accompanied by scores of civilian vehicles with goods and fuel for localities that were still holding out against the Angolans. They took four days to cover the 350 miles (550 kilometers) to Negage via Lucala, Vila Salazar, and Camabatela, leaving supplies and reinforcements along the way. By July 1, 1961, it was estimated that Portuguese troop strength in Angola had reached 17,000.

Helio Felgas, the Portuguese historian of this period, affirms that their forces reoccupied the whole northwest area in less than four months. This period began with the taking of the post of Lucunga on June 13 and ended October 7, during which time fifty posts and commercial settlements, spread over three districts and occupying an area more than twice the size of Portugal, were reconquered. Many others were reinforced and the frontier area was garrisoned. On October 7 the governor-general, referring to the reconquest, said: "If we can divide the war into distinct phases, we would say that we have terminated the military operations and are beginning the next phase of police operations, although this will still be in a military manner."[46]

In the period 1961-1965, the size of Portugal's armed forces in Angola increased from 9,000, including 2,000 to 3,000 Europeans, to 50,000 officers and men. These regular military forces were reinforced by Forcas Militarizadas (mililarised forces), which included the OPVDC, PSP, and PIDE. The Provincial Organisation of Volunteers and Civil Defense (OPVDC) was a militia which served as an auxiliary to the regular armed forces with special responsibility for protection of life and property against guerrilla attacks. The OPVDC had a permanent staff of military commanders. The Public Security Police (PSP), which had performed normal police duties in towns and cities before the war, took on special paramilitary duties, protecting plantations in the war zone and patrolling highways and rural areas. The International Police for the Defense of the State (PIDE) had sent its First agents from Lisbon to Luanda in 1957 and by 1965 had about 500 agents in Angola. This, of course, did not include the paid informants who were many times more numerous than the actual agents. In addition, the militarised forces included the judicial police and railroad brigades.

The military response to the nationalist attacks can be measured by the fact that in 1969 slightly more than half of the total European male population between the ages of twenty and sixty-Five were engaged in either military or paramilitary activities.[47]

The military set itself to fulfil a threefold mission: to secure the borders, maintain internal security, and conduct a social action program to gain or maintain the loyalty of Africans through psychological warfare. To fulfill this third objective, military personnel assisted the expanding educational system by building schools and teaching in classrooms, particularly in war zones. Some health services and first aid were also provided by military personnel.

Strategic Hamlets

To facilitate both military and psychological warfare, the Portuguese forced the Angolans to settle in strategic hamlets. Portugal had earlier employed "rural concentrations" in the north of Angola in the fight against sleeping sickness (trypanosomiasis). Bakongo were forced to abandon their inaccessible villages and build houses along the main roads so nurses could innoculate the population against the disease. This system was adapted in 1961 to the pattern of strategic hamlets used against guerrilla fighters in Malaya, Philippines, and Vietnam. Military officials argued that concentrating the Angolans into larger villages alongside the roads patrolled by the military would deny the insurgents the aid and comfort they formerly received from the local populace. Civilian officials supported the plan, maintaining that strategic hamlets provided the opportunity to extend medical, educational, agricultural, and sanitary services to the people.

After the Portuguese had regained control of the towns, administrative posts, and plantations, the strategic hamlets became. the central focus of the military program in the north. The government constructed 130 to 150 hamlets with the capacity for about 2,000 persons each.[48] The estimates of the population of the northern area in general and the strategic hamlets in particular is disputed. According to the 1960 census, the Zaire and Uige districts had a total African population of 503,318. Most of the people fled to the Republic of the Congo or hid in the forests between 1961 and 1965. The Portuguese claimed that as many as 200,000 had returned and were living in the hamlets, but the exact number in the hamlets is impossible to ascertain.

Reforms in Angola

Recognising that the conflict in Angola could not be won by military means alone, the Portuguese mobilised politically almost as rapidly as they did militarily. Reforms were instituted to respond to the three main charges against Portuguese colonialism. To counter the charge that Africans were second-class citizens in Angola, the Portuguese government revoked the Statute of Natives (Estalulo dos Indigenas, Decree Law No. 39,666) of May 20, 1954. By a decree (No. 43,893) of September 6, 1961, the distinction between "civilised" and "noncivilised" was legally abolished. To replace the native tax book, the identity card that had been the sign of citizenship, and therefore restricted to whiles and assimilated blacks, became available to all.

However, most rural Angolans found this reform more bother than benefit. The government sent teams of functionaries into remote areas to take pictures, collect fingerprints, and register the vital statistics necessary for the new identity cards. People were expected to pay for services in time and money, and when they finally received the card, it guaranteed no new privilege. The special head tax levied on Africans was also abolished, and a new "general minimum tax" (Imposto Geral Minimo) was instituted, which, however, doubled the tax for the former *indigenas.*

The Portuguese next reformed the educational system, recognising it as a weapon in the struggle between Portuguese and Angolan nationalism. Believing that this weapon should be in the hands of the government, the Portuguese moved in 1961 to assume direct responsibility for the education of the total Angolan population instead of leaving African education to the missions. The first task was to train more teachers and the most urgent need was among the rural Africans. Therefore, in 1962, vacation courses of two and a half months were established to train *monitores* to teach the first year of the rural education course. The next year the government repeated the First-year course and added a second-year course in seven centers with 791 students.

By 1965 each of the fourteen districts had a *monitores* course with a total of 2,413 students.[49] Since these students became *monitores* or teachers on government salary after completing the first two-and-a-half-month course, this new program almost doubled the number of teachers in Angola in the first five years of the war.

To prepare primary teachers with more adequate training, the government established two more levels of normal schools: *escolas de habilitaqdo* and *escolas de magisterio.* The former received students who had completed primary school and gave them a four-year program which included community development courses as well as the rudiments of an academic education. The six *Ksrolns de habilitacao* established by 1965 were administered by the Catholic Church and had 649 students. At a higher level, the education services established a two-year program at three *escolas de Magisterio* for students who had already completed their fifth year of secondary school. These three schools had 205 students. The new teacher training programs allowed an increase of 81 per cent from 1961 to 1965 in the number of primary pupils, from a total of 105, 781 to 191.693.[50]

To cap this educational development, which was accelerated in response to the war, the government established the University of General Studies in 1963 with three campuses: Luanda (faculties of arts and medicine); Sa da Bandeira (faculty of edu-cation); and Nova Lisboa (agronomy and veterinary science). In 1963 the three campuses had 314 students and by 1966 they almost doubled the number to 600, practically all whites.[51]

The educational reform was qualitative as well as quantitative. Until 1961 all primary textbooks came from Portugal and described exclusively European geography and customs. Parrot pedagogy prevailed. Some educators had been preparing new curriculums and texts, but they did not receive official support until March 1961, when the government recognised that new materials with illustrations and vocabulary from the daily life of the students were essential if mass education were to succeed. The new books still looked at Angola through Portuguese eyes, but some effort was made at least to look at Angola. Prewar hooks were exclusively Portuguese; postwar books were colonial-Angolan.

The Portuguese expanded the educational system in Angola on the assumption that this reform would be a significant part of a counterinsurgency program. Since Africans complained of not having access to education, the provision of schools, teachers, and new books should, according to Portuguese analysis, produce loyalty to Portugal. However, the experience in Angola would seem to support those who contend that social and economic improvements may be more subversive than supportive of the established regime. Rather than satisfying the population's expectations and desires, the government's efforts, which the people never judged to be sufficient, exacerbated the frustrations and further alienated the people.[52]

The third reform that Portugal instituted in response to the outbreak of war was the elimination of forced labour. African laborers were no longer recruited forcibly through government administrative officers. Instead, the government licensed private labour recruiters to go into the villages and enlist men to work in coffee or sugar plantations, fisheries, mines, and the like. Even without the direct coercion of the administrative officials, the private recruiters succeeded in supplying the number of workers required. The recruiters could count on the Africans' constant need of cash income to pay taxes and buy the necessities of life. It was difficult for the Africans who had been forced all their lives to obey the administrative officials lo distinguish the new recruiters with official licenses from Portuguese administrators.

Nationalist Reaction to Reforms

Portugal instituted reforms in 1961 to correct three of the evils against which the Angolans rebelled: the legally inferior status of the *indigena,* lack of educational opportunities, and forced labour. Angolans were pleased to take advantage of new educational opportunities, more employment openings, and some slight administrative benefits. However, they did not consider that these reforms had fundamentally changed the unjust relationships between the Portuguese and the Angolans. One thing that was not changed by the reforms was the throttle on free speech. No one in Angola could publicly criticise the government programs or propose reforms.

Only the Angolan nationalist leaders in exile could criticise the reforms and express the more radical view that the time had passed to reform colonialism: it must now be discarded in favour of self-determination and political independence. In fact, the nationalist criticism considered the Portuguese reforms not only ineffective and hypocritical, but positively evil. Angolan nationalists held that by signing these decrees and making speeches, the government convinced the Portuguese that justice was being done. The exiles feared that even some Angolans would be lulled to sleep by these palliative measures, and the reforms would salve the consciences of the Western powers which were supporting Portugal.

According to the nationalist leaders, the worst feature of the reforms was that they concealed the real issue—a conflict of nationalisms. Portuguese nationalism had reluctantly opened itself to receive Angolans as citizens within the Lusitanian nation, but they were still second-class citizens with restricted educational and economic opportunities. Angolan nationalism protested not simply against forced labour, but against an economy that was geared to the enrichment of Portugal and other European or American investors. They demanded not only more schools, but an educational system that would teach Angolans the values of their traditions and the fads about I heir land and society.

In their rejection of reform, the Angolan nationalists were supported by the United Nations. Through a historically significant coincidence, the Angolan nationalist movements were being formed just at the time that Portugal became a member of the United Nations. Between 1955 and 1960, Angolan nationalism benefited as the United Nations took an increasingly active role in defining the relationship between members and their non-self-governing territories.

Role of the United Nations

Angola became the test case when the General Assembly approved a list of twelve principles which declared that *prima facie* there is an obligation to transmit information in respect to a territory that is geographically separate and is distinct ethnically and/or culturally from the country administering it (Resolution 1541 XIV, December 15, 1960).

With the outbreak of the war in 1961, Angolan colonialism was transformed from a legal case to an issue of international urgency. Just after the attempt to free Luanda prisoners on February 4,1961, Liberia and twenty-six other African and Asian countries requested an urgent meeting of the United Nations Security Council. Portugal protested that the rebellion was a domestic affair, while African and Asian delegations argued that the "juridical fiction" of Angola being an integral part of Portugal should not impede the Security Council from consideration of the question.

The Security Council agreed to discuss Angola at a special meeting (March 10-15), where Ceylon, Liberia, and the United Arab Republic introduced a resolution calling on Portugal to implement Resolution 1514 (XV) on the Granting of Independence to Colonial Countries and Peoples. On March 15, 1961, the very day the rebellions broke out all across northern Angola, the resolution was rejected because it failed to secure the required majority. (The vote was five in favour—Ceylon, Liberia, USSR, United Arab Republic, and United States—and none against, with six countries—Chile, China, Ecuador, France, Turkey, and the United Kingdom—abstaining.)

Following the events of March 15, forty African, Arab, and Asian nations brought the question of Angola before the United Nations General Assembly. On April 20 the General Assembly, with only Portugal and South Africa voting against, adopted a resolution (1603 XV) similar in its operative provisions to the one rejected in the Security Council. It stated that the failure to. "act effectively and in time for ameliorating the disabilities of the African peoples of Angola is likely to endanger international peace and security." It called upon Portugal to "consider urgently the introduction of measures and reforms" in order to implement the provisions of the declaration on ending colonialism, and it established a Five-member subcommittee on Angola to report on the situation.

The United Nations played a more important role for Angolan, Guinean, and Mozambican nationalism than for other African nations. Portugal had not provided opportunities as Britain, France, and even Belgium had done for the discussion of political issues by the leadership of their colonial people. After the Republic (1926), any expression of African nationalist aspiration was prohibited in Portugal or in any of its colonies. Although, nationalist leaders from other colonies were arrested and restricted in their political activities, they were allowed to form parties, publish literature, and, up to a point, criticise the colonial regimes. The United Nations, therefore, provided the essential forum for the articulation of Angolan nationalism when Portugal banned it.

Development of National Movements in Angola

The initial Angolan military successes and the international recognition of Angolan aspirations put pressure on the two main Angolan political parties to become more truly national movements. To this end, the parties sought to be more inclusive in their leadership and to form united fronts.

The UPA, which was firmly rooted in the Bakongo and depended on the leadership of Roberto, Pinock, and Nekaka, reached out to include important non-Kongo elements. Rosario Neto (no relation to Agostinho Neto), a Kimbundu exile, opened the UPA office in Leopoldville at the time of Congolese independence in 1960 and became vice-president. Joao Batista, a Cuanhama corporal in the Portuguese army, fled from his post in northern Angola in 1960 and became a UPA commander. Alexandre Taty, a Cabinda Catholic seminarian, became second vice-president of UPA, and a prominent Luanda mestico, Anibal de Melo, was chosen to be the party's political director. In late 1961, Jonas Malheiro Savimbi, an Umbundu student who had fled in 1960 from Lisbon to Switzerland because of harassment by the PIDE, took the post of secretary-general of UPA. Savimbi's entry moved the UPA toward its goal of becoming a national party by providing prominent representation of the largest ethnolinguistic group and counteracting UPA's anti-intellectual image. Therefore, by the end of 1961, UFA could claim to be a national party, at least on the basis of its representative leadership.

UPA next moved to extend its constituency support from the BaxiKongo in the area of Sao Salvador to include other peoples of the same ethnolinguistic group. The Bazombo to the east had formed a legally recognised mutual aid society, the Association Muluellc des Ressortissants de Zombo (ASSUM1ZO), in Leopoldville in 1956. After Congolese independence, AS-SIMIZO transformed itself into a political party, the Alliance des Ressortissants de Zombo (ALIAZO), which was a nonviolent and conciliatory alliance reflecting its leaders' Christian training and middle-class values. Under nationalist pressure, ALIAZO dropped its ethnic label and became the Partido Democratico de Angola (PDA) in January 1962. It aspired to play the role of mediator between UPA and MPLA but, when it failed in this, PDA joined UPA on March 27, 1962 to form the Frente Nacional de Libertacao de Angola (FNLA), which issued the following statement of objectives:

> To direct the struggle for Angolan national independence on the basis of fraternal collaboration among all Angolan ethnic groups... To install... a democratic regime that will respect the provisions of the Universal Declaration of Human Rights, that will institute agrarian reform... a planned economy, and industrialisation of the country... to adopt a policy of nonalignment... [53]

The FNLA could hardly be considered a "national" front, however, since at the base the UPA and PDA represented only two of the peoples belonging to the Kongo ethnolinguistic group.

The MPLA followed the same process of including leadership from outside its urban-Kimbundu-mestico base in naming Antonio Jabes Josias, one of Holden Roberto's former associates from Sao Salvador, to the president of its Congo committee. The committee also included Jorge M. Freitas, earlier connected with Barros Nekaka's group in Leopoldville. However, the MPLA placed more emphasis on uniting various Angolan groups to give it a national character than on seeking individual leaders from various regions or communities. This approach was to its advantage since it had confidence that its better-trained leadership would assure a dominant position for MPLA in any united front. The MPLA achieved a short-lived front at the end of 1960 when representatives of MPLA, UPA, ALIAZO, and a small Cabindan movement, AREC (Association des Ressortissants de l'Enclave de Cahinda), met in Leopoldville and formed the Front Commun des Partis Politiques de 1'Angola (FCPPA). A power struggle took place within UPA between those who favored the united front and those who opposed it. Holden Roberto led the latter group, contending that meaningful unity depended upon a real consensus of political views and that Angolan unity was "total as far as elements of the population on the field of battle [are] concerned.... There is no other kind of unity."[54]

Internationally, the MPLA pressed for a common front in 1961 at the Third All-Africa People's Conference in Cairo, which warned against "imperialist or neocolonialist" maneuvers tending to provoke "divisions amongst the people," and at the Council of the Organisation of the Afro-Asia Peoples' Solidarity Conference held in April 1961 in Bandung. The MPLA used the meeting of the nationalist movements for Portuguese colonies in Casablanca to put pressure on the UPA to join a coalition. At this meeting the Conferencia das Organizacoes Nacionalistas das Colonias Portuguesas (CONCP) was formed. Discussions between the MPLA and the UPA, ALIAZO, and the Mouvement de Liberation de l'Enclave de Cabinda (MLEC) did not result in coalitions or united fronts.

The two major parties also attempted to extend their influence and support through auxiliary labour, student, and health organisations.

Government-in-Exile

The most daring initiative taken by Angolans to create a national instrument to oppose Portugal was FNLA's formation of a government-in-exile a week after UPA and PDA had created the Frente Nacional de Libertacao de Angola (FNLA) in April 1962. The Governo Revolucionario de Angola no Exilio (GRAE), which originally was to be located inside Angola, was established instead in Kinshasa (then Leopoldville), since no area in Angola was securely held by Angolan nationalists. Holden Roberto assumed the presidency and Manuel Kunzika, president of PDA, became the First vice-president of GRAE. Jonas Savimbi occupied the position of foreign minister, which was the most strategic position after the presidency, since one of the main purposes of GRAE was to gain international recognition for the FNLA and the Angolan war of liberation. When the Organisation of African Unity (OAU) was formed a year later, in May 1963, GRAE received its official recognition and that of some twenty African states.

The OAU recognition of GRAE was not only the high point of FNLA's political fortunes, but also raised new and exaggerated expectations among its militants and sympathizers. GRAE expected greater financial support through the OAU's Liberation Committee, but actually received less than it had been receiving previously through bilateral assistance. Holden Roberto's prediction of military victory within two or three years also led Angolans to expect GRAE's forces to carry the attack on Portuguese colonialism to all regions of Angola. Umbundu who had joined the GRAE army with the hope of penetrating their region in central and southern Angola became disillusioned and mutinied when Roberto seemed to be waging a "border war." Tension mounted within GRAE when Roberto had some sixty of the mutineers arrested and put into Congolese jails.

The dissent and rebellion within GRAE assumed more serious proportions with the resignation of three top non-Kongo leaders. At the OAU conference in Cairo in July 1964, Jonas Malheiro Savimbi resigned his post as minister of foreign affairs. Then Dr. Jose Joao Liahuca, the director of the GRAE health and welfare agency, SARA, and Jose Kalundungo, chief of the general staff of the GRAE army, submitted their resignations. All three were Umbundu and attributed their frustrations to what they considered Holden Roberto's tribal orientation. Savimbi recalled that the Executive Committee of the UPA, the propelling force behind the GRAE, was composed of nineteen members, of whom eighteen were Kongo and of these, twelve were from the traditional Kongo capital, Sao Salvador, the home of Holden Roberto. Kalundungo argued similarly: "To show you Mr. Holden's attachment to tribalistic principles, we need only tell you that of the twenty-two officers trained in Algeria, only six belonged to ethnic groups different from his own."[55]

The dissidents argued that Holden Roberto and his organisations UPA/FNLA/GRAE were not only crippled by tribalism but also by inefficiency and undue dependence on American assistance. They made these arguments not so much on the basis of ideology but because of the practical effects of these policies. The war was stalled and nothing was being done to liberate the majority of Angolans who lived in central or southern Angola. Savimbi was undoubtedly articulating the convictions of his colleagues from central Angola when he said, "The guerilla army should live and progress into the interior with the total support of the population."[56] In a matter of months, Savimbi would begin mobilising another movement with the goal of pushing into the interior.

TABLE 1

Casualties in Angolan fighting, 1963-1965

Year	Killed	Wounded	Imprisoned	Total
1963	840	350	2737	3927
1964	749	469	1130	2348
1965	548	465	780	1793

Source: "BAC 5.6 boletim anti-colunial Feb. -Mar, 1973" (Lisbon, mimeographed), p. 13.

GRAE suffered another reverse in mid-1964 when Holden's long-time friend Cyrille Adoula was replaced as prime minister of the Congolese Republic by Mouse Tshombe, who had close ties with Portugal. The internal weakness of the two principal movements, MPLA and FNLA, during 1964 and 1965 is reflected in the lower level of military activity. According to the Portuguese military command in Angola, the number of Angolan casualties declined, as shown in Table 1.

In 1964, the MPLA began to recoup its fortunes, while GRAE was under heavy attack from Savimbi and other influential dissenters. The overthrow of Fulbert Youlou, president of Congo Brazzaville, by the revolutionary government of Alphonse Massamba-Debat provided the MPLA with a base from which it could operate much more freely. Russia and Eastern Europe provided materiel, while Cuban advisors established a training base at Brazzaville. The most active and best educated of the-young militants were sent for military training and other study to Eastern Europe.[57]

Economic Response to the War: 1961 -1965

Salazar, who was basically an economist, realised that a prompt military and political reaction was not sufficient to defend Angola. Comprehensive and rapid development of Angola was needed for Portugal to maintain political control. In June 1961, Decree Law No. 44016 established the outline of a new program for economic development in the overseas provinces and the integration of the financial and production structures of each province into an Escudo Area Common Market.[58] The outline was filled in gradually from 1961 to 1965 and, as we will see below, in the latter year the Portuguese made a more dramatic response to the economic pressures brought by the colonial wars.

Both military and economic responses to the nationalist threat demanded a more rapid expansion of the infrastructure. The total mileage of roads, 20,000 (35,000 kilometers) in 1961, which made it theoretically possible for Portuguese officials to reach all corners of Angola, was impressive. However, only 435 miles were paved. By May 1966, 2,190 miles (3,504 kilometers) were paved, 504 were graded and ready for paving, and 1,287 miles (2,059 kilometers) were improved roads with some engineering. More contracts had also been let to achieve the goal of uniting the capitals of all the districts by paved roads, which was seen as both a military and an economic necessity by the government.[59]

The war stimulated the development of the air network within Angola but isolated the colony even more from the outside world. For internal flights the domestic airline, DTA, purchased two Fokker Friendships (F-27), which speeded up the longer domestic flights. However, Air France and Sabena discontinued their regular flights to Angola. Only Portuguese Air Transport (TAP) and South African Airways (SAA) connected Angola to a limited outside world: Rliodesia, Mozambique, and South Africa on the continent and Portugal in Europe.

Agriculture was the basis of Angola's economy, so any economic reform had to deal first with agriculture. Within that sector the most urgent demand for change came from the Cassange region, where the compulsory production of cotton had caused the peasant rebellion in 1960-61. Immediately following the outbreak of the war in March 1961, compulsory cotton cultivation and cotton concessions were abolished. Then, as part of the overall economic reform, the Portuguese government established a Cotton Institute in Angola to replace the board in Lisbon which had regulated the trade before 1961.

Similarly, the Lisbon government substituted coffee and cereal institutes for trade boards that had operated out of the Portuguese capital in the prewar period. The institutes dealt with virtually all commercial aspects of these three crops, including marketing, price fixing, crop storage, and quality control, and also gave technical assistance to growers. New research facilities were provided to promote agricultural development. The Institutes and research centers served commercial agriculturalists, who were almost exclusively European. Some of the government agriculturalists wished to promote the development of the traditional sector of agriculture, but their lack of appropriate structures for extension work and their ignorance of the Angolan languages and cultures, together with limited resources, restricted severely their moving beyond good intentions.

In April 1961, the government gave emergency aid to the coffee farmers in the northwest, who were most seriously affected by the uprising, by establishing an agricultural and livestock credit fund. In 1964 its function was extended by law to include the promotion of agricultural development in general.

Portugal instituted these economic reforms to strengthen itself to bear the burdens imposed upon it by the wars in Angola,

Mozambique, and Guinea. However, the impact of the reforms was not nearly as beneficial to Portugal as the increased income from mineral production. Iron and petroleum had been explored before 1961, but only came into significant production after the outbreak of the war in Angola.

TABLE 2

Angolan foreign trade, 1961-1965

Year	Exports	Imports
1961	$135,593,850	$114,369,150
1962	149,250,150	136,428,810
1963	163,935,450	147,402,300
1964	205,363,200	165.000,150
1965	201,155,850	196,040,600

Source: Allison Butler Herrick ct al., *Area Handbook Angola* (Washington, D.C., 1967), p. 320.

Iron had been mined since 1957 and by 1965 it constituted a major export item. In 1959, iron ore production totaled 349,000 metric tons and by 1964 it reached 905,000 metric tons. In a more dramatic fashion, the production of petroleum increased from 9,000 metric tons in 1956 to 904,737 metric tons in 1964. Over half was processed in the Luanda refinery.[60]

The attacks on the coffee plantations in the north, the flight of whites to Europe, and the general atmosphere of uncertainty following the uprisings in 1961 disrupted local economies. However, government statistics indicate that Angola's foreign trade increased steadily from 1961 to 1965, with only a slight decline in exports in 1965. Even in that year Angola had a favorable balance of trade, as Table 2 shows.

Communications

Each side in the colonial war felt the need to tell its story to the widest audience possible. The vast majority of Angolans were entirely dependent on direct and informal oral communication for information. Radio was the most important channel of public communication. The Portuguese had eighteen stations which they controlled through government subsidies and censorship to assure that only the official view of the news was transmitted. The number of licensed receiving sets increased 25 per cent from 1961 to reach a total of 73,000 in 1964.[61]

An estimated 25 per cent of the Angolan population understood some Portuguese. One or two stations broadcast several hours weekly in African languages, but they were listened to more as a curiosity than as a source of information by Angolans. The government station in Luanda also beamed programs in French to the Congo and in English to South-West Africa.

The African nationalists broadcast to Angola over the respective host government-owned stations: MPLA from Brazzaville and FNLA from Kinshasa. Programs from Russia, South Africa, Great Britain, West Germany, and the Netherlands and the Voice of America were some of the foreign broadcasts that reached Angola with regular news and entertainment, sometimes in Portuguese.

Angolans differ over which is their national day—February 4 or March 15—but all agree that 1961 was the year in which the decisive war began between Angolan and Portuguese nationalisms. The years 1961-1965 constituted the first phase of that war of independence. If the history of Angola is one of five centuries of conflict, how did this conflict differ from those of the previous centuries?

First, for the first time Africans revolted against colonial rule in the name of Angola. The Kingdom of the Kongo had fought to assert its own authority repeatedly since the first Portuguese arrived in 1482. The Kimbundu, organised into a variety of political units, had resisted Portuguese conquest and allied themselves with or opposed the Bakongo to the north according to their political or commercial interests. The Bailundo revolted against the abuses of the Portuguese in 1902 and although they sought alliances and support from Huambo, Bie, and Chiyaka, they had no colonywide plan or vision.

The Portuguese tried to deny the existence of Angolan nationalism, claiming that the war was simply a series of tribal skirmishes. Official news stories stressed the conflict between the Bakongo and "loyal Bailundos." The Cuanhamas, who were drafted in the south, were sent to the northern front and praised for their heroic feats against the Bakongo. The Portuguese refused to admit that Angola might be a nation and not simply a colony or an overseas province of the Portuguese nation.

The Portuguese introduced a new patriotic song which ended:

> *"Angola é nossa. Angola e Portugal"* ("Angola is ours. Angola is Portugal"). However, when the Angolans sang lustily the line "Angola is ours" and whispered "Angola is Portugal," the song was banned. Even the Portuguese began to admit to themselves, if not publically, that the real enemy was not simply rebellious tribes but Angolan nationalism.

The second distinctive characteristic of the 1961 war was the combatants' sense of its being a life-and-death struggle. The Portuguese feared that the loss of their African colonies, especially the richest, Angola, would mean the economic end of Portugal, already the poorest nation in Western Europe. On the other side of the battle line, the Angolan nationalists knew that their only alternatives were independence or permanent exile. Compromise or reconciliation were no longer acceptable options.

Third, the 1961 war was internationalised in a unique way. Other countries had intervened militarily in the territory now known as Angola on previous occasions, but they were only using it as a battleground to grab some local advantage. Even when the nations met in Berlin (1884-85), they were concerned about keeping trade open in the Congo basin and did not recognise the existence of Angola as a political entity. After 1961, various countries intervened to try to shape Angola according to their interests. The United States and Western Europe spoke in favour of self-determination for Angola, but preferred it to continue as a Portuguese colony to any of the alternatives that they could see. South Africa and Rhodesia had no great respect for the Portuguese, but feared Angola as an independent, black-ruled nation. Newly independent African nations sympathised strongly with Angolan nationalism, but their practical assistance was limited to the provision of diplomatic channels, bases in neighbouring countries, and token military financial contributions. The socialist countries encouraged Angolan nationalism by furnishing arms, training, and finances as a means of attacking the West.

The life-and-death struggle of two nationalisms, supported by different international interests, had reached a stalemate in 1965. By that time, Portugal had succeeded in recapturing control of all the towns, administrative posts, and plantations in the north, and the Angolan economy was growing steadily. Angolan nationalists, with the added pressure from African nationalist movements in Guinea and Mozambique, were forcing Portugal to spend almost half its national budget on defense. Fifty thousand Portuguese troops were tied down in Angola alone, and Portugal was under increasing pressure from the international community to grant independence to its colonies.

Both the Portuguese and Angolans conceded that the struggle would be long and expensive. Yet, each claimed that victory was certain. To prepare for this prolonged struggle to achieve ultimate victory, each side in 1965 was planning new offensives.

NOTES AND REFERENCES

1. Wheeler and Pélissier, p. 119.
2. *"Memagem do povo negro de Angola dirigida as Nayies Unidns para: Sun Excelencia Presidents da Republics dos Estados Unidos da America do Norte, Washington."*

3. John A. Marcuin, *The Angolan Revolution,* Vol. I: *The Anatomy of an Explosion* (Cambridge, Mass.: The MIT Press, 1969), p. 300.
4. *Musstque* means sandy, arable land. The plural is used for the extensive areas surrounding the European city of Luanda where the Africans lived and cultivated small plots of manioc and other food crops. Oscar Ribas, *Tudo isto acuntereu: Romance autobiografico* (Luanda: Edicao do Autor), p. 630.
5. *Mar cum*, I, 330-31.
6. Agostinho Neto, *Sacred Hope,* trans. Marga Holness (Dar es Salaam: Tanzania Publishing House, 1974), p. 1.
7. *Ibid.*, p. xxv.
8. *Ibid.*, p. xxvi.
9. *Ibid.*, p. xv.
10. *Ibid.*, p. 68.
11. *Ibid.*, p. xxx; and Marcum, 1, 39-40.
12. *Neto*, p. xxxv.
13. Marcum, 1, 263.
14. *Ibid.*, p. 40.
15. Mario dc Andradc, *Antolugia tematica de poesia africana* (Lisbon: Livraria Sa da Costa Editora, 1975), p. 6, translated by L.W.H.
16. *Ibid.*, pp. 122-23; translated by permission of the publisher.
17. Marcum, 1,41.
18. *Ibid.*, pp. 41-42.
19. *Ibid.*, p. 56.
20. *Idem.*
21. *Ibid.*, p. 62.
22. Ronald H. Chilcote, *Emerging Nationalism in Portuguese Africa: Documents* (Stanford, California: Hoover Institution Press, 1972), pp. 44-48.
23. *Ibid.*, pp. 43, 54, 63, 65; and Marcum, I, 63.

24. Marcum, 1, 64-65.
25. *Ibid.*, p. 65; and Pierre A. Moser, *La revolution angotaue* (Tunis: Societe l'Action d'edition et de Presse, 1966), p. 66.
26. Marcum, 1, 169.
27. Libertacao nacional: Textose documentos do MPLA sobre a revolucaoo angolana *(Edicoes Maria da Fonte, 1974), p. 33.*
28. Henrique Galvao, *O assalto as"Santa Maria,"* trails. Manuel Pires de F. Matos (Lisbon: Edifies Deltbs, 1973), p. 147.
29. *Ibid.*, p. 217.
30. Rene Pelissier, "Resistance et revokes en Angola (1845-1961)," vol. 3 (unpublished manuscript), p. 1225.
31. Marcuin. I, 135.
32. *Ibid.*, p. 141.
33. *Ibid.*, p. 142.
34. Idem.
35. *Pereira da Costa,* Ummes de terrorismo (Angola: Marco-Abril de 1961) (Editorial Polis, 1969), p. 13.
36. *Jeffery M. Paige,* Agrarian Revolution: Social Movements and Export Agriculture in the Underdeveloped World *(New York: Free Press, 1975), p. 274; and Eduardo dos Santos,* Maza: Elementos de etno-historia para a interpretacao do terrorismo no noroeste de Angola (Lisbon: Edicao do Autor, 1965) pp. 45-50.
37. Paige, p. 275.
38. *Ibid.*, p. 277.
39. Marcum, I, 134.
40. Chilcote, p. 83.
41. Marcum, I, 124-26. The name Maria's War came from the mispronunciation of the name of the leader, Antonio Mariano.
42. Pélissier, III, 1282.
43. Marcum, I, 125.
44. Pélissier, III, 1366-68.

45. Hélio A. Esteves Felgas, *Guerra em Angola* (Lisbon, 1961), p. 79.
46. Felgas, p. 204.
47. Gerald J. Bender, "The Dilemmas of Counterinsurgency: The Portuguese Strategic Hamlet Program in Angola" (unpublished research paper), p. 19.
48. *Ibid.*, p. 30.
49. Herrick et al., *Area Handbook fur Angola,* p. 135.
50. *Ibid.*, p. 126.
51. *Ibid.*, p. 133.
52. Bender, *Dilemmas,* pp. 8-9.
53. Statement of the objectives of FNLA, in Chilcote, pp. 102-5.
54. Marcum, I, 309.
55. Chilcote, p. 162.
56. *Ibid.*, p. 160.
57. Wheeler and Pélissier, p. 216.
58. Herrick *et al.,* p. 357.
59. *Ibid.*, pp. 332-33.
60. *Ibid.*, pp. 308-9.
61. *Ibid.*, p. 242.

8

Final Phase of the Angolan Nationalism

Politico-Military Clashes between Portugal and Angola

Angolan and Portuguese fought each other to a standoff as they clashed militarily and politically from 1961 to - 1965. Portugal succeeded in confining the Angolan nationalists to a few refuges in the "rotten triangle" in the hills of northern Angola. Yet, to do this Portugal had to maintain an expeditionary force in Angola proportionately mush larger than that of the United States in Vietnam at the height of the Indochina war. In addition, Lisbon had to support the military, economic, and psychological pressure of more violent and disciplined attacks by PAIGG in Guinea and FREIIMO in Mozambique. This required the Portuguese government to spend nearly half of its national budget on the three colonial wars.

The two Angolan nationalist movements leading the attack on Portuguese colonialism had suffered various political and military defeats in the first four years of the war. Yet, they were far from conquered. The Angolans' strength lay more in the support they enjoyed both inside Angola and in the international community than it did in military power.

The stalemate of 1965 prompted both sides to prepare new initiatives to carry on the war to victory. In the last phase of the history of Portuguese Angola, however, the more crucial struggle was the internal conflict within each nationalism rather than the external clash between Portugal and the Angolan movements.

Within Angolan nationalism a new movement, UNITA. appeared which fragmented even more the forces facing Portuguese colonialism. The Angolans spent more time and energy fighting among themselves, or seeking a solution to their internecine warfare, than they did opposing their main enemy, Portugal.

Similarly, Portuguese nationalism was racked by dissension and internal conflict. Politically, the opposition maintained pressure on the regime in Lisbon by presenting candidates at all elections, although in most cases they withdrew on the eve of the elections in frustration at the restrictions placed on them. Economically, the regime's insistence on the vital importance of the colonies was challenged by commercial and industrial leaders who advocated concentrating economic interests in Europe rather than in Africa.

Religiously, opposition to the Salazar-Caetano regime appeared in the Catholic Church both in the metropole and in the colonies. Finally, the opposition became so strong within the Portuguese armed forces that the "movement of the captains" executed the coup on April 25. 1974, which not only ended the fifty years of authoritarian rule in Portugal but gave victory to Angolan nationalism in its struggle against Portuguese colonialism.

MPLA's New Front

The FNLA/Zaire alliance had effectively excluded MPLA from a major military role in the northwest region of Angola so it looked to Zambia in the east as a base for a new front. In 1964, the MPLA opened an office in Dar es Salaam, where it could work more closely with FRELIMO, its CONCP ally, and also have access to a friendly port for the importation of materiel.

When Zambia became independent in October 1964, the eastern border of Angola became accessible so a new MPLA office was established in Lusaka. MPLA ordered its personnel into the Mexico and Cuando Cubango districts of eastern Angola in 1965 to begin building a "minimum network of political cooperation."[1] Some military supplies began to flow from Dar es Salaam to Lusaka, and in May 1966, MPLA reported firing its first shots on the eastern front. The Portuguese Defense Minister, General Gomes de Araujo, returned to Lisbon from an inspection tour in Angola in September 1966 confirming that a new front had indeed been opened in the east by MPLA units infiltrating from Zambia.[2]

UNITA: A Third Liberation Movement

Another initiative undertaken by Angolan nationalism in 1966 was the creation of a third liberation movement, the Uniao Nacional de Independencia Total de Angola (UNITA), which was organised in March 1966 in the village of Muangai in eastern' Angola, 300 miles (480 kilometers) from the Zambia border. Jonas Savimbi had been seeking a new role for himself in the struggle against Portuguese colonialism in the twenty months between his resignation as a foreign minister of GRAE in July 1964 and the founding of the third major Angolan liberation movement in March 1966. His search entailed a long trip to North Vietnam, North Korea, and China which was arranged in part through the diplomatic assistance of Ahmed Ben Bella of Algeria. Savimbi had to explain to Chairman Mao Tsetung and Premier Chou En-lai why he had opposed Viriato da Cruz, who had the backing of China when he left the MPLA and sought to work in the FNLA in 1962-63. If Savimbi's position at that time was displeasing to the Chinese, he could at least assure them that he now intended to carry on a people's war inside Angola. On his return to Africa, Savimbi talked with Agostinho Neto and Daniel Chipenda about possible collaboration with the MPLA, but evidently decided instead to form a new movement.

In the midst of this travel, Savimbi was still fulfilling his final requirements for his degree in political and legal sciences, which he received from the University of Lausanne in July 1965. He had started his educational career in a mission school, as did most rural Angolans. His father, Lot Malheiro Savimbi, who was a lay leader of the Protestant community in central Angola, had been graduated in 1921 from Currie Institute, a male training school in the Dondi Mission. The mission expected that all graduates would receive work assignments with their diplomas, but Lot Savimbi disappointed the missionaries and church leaders when he took his diploma and went off to work on the Benguela Railway. However, he soon proved to himself and to the church that he could be just as useful a Christian working as a telegraph operator or stationmaster on the railway as he could by serving the church as pastor, teacher, or nurse. When Lot Savimbi retired after twenty-five years of service on the railway, he became mission school inspector and, finally, director of the Chilesso Mission at the same time that his son, Jonas Savimbi, founded UNITA.

Jonas Savimbi's travels had convinced him that he could find allies in Asia and Africa for a new initiative against Portuguese colonialism, but it was more important to find the Angolan constituency that would support him. First he identified colleagues from central Angola who had left GRAE with him and who were helped across the Congo River to Brazzaville by MPLA. Twenty-four of these defectors, predominantly Umbundu, writing as the Amigos do Manifesto Angolano (Amangola), issued a statement in December 1964 calling upon exiled Angolans to move back inside their country and mobilise the masses for guerrilla warfare.[3] MPLA supported Amangola until it became clear that the dissidents from the FNLA were not disposed to apply for membership in the MPLA.

A second constituency open to Savimbi's blandishments was the group of exiled Angolan students in Western Europe and North America. Many of the students active in the Uniao Nacional dos Estudantes Angolanos (UNEA), which supported GRAE, had become disillusioned with the lack of military activity by both major movements and even more disappointed with the constant conflict between the FNLA and MPLA. Consequently, Savimbi found a student constituency ready to listen to his criticisms of the two movements and anxious for some new initiatives. UNEA took a position of nonalignment in relation to the two movements and called for unity of all Angolans.

Savimbi found a third constituency in Zambia among the Angolan refugees who had been active in the UPA/GRAE office in Lusaka. They were mainly Lunda-Chokwe and Ganguela (Luenas and Luchazes) from eastern Angola who were disappointed with the inactivity of the two movements in their home territories.

After contacting potential allies and assessing the strength of a new Angolan constituency, Savimbi began to formulate the rationale for a new party. In a letter to former missionaries of the United Church of Christ, he set forth the gist of his political thinking:

> Only the Angolan people within the country is capable of freeing itself from foreign domination.... The unity of Angolan forces really dedicated to the liberation of our country is the most important condition for victory.... This unity has to result from an equilibrium of all Angolan nationalist forces.... this equilibrium will mobilise our People against the enemy in a popular and proportional representation of all the social groups.... Angolan society is divided into tribes, into clans, and classes. There cannot be any durable solution for Angolan divisions if the social structure is not considered.... The MPLA only includes representatives of the "Kimbundus". GRAE only contains "Kikongos." These two parties together still leave outside the political struggle more than half of the population.... It is necessary that a new political formation representing other Angola forces should be constituted.... Today it is internationally known that the MPLA is affiliated with pro-Communist ideas and methods.... Sr. Roberto Holden was

> supported by western forces.... It is vital to avoid a direct or indirect confrontation of the great powers on our soil.[4]

When Savimbi reached Zambia in October 1965, he persuaded Kenneth Kaunda to invite Holden Roberto and Agostinho Neto to Lusaka for discussions regarding a united front of all Angolan forces. When they declined the invitation, Savimbi proceeded with his plans to form a third movement. In March 1966, Savimbi hiked into Angola and held a conference in Muangai at which UNITA was formed. Not much was heard about UNITA, however, until Christmas Day, 1966, when several hundred UNITA partisans attacked the border railroad town of Teixeira de Sousa.[5] By casualty count, UNITA would have to consider the attack a defeat since it lost perhaps 300 of its ill-armed and ill-trained soldiers, while only six or seven Portuguese were killed. However, by interrupting the Benguela Railway and stopping Zambian and Zairean copper shipments for a week, UNITA had forced the world to take notice of its entry into the Angolan war.

UNITA Expelled From Zambia

Savimbi returned to Lusaka in February 1967 and then flew on to a meeting of African leaders in Cairo. In March, during Savimbi's absence, UNITA forces twice derailed trains, closing the Benguela Railway to Zambian copper traffic for several weeks. To avoid Zaire's and Zambia's anger, the MPLA and FNLA were quick to dissociate themselves from the rail disruptions. When Savimbi returned to Lusaka in June 1967, he was arrested and expelled from Zambia. He then found himself back in Cairo, where he had resigned from GRAE three years before and had begun the pilgrimage that led him to found an Angola-based movement. Some observers predicted that without Savimbi, UNITA could not survive,[6] but it did, and Savimbi slipped back into Angola a year later. From June 1968 until April 1974, Savimbi made a virtue of necessity and led UNITA in its struggle against Portugal from the bush of eastern Angola.

Savimbi has always been the uncontested leader of UNITA. One sign of his leadership has been his ability to attract strong nationalists from other regions and other ethnolinguistic groups. The secretary-general of the movement and political commissar of its guerrilla forces was a Cabindan, Miguel N'Zau Puna. Born about 1939,[7] Puna attended a seminary in Malange, then worked for the port administration at Noqui before going to Tunisia, where he studied agronomy for five years. He returned to Angola with Savimbi in 1968 and played key roles in UNITA as political strategist and military commander. Jose Samuel Chiwale, born about 1944 in Huambo, taught school and in 1965 went to China for military training.

In the early 1970s, Chiwale emerged as UNITA's top military leader.[8] Samuel Chitunda was the *nom de guerre* of Samuel Piedoso Chingunji, born about 1938 in Bie. He received his military training in the Portuguese army, in which he became an officer.[9] Jorge Isaac Sangumba, UNITA's principal external spokesman, earned a university degree in New York and then established a modest office in his apartment in London. Smart G. Chata, a Chokwe, was elected one of three vice-presidents.

The recruitment of these leaders reflects the development of the mid-sixties as Angolan nationalism reached out to enlist more peoples of Angola in the political struggle against Portuguese colonialism.

Portugal's Economic Initiative

Portugal's new initiative against Angolan nationalism was economic rather than military. In 1935, Salazar had laid the foundation of his economic system, which was designed to exclude or severely limit foreign investments and to exploit the colonies for the benefit of the metropole. The colonial wars forced Salazar to change this policy and by Decree Law 46,312 in April 1965 the door was opened to foreign capital.[10] This new policy plus the stimulation of the increasing military expenditures gave Angola its most rapid economic growth, which benefited principally the Europeans although some of the prosperity trickled down to a few of the more privileged urban Africans.

Angola's gross internal product increased more than threefold from $850 million in 1963 to $2,800 million in 1973[11] as a result of both private investment and government action. The government's Third Development Plan (1968-73) invested 41.8 per cent of its $962 million budget in extraction and mining, 12.5 per cent in transportation and communications, 8.9 per cent in social services, and 8.3 per cent in agriculture, forestry, and stock raising.

The private sector produced the dramatic economic growth that reinforced Portugal's will and ability to sustain its defense against African nationalists. In 1966, as MPLA and UNITA were opening the new military fronts in the west, the Gulf Oil Company found oil in the waters off the Cabinda enclave and in December signed a contract giving Cabinda Gulf Oil, a subsidiary of Gulf Oil, exclusive rights to prospect and exploit in the area. The company was required to invest at least $2.8 million during 1967 and 1968.[12]

By the end of 1972, the Cabinda Gulf Oil Company had invested $209 million in Angola, and in the same year Gulf paid $61 million in income taxes and royalties to the Portuguese authorities,[13] representing 13 per cent of the total Angolan provincial budget for the year and 60 per cent of the province's 1972 military expenses.[14] Rebocho Vaz, governor-general of Angola, indicated how keenly aware the Portuguese were of the importance of a protected supply of oil for their war effort:

> As you know, oil and its derivative's arc strategic materials indispensable to the development of any territory; they are the nerve-center of progress, and to possess them on an industrial scale is to ensure essential supplies and to dispose of an important source of foreign exchange.

> Apart from this, in the mechanised wars of our times, its principal derivative—petrol—plays such a preponderant part that without reserves of this fuel it is not possible to give the Army sufficient means and elasticity of movement. The machine is the infrastructure of modern war, and machines cannot move without Fuel. Hence the valuable support of Angolan oils for our armed forces.[15]

The economic support of the Portuguese war effort increased as the production of petroleum multiplied more than tenfold in five years, from 537,152 tons in 1967 to 7,055,144 tons in 1972. By 1973 petroleum had surpassed coffee as Angola's most valuable export. Not only Gulf, but two other companies with European capital, Petrangol and Angol, also signed contracts with Portugal for exploitation of oil in Angola, contributing to an increase in production. Churches and other voluntary organisations in North America and Europe protested against Gulfs investment in Portugal's war effort, but the adverse public opinion that these campaigns generated was not sufficient to discourage other corporations from seeking opportunities to invest in Angolan oil. Exxon, Texaco, Sun Oil, the Amerada Hess Corporation, and the Cities Service Company were all negotiating contracts which had reached various stages of agreement by the time Portuguese rule of Angola came to an end in 1974.

The production of iron, like that of petroleum, became significant in Portugal's economy in the mid-sixties and increased steadily as the nationalist military and political pressure escalated. The value of iron production rose from $1.4 million in 1967 to $45.8 million in 1970.

In value, the production of diamonds rated above iron. It had maintained a steadily growing production rate for many years but did not multiply as dramatically as oil and iron during the escalation of the war. Yet, during this critical period in Portugal's effort to provide economic support for its war, the value of diamond production increased from $40.8 million in 1967 to $59 million in 1971.[16]

Almost as dramatic as the increase in exploitation of minerals and agricultural produce was the growth of the manufacturing sector of the Angolan economy. During the period from 1962 to 1972, the respective gross production value increased more than fivefold, rising from $7,475,000 to $39,748,000. In the period from 1968 to 1972, the annual rate of industrial growth reached about 20 per cent.

The only part of the economy that did not grow to meet the challenge of Angolan nationalism was the subsistence sector. This, of course, reinforced the arguments of the liberation movements. According to their analysis, the Portuguese were exploiting Angola's raw materials to profit the metropole and the foreign nations that had increased their financial investments in the colony. The Angolan economy, following the typical colonial pattern, was directed toward exports; by 1970 the export value was about $74 per head, representing about double the African developing countries' average, surpassed only by Zambia with its copper exports. Three years later, Angola's exports had jumped to $124 per capita. However, the subsistence sector, upon which most Angolans depended, remained stagnant at about $70 per capita[17] for the twenty years from 1953 to 1973.

Economic Opposition to the Portuguese Colonial Policy

Angola's economic growth in the late sixties and early seventies seemed to justify Portugal's determination to keep control of its largest and richest colony. Yet, as the cost of the colonial wars escalated, the debate sharpened within Portuguese nationalist circles over whether Portugal should orient its economy toward Europe or Africa. The Salazar-Caetano view of Portuguese nationalism conserved the anachronistic principle that the sending of inferior products to the protected colonial markets and receiving of raw materials at depressed prices was sound economics. Portugal should have learned from its experience in prolonging the slave trade through the nineteenth century that such colonial dependence actually stunts the growth of both the metropolitan and the colonial economies. Opposition to this colonialist economic position did appear among some young technocrats, who became known as Europeanists since they saw the economic future of Portugal in Europe rather than in Africa. When Caetano succeeded Salazar as prime minister in 1968, he appointed some of these technocrats to important government posts, which strengthened the "Europeanist" opposition.

However, under pressure from the conservative "colonialists" the technocrats were forced out of the government by 1972 and many of them became associated with a group established two years earlier, called SEDES (Association for Social and Economic Development). In a booklet entitled *Portugal para onde vais?* SEDES outlined the economic options that would vie for acceptance: (a) Western European capitalism; (b) elite capitalism (e.g., the Caetano regime); (c) Western socialism (e.g., the USSR and Sweden); and (d) another kind of socialism (e.g., decentralisation along the lines of China or Tanzania). In the opinion of one observer, "SEDES favored the fourth option and they clearly had considerable influence on the opposition forces, including the MFA and General Spinola himself."[18]

Colonialists *Vs.* Europeanists

The conflict between the "colonialists" and "Europeanists" was not simply one of economic theory or analysis. The Portuguese economy, without waiting for the resolution of the theoretical argument, shifted from its dependence on the colonies as trade with Europe expanded. From 1959 to 1972, Portugal's exports to the European Free Trade Association and European Economic Community (EFTA and EEC) increased from 40.3 per cent to 61.3 per cent, while its exports to the colonies were declining more precipitately, from 29.8 per cent to 14.7 per cent. Portugal's imports moved in the same direction, from the colonies to Europe, but not as sharply as exports.[19] Curiously, although these statistics appeared in the Lisbon newspaper *Expresso* on April 20, 1974, just five days before the coup, few observers recognised that the economic foundation of the "colonialist" position had been so drastically eroded. In fact, the capitalists who were assumed to be principal supporters of the colonial wars had recognised before the politicians and the foreign analysts that the cost of colonialism was too high. Guinea, which was almost a fief of CUF (Companhia Uniao Fabril), Portugal's largest conglomerate, was the most striking example of the economic futility of the colonial war. PAIGC, the most effective of the anti-Portuguese nationalist movements, caused Portugal to escalate its defense budget for that tiny West African colony until it reached hundreds of millions of dollars per year by the 1970s.[20]

At the same time, Guinea's balance of trade showed a steadily increasing deficit as exports remained stable and imports rose rapidly to meet defense demands. The Guinea-Bissau economy was tiny, even by Portuguese standards, but its economic crisis had a critically important impact on the struggle within Portuguese nationalism between "colonialists" and "Europeanists." The Mello brothers, who were the principal owners of CUF and two of the most prominent capitalists in Portugal, realised that it no longer made economic sense to continue their support of the Caetano regime. According to the same observer, "Once these men and others in the large business sector adopted the position that their best interests were served by expanding trade abroad rather than with the colonies, the wars became liabilities rather than assets. And once these business oligarchs got off the Caetano bandwagon, the regime was in very serious trouble."[21]

Political Opposition

The disaffection of crucial economic interests within Portuguese nationalism was not commonly recognised until the Salazar-Caetano regime fell. The political opposition was more visible since it surfaced during each electoral period.

Salazar always identified his political program with Portuguese nationalism and defined the purpose of his dictatorship as being "the establishment of a political, economic and social nationalism... dominated by the uncontestable sovereignty of the Strong State."[22] Therefore he counted any opposition to his program or policies as antinational and antipatriotic. The political police (PIDE), the Portuguese youth movement (Mocidadc Portuguesa), the volunteers of the Spanish Civil War who had formed the Legiao Portuguesa, and the official censorship, all were organised to protect the New State and eliminate all opposition. Nevertheless, opposition persisted.

Unity of Democratic Forces in Portugal

The republican and democratic forces in Portugal had been encouraged by the Allied victory in Europe in 1945 to form the Movement of Democratic Unity (MUD), which hoped to start in Portugal "a legal and orderly revolution in the internal political system with the affirmation of principle and ideas which rule gloriously in the countries of the most advanced civilisation."[23] The government dissolved parliament and announced free elections for November 1945.

However, the opposition soon recognised that it needed more than the month allowed for the campaign to properly organise its ranks, and MUD petitioned the president to delay the elections for at least six months. When the petition was denied, the opposition decided to abstain and all the candidates of the official party, Uniao Nacional, were elected as they had been in 1934, 1938, and 1942. Shortly after the election a wave of persecution against those who had supported MUD swept hundreds into prisons and others—including military officials—out of their government employment. It appeared that Salazar had not expected such strong opposition.

The united political opposition made its greatest show of strength in the presidential election of 1949, but it still lost.

MUD nominated the elderly general Norton de Matos, who had been governor of Angola for two terms in the republican period. As had consistently happened, on the eve of the election the opposition withdrew because the government refused to change its regulations to allow for the free registration and voting by opposition supporters. However, in various regions of Angola where Norton de Matos' prestige was high and the opposition went to the polls, the opposition won majorities.[24]

The presidential election of 1958 not only produced a strong opposition candidate, General Humberto Delgado, but even revealed dissension within the regime. President Craveiro Lopes was not a candidate for reelection, either refusing because of disagreements with Salazar or being rejected by the dictator. Salazar chose his navy minister, Americo Tomas, as the official party candidate. He was opposed by Delgado, an air force officer and general director of civil aeronautics who attracted considerable support by his charismatic style. Contrary to the usual practice of opposition candidates, Humberto Delgado did not abstain at the last minute and he maintained that he had won. However, the official results gave Delgado only one-fourth of the-votes and the regime followed its usual practice of punishing prominent opposition leaders. Delgado was dismissed from his government position and sought asylum in the Brazilian Embassy.

The repression of the opposition to Salazar's nationalism increased when Humberto Delgado was assassinated by the political police in 1965 and Mario Scares, the Socialist leader, was deported to Sao Tome.[25] The increasingly senile Salazar seemed to have lost control of the country to his own creations, the censor and the political police. In the late sixties the legal opposition, which had courageously albeit futily protested at each election period, became more frustrated and hoped for a change by means other than protest or elections.

In September 1968, change came in an unexpected way. Antonio Salazar fell and suffered a cerebral hemorrhage from which he never recovered. President Americo Tomas called Marcelo Caetano to assume the post of prime minister.

One political anecdote at the time of transition from Salazar to Caetano described the latter as a driver who gave a signal to the left but turned right.[26] The signal was seen in the call to Mario Scares to return from exile and the readmission of many other political refugees; in the placing of PIDR under the restraint, of the justice ministry; and in the slight modification in the powers of the censor. Also, the political opposition was allowed to hold a congress, and previously banned books began to appear. The signal that was watched most closely was the election of November 1969. For the first time in forty-four years the opposition went to the polls in Portugal and even participated in the inspection of the votes. A few independent candidates were allowed to run for the National Assembly on the official party ticket and, of course, they won.

These new "liberal" legislators were some of the first to recognise that Caetano had given a false signal. The conflict between the new prime minister and the opposition centered on the colonial question. He devoted more than half of his first policy speech to African questions, affirming that: "Portugal cannot abandon her people, of whatever color or race, to the whims of violence, to the fury of resentments, to tribal hatreds, or to the devious maneuvers of international politics.... We defend not one civilisation, but civilisation itself."[27] Caetano became more rigorous than his predecessor in suppressing any discussion of Portuguese colonialism or of alternate solutions to the African wars.

The political opposition increased as the burden of the colo-nial wars became heavier, and the government allowed a Con-gresso Democratico to meet in Aveiro in April 1973, six months before the electoral campaign. Although, discussion of the colonial war was still officially prohibited in Portugal, most of the speeches and the resolutions at Aveiro dealt directly or indirectly with the war and linked the establishment of democracy in the metropole with the decolonisation of the African territories.

Political Opposition in Exile

The Portuguese political opposition, frustrated within the system, also became active underground and in exile. General Humberto Delgado had helped to form the Frente Patriotica de Libcrtacao Nacional (FPLN) in Algeria. This "front" was rent by internal strife, principally between Delgado's supporters, who proposed to infiltrate the Portuguese military and government through an internal underground, and the Portuguese Communist Party's strategy, calling for a long struggle leading toward a mass "popular uprising."[28] The Communists won control of the FPLN and the Algerian government ejected Delgado from his FPLN office. Within a few weeks, the slain body of the former air force general was discovered in Spain near the Portuguese border.[29] Under Communist leadership the FPLN continued its publications and broadcasts from Algeria, but Delgado's judgment was vindicated by the events of 1974, when the regime was overthrown by an underground movement within the military itself.

Religious Opposition

The opposition to the Lisbon regime came from elements in the Catholic Church as well as from economic interests and politicians. During the 1958 presidential elections, when Humberto Delgado was leading a strong political opposition, the Bishop of Porto, Dom Antonio Ferreira Gomes, not only[30] wrote to Salazar insisting on governmental changes but even had the temerity to circulate the letter. The bishop went into exile, but this did not stifle the Church's criticism of the Salazar regime. In fact, opposition was stimulated the next year when Pope John XXIII announced his intention to call an ecumenical council for the updating, *aggiornamento,* of the Catholic Church. The open style encouraged by Pope John and many of the texts enacted by the council threatened the conservative Portuguese ecclesiastical and political hierarchies. Strong supporters of the Vatican Council became suspect. The hierarchies feared, for example, three Holy Ghost fathers in Lisbon who, with the encouragement of Vatican II, freely expressed their progressive ideas. Inexplicably, the Portuguese officials sent the three missionaries to Angola rather than disciplining them in the metropole. Indeed, they gave them strategic ecclesiastical positions in the colony where the war was escalating. Padre Jorge Sanches became rector of the largest seminary, Cristo Rei in Nova Lisboa, and Padres A. F. Santos Neves and Waldo Garcia, a Spaniard, were assigned to his staff.

Inspired and supported by the Vatican Council documents, the three progressive missionaries opened up theological, political, and sociological doors, not only to the seminarians with whom they worked daily, but also to many clergy and lay members of the Church. The bishop of Nova Lisboa, Dom Daniel Junqueira, with considerable misgivings, allowed the three priests to establish the Institute Superior Catolico, which sponsored various lecture series and ecumenical encounters. The impact of Sanches, Waldo, and Santos Neves, and indirectly of the Vatican Council, was felt especially by the younger clergy. Twenty-two Holy Ghost missionaries in Angola signed a statement sharply criticising the Church's support of the Portuguese colonial system:

> What is the point of a society of baptised Christians... which lets a rich communal life, such as the African peoples enjoyed, go to rack and ruin?... How can such a society witness to brotherly love and poverty when it parades a style of life which shows an imposing, impressive, official and intimate connection with the powers of this world, and is conditioned by these powers? How can a church witness, as the Gospel demands, to understanding and peace, when, in an armed struggle that has been going on for nine years already, it does not publicly try to bring the opposing parties together round the negotiating table? How can people believe in the disinterestedness and full freedom of the bishops when public opinion can only see them as State officials with the same privileges

as these high officials of the State in matters of salary, housing, transport, protocol and even retirement pension?

We feel that, as Portuguese, we have a special responsibility as preachers of the Gospel in this land where we want to stay.... We cannot, in conscience, accept a system of missionary activity such as it exists here at present, and to give it active support would constitute a grave mistake.[31]

The hierarchy, which had deported the three progressive missionary priests from the metropole to Angola, expelled them from the colony in 1968-69: Padre Sanches to the offices of the General Council of the Congregation in Rome, Santos Neves to Paris, where he later left the priesthood, and Waldo Garcia to Spain. The latter wrote an article describing the "Two Churches of Angola": one white, Portuguese, self-satisfied, the other black, African, suffering. Since the hierarchy belonged to the first of these churches, it did not allow the second to speak, which led to the defection of some of the more progressive seminarians and priests. The loyalty of the hierarchy to Portuguese colonialism hid the fact that more Catholic than Protestant missionaries were expelled from Angola during the war of liberation. Santos Neves became the chief publicist for the religious opposition by publishing five books between 1968 and 1975, composed principally of the papers, lectures, and reports of the short-lived but fecund Institute Superior Catolico de Nova Lisboa.[32]

The erosion of the support of Portuguese colonialism by the Roman Catholic Church became most visible on July 1, 1970, when three leaders of liberation movements from Portuguese colonies were received by Pope Paul VI in the Vatican. Agostinho Neto of MPLA, Amilcar Cabral of PAIGC, and Marcelino dos Santos of FRELIMO, who had been attending an International Conference in Support of the Peoples of the Portuguese Colonies in Rome, stayed over for the privately arranged interview. This outraged the Portuguese government, which had diplomatic relations with the Vatican through the Concordat. Prime Minister

Caetano tried to assert that this audience implied no recognition of the movements:

> Taking advantage of a routine event in the Pontiffs life, namely the weekly collective audience given to visitors, the terrorists insinuated themselves into the Pope's presence as Catholics and Christians, engaged him in a discussion which could scarcely be heard and later used this for spectacular effect with the aim of compromising our country.[33]

Radio Vatican, however, did not agree with this interpretation and answered:

> That the audience of the leaders of the three movements struggling against Portuguese authorities in Africa was only able to take place by prior consent; that the delegates of the Decolonisation Committee of UNO had attended the anti-colonialist conference in Rome, in company with the leaders of the liberation movements; that the attitude of the Church towards the independence of the new nations remains unchanged and is well known through the documents of the Council, the encyclicals and the allocutions of Paul VI."[34]

Although, the Portuguese government withdrew its ambassador from the Vatican over this incident, it still had confidence in the Catholic hierarchy. A council on counter subversion in the Huila district of Angola expressed this confidence in a report:

> We believe that the bishops of Angola have manifested very well their patriotism and their dynamic will for the expansion of the Catholic faith among the masses, with the accent on civilising in the constructive sense of portugalisation.[35]

The same Council gave a negative evaluation of the influence of the Protestant Missions:

> In meetings of the District Council we have often spoken about the pernicious influence which the Protestant missions exercise through individuals who made harmful statements and propaganda. These are foreign agents who exert influence over the native masses.

> They generate admiration and enthusiasm for certain anti-Portuguese ideologies and movements. They surreptitiously undermine the idea of Portuguese citizenship. They create mentalities in the service of ideas inimical to Portugal. At best, they limit themselves to propagating a religious ideology not in conformity with our tradition. They neutralise our efforts for portugalisation and occupy key positions which make it easy for them to implant ideas contrary to our interests.[36]

For the Portuguese authorities, the crowning proof of the Protestants' subversive influence was the identification of the major mission-church agencies with the three liberation movements. Holden Roberto, named after a British missionary, was educated in Baptist Missionary Society schools. However, the tie between the FNLA, the Baptists, and the Bakongo was not simply in the person of Roberto. After the outbreak of the revolt in northern Angola in March 1961, hundreds of thousands of refugees fled to Zaire, not only as individuals but in village groups. It was the church which provided the necessary cohesion to keep the bands together as they fled the military zone. It was also a Baptist mission in the lower Congo which provided food, clothing, tools, and seed as well as moral and spiritual support to the refugees.

Agostinho Neto was the son of a Methodist pastor and studied medicine with a scholarship from the Methodist Church. The Rev. Domingos da Silva, a Methodist minister, was vice-president of the MPLA, and Deolinda Rodrigues de Almeida, a cousin f Neto and also a Methodist Crusade scholar, held several importa it posts in the party before she died or was killed in the war. T ie arrest and expulsion of four American Methodist missionaries in 1961 for allegedly "running a school for terrorists, teaching courses with hidden meanings, and importing refrigerators filled with guns" certainly identified the Methodist missions with the liberation struggle in the minds of the Portuguese and of the Angolans.

Agostinho Neto, while on Methodist scholarship support in Lisbon, admitted to the mission board that he no longer considered himself a Christian believer. The MPLA also explicitly refuted religion and supernaturalism in its third-grade science book.[37] Nevertheless, the Portuguese knew that the sympathies of the Methodist Church in Angola were with the MPLA and in 1966-67 imprisoned many of the church's leaders, including a number of women, whom they suspected of giving financial aid to the movement.

Jonas Savimbi grew up in the Chilesso Mission and like the other liberation leaders studied abroad with a church scholarship. The Portuguese council of counter subversion considered the influence of the Dondi Mission nefarious.

Military Opposition

Civil and religious opposition within Portuguese nationalism persisted through the Salazar-Caetano regime, but it was not able to change the system. Military opposition to Salazarist nationalism also appeared regularly and finally it won the victory for anticolonial, democratic, socialistic nationalism. It was the Movement of the Armed Forces that played a crucial role in overthrowing the regime.

In 1946, a military revolt broke out in the north of Portugal, and although it was easily crushed by the government's forces, military opposition to Salazarist nationalism persisted. The next year another military plot was discovered in which even President Antonio Carmona was suspected of participating.

After the government declared Americo Tonias victor over Humberto Delgado in the 1958 election, the air force general pled with four other generals who were chiefs-of-staff to impede the inauguration of Tomas, They did not respond, but other lower officers and civilians formed the Movimento Militar Independente, which laid plans for a military coup. The Portuguese Communist Party was part of the movement but withdrew shortly before March 12, 1959, the date set to take control of the military establishments, radios, and newspapers. At the last minute, the authorities suspected some subversive activity and just before the zero hour put the strategic barracks and headquarters on alert. When faced with the necessity of actually entering into combat, the leaders cancelled the coup and several of them were arrested.[38] Delgado's political charges during the campaign and the attempted coup made the armed forces sensitive to the criticism that the Portuguese military was a pretorian guard defending a dictatorship that it detested.[39]

In 1961, important elements in the military saw the specter of colonial war on three continents. The Minister of National Defense, General Botelho Moniz, told Prime Minister Salazar that the armed forces would confront "a suicide mission from which we could not come out alive."[40] As early as August of 1960, the conflicting views regarding the colonial situation became evident within the Portuguese military. One side included the Minister of Defense, Botelho Moniz, and Colonel Costa Gomes, Subsecretary of the Army, who believed that a political solution leading to self-determination was the only way to avoid this suicide. The most articulate spokesman for the "intransigent military defense of the colonies"[41] was Kaulza de Arriaga, Subsecretary for the Air Force, who discovered the plot to oust Salazar in March of 1961. Salazar appointed himself as minister of defense, which removed the danger of the coup being led by Julio Botelha Moniz, and immediately implemented the hard line in Angola by sending troops *ja em forca,* "in full force."

The support of the armed forces for Salazarist nationalism suffered another blow with the Indian conquest of the Portuguese enclave of Goa, Damao and Diu in December 1961. Salazar had exhorted the Portuguese to resist the invasion, but did not supply troops or supplies. The military opposition to the regime always presented itself as faithfully patriotic—but rebelled at being the scapegoat for the regime's ineptitude.

Movement of the Armed Forces

The Movement of the Armed Forces, which finally ended fifty years of fascist nationalism in Portugal, started out as an elitist revolt of career officers and in nine months had become a revolutionary force which established a new anticolonial, democratic, and socialist nationalism.

In July 1973, the Portuguese government issued a decree to increase the supply of career officers to the infantry, artillery, and cavalry. The Military Academy was not attracting students and by 1973 only 72 of the 423 places in the school were Filled. Therefore the government issued Decree 353/73, providing that drafted noncareer officers who were mostly students or professional men could become regular officers if they studied for two semesters at the academy. Career officers protested the decree which, they felt, discredited their professional training and prestige. After several weeks of pressure from the officers the government issued a revised decree which did not change the essence of the previous ruling but protected the majors and superior officers.

A group of career captains met August 21, 1973, and formed the first cell with the idea of organised, continuing action against the decree. Simultaneously, meetings were being held by officers in Guinea. The first mass meeting of the captains was held September in Evora, Portugal, with 136 officers present. They considered demonstrating against the government in Lisbon and formulated a statement to be presented to the prime minister. All the officers signed the document in Evora and another 190 added their names later. The petition was sent to the colonies, where officers supported it with their signatures.

The officers in Angola took the most radical action. Each one agreed to write his personal letter of resignation and also to sign a joint letter of resignation to take effect if and when the decrees were implemented. The Angolan meeting was also distinguished by the fact that the career officers invited noncareer officers to attend and lend their support.

On September 14, 1973, the military governor of Lisbon issued an official note warning officers against any unauthorised actions, but this did not deter the protests. In fact, the very next day the first information bulletin of the "Movement" was sent out to military units in the metropole and the colonies. The number of officers who committed themselves to resign if the decree were enforced increased rapidly and by October 30, 1973 there were 598, with the metropole accounting for 368, Angola 120, Mozambique 60, and Guinea 50.[42]

The rapid development of the movement was not only numerical but ideological. After three months of almost exclusive preoccupation with their own privileged status as career officers, the movement in November 1973 suddenly plunged into radical criticism of the regime's politics and especially of the colonial war. A lieutenant colonel affirmed: "We must awake from this nightmare. We must end, once and for all, this damned colonial war, which is consuming everything, including the dignity of military professionals of a civilised nation."[43]

A week after listening to this call to action the "captains" met in Obidos in Portugal and voted on three alternatives: immediate revolution; revolution after a more or less extended period of preparation; or revolution as the last resort after exhausting all means of negotiation with the government. The third alternative of revolution as a last resort received the most support, but the option of immediate revolution gained enough votes to surprise everyone.

What produced this rapid ideological shift from a conservative struggle to protect the prestige of the military profession to radical criticisms of the regime and its colonial war? First, the high command, which became known as the "Rheumatic Brigade," had become so decrepit that it not only alienated the career officers by its First decree, and then the noncareer officers by its second, but offended the whole of the military by its ineptitude. Second, some political radicals were in the movement from the beginning and took advantage of the government's mistakes to lead the elitist protest to a revolutionary revolt. Third, most of the noncareer officers had come out of the radicalised academic or university communities of the metropole; when they joined the movement toward the end of 1973, they strengthened the few radicals who had been active from the beginning.

The dissension within the Portuguese armed forces did not relied serious military problems (or them in Angola. In fact, in eastern Angola the Portuguese had successfully carried out "Operation Attila" in 1972-73, using napalm and defoliants in scorched-earth assaults on nationalist villages. By May 1973 the Lisbon press carried articles confidently describing the decline in insurgent activity in Angola.[44] It was only in Guinea and Mozambique that PAIGG and FRELIMO were challenging the Portuguese militarily and politically.

Angolan Military Weakness

The Angolan armed forces, on the other hand, had suffered serious fluctuation in their fortunes during the thirteen years of the war of independence, and in 1973 they were at a low ebb. The MPLA's army, EPLA (Exercito Popular de Libertacao de Angola), had reached its peak strength in eastern Angola in 1970-71 when it carried out some 59 per cent of the nationalist actions against the Portuguese. Guerrilla forces in Vietnam inspired the MPLA and it named two of its principal bases Hanoi II and Ho Chi Minh. At Hanoi II, Dr. Americo Boavida, the head of the medical services of MPLA, was killed during a Portuguese air attack in 1968. Ho Chi Minh surrendered to the Portuguese in 1972. EPLA suffered especially from Operation Attila. Whether as cause or effect, the military reverses were accompanied by political and diplomatic setbacks. In 1972-73, Agostinho Neto transferred 800 EPLA troops from the eastern front to Congo-Brazzaville and the Soviet Union withdrew support from MPLA. On the eve of the Angolan nationalist political victory the MPLA military was at its weakest.

ELNA (Exercito de Libertacao Nacional de Angola), the FNLA's military arm, had the logistic advantage of exclusive access to Angola across the Zaire border. Its major external base, Kinkuzu, in the Lower Congo district of Zaire, also enjoyed a favorable location and the protection of the Zaire government. However, these advantages contributed to the relative passivity of the ELNA forces, which were numerically larger than either of the other major movements. As Jonas Savimbi and the other rebels charged in 1964, the FNLA fought a frontier war and did not use its logistical advantage to press aggressively into the interior of Angola. The FNLA did open an eastern front north of the UNITA-MPLA operational zones but, as in the north, sent patrols into Angola from a staging base in Zaire, near Kolwezi.

Portugal in 1969 raided Mpinda, a Zairean border village that FNLA used as a rest camp and staging base. The Zaire authorities then shut down three border camps and pulled the ELNA forces back to Kinkuzu from which it was more difficult to launch incursions into Angola.[45] ELNA actions declined and the Zaire frontier was reopened to local trade.

The FNLA's military strength was struck another blow in 1972 when troops mutinied and Zairean forces had to intervene to rescue Holden Roberto from almost certain overthrow.[46] This placed the FNLA under closer Zairean tutelage and the Zaire army more actively reorganised, retrained, and equipped the FNLA forces. At the same time the number of ELNA soldiers increased as large-scale recruiting—almost conscription—took place among the large Angolan refugee population in the Lower Congo. On the eve of the Angolan nationalist victory, the FNLA was able to mount an impressive parade of troops in smart uniforms before diplomatic representatives from twenty-two countries who had been flown to Kinkuzu by Zairean helicopters.[47] Yet, the number and appearance of the FNLA troops were misleading. They proved disorganised and ineffective when the civil war broke out in 1975.

UNITA's military arm, FALA (Forcas Armadas de Libertacao dc Angola), suffered for lack of an outside base and arms suppliers. Some of the Chokwe troops that had formed the core of UNITA's initial attack on Teixeira de Sousa on Christmas Day, 1966 defected to FNLA and MPLA when UNITA was not able to supply them with arms and munitions.

In 1972, UNITA claimed 4,000 "well-trained men and women,"[48] though a Portuguese estimate of April 1974 went as low as 300 and a report published by the International Institute for Strategic Studies in London credited UNITA with something over LOOO.[49] Out of necessity, UNITA emphasised political education and self-reliance. "To liberate territory is of no interest to us, we want to liberate consciousness.... The army and the armed struggle are in a way secondary, for one does not conduct a nationalist war in the absence of national consciousness."[50] Foreign journalists who walked into Angola in August 1973 and attended the Third Congress of UNITA seemed to confirm that UNITA had established "a nation within a nation" although their military strength was minimal.[51]

Internal Contradictions of the Angolan Liberation Movements

Inter movement conflicts in Angola weakened Angolan nationalist forces so that they were not able to present the threat to the Portuguese authority that PAIGC and FRELIMO offered in Guinea and Mozambique. For example, the MPLA and FNLA could not exploit the advantages they had over the Portuguese of popular support and rugged terrain because of their internecine warfare. Since the FNLA's alliance with Zaire gave them control of the border, it was able to apprehend the MPLA soldiers as they moved in and out of northern Angola. In March 1967, FNLA forces captured a group of twenty MPLA militants, including five women, returning to Zaire from northern Angola. The most famous of those captured was Deolinda Rodrigues de

Almeida, a member of the MPLA Executive Committee, whom Roberto imprisoned at Kinkuzu, where it is presumed that she was executed.[52] Later, Commander Joao Goncalves Benedito, another member of the MPLA Executive Committee, was ap-prehended with nine other militants and also imprisoned in Kinkuzu, never to be seen again.[53] In 1968, Agostinho Neto claimed that the FNLA was keeping nearly 100 MPLA militants in Kinkuzu, which became as infamous as a prison as it was famous as a military base.

The FNLA also blocked attempts by the MPLA to reinforce its northern front, and as a result the northern headquarters base of BRNO fell to the Portuguese in 1968. "According to Portuguese officers, hatred between the two forces was such that MPLA informers 'often' disclosed FNLA positions and let the Portuguese wipe out an FNLA unit."[54] UNITA claimed to have captured arms from both the Portuguese and MPLA troops since it had no regular external supply. "In 1972 an MPLA deserter alleged that his unit had, in fact, done most of its fighting against UNITA."[55]

Not only this intermovement conflict, but also intramovement dissension weakened the Angolan nationalism in its struggle with Portuguese colonialism. Holden Roberto kept control of the FNLA by ruthlessly eliminating anyone who challenged his command, and survived the two major challenges to his leadership: the Umbundu revolt and resignations led by Jonas Savimbi in 1964 and the Kinkuzu mutiny in 1972. MPLA's dissensions are associated with three names: Viriato da Cruz, Mario de Andrade, and Daniel Chipenda. Viriato rebelled against MPLA policy in 1963 and, after trying to align himself with FNLA, went to China, where he died in exile. Mario de Andrade abandoned his active role in MPLA in the mid-sixties and in February 1974 led the "active revolt" of a group of intellectuals who criticised Neto's leadership. Daniel Chipenda, the Umbundu who had been one of the principal leaders on MPLA's eastern front, revolted when

Neto made an agreement with the FNLA and withdrew most of the MPLA forces from the east. Chipenda led what was called the Eastern Revolt and almost gained control of the movement as the colonial war came to an end.

Perhaps, because UNITA was smaller and more concentrated it was less subject to factionalism. However, some assassination attempts on Jonas Savimbi were reported.

Efforts Toward Unity

Even the search for unity by the Angolan nationalist movements became a cause for contention among them. Each movement professed to advocate a united front against Portuguese colonialism but claimed a position within the front that the other parties would not accept. As the name indicated, the FNLA considered itself already a front and that the other movements should merely join the UPA and PDA in the Frente Nacional. Holden Roberto and most of the FNLA leaders feared that a truly united front would be dominated by the MPLA because of its greater political sophistication. The MPLA also assumed its superiority and so initiated unity negotiations which usually broke down due to Roberto's intransigence. UNITA was a tireless advocate of unity since such negotiations would at least have given it the recognition that it lacked both on the part of the other movements and internationally.

The Organisation of African Unity (OAU) succeeded in gathering representatives of MPLA and FNLA around a common table to sign two agreements, but both attempts aborted before they produced a united front. Under the auspices of the OAU Conciliation Committee, MPLA and FNLA signed an accord on October 13, 1966, calling for a political as well as military cease-fire and a release of prisoners, but the agreement was promptly repudiated by Roberto. In 1972, the OAU made another serious effort at reconciliation through four African presidents, Kenneth

Kaunda, Joseph Mobutu, Julius Nycrere, and Marien Ngouabi. Only the F'NLA and MPLA were involved since the OAU did not recognise UNITA.

Both the FNLA and the MPLA were weak in 1972 and considered that cooperation with the OAU's reconciliation efforts could give them advantages. MPLA had suffered from Portugal's offensive in eastern Angola and needed access across the Zaire border to its constituency in the northwest. The Kinkuzu mutiny had weakened the FNLA and it sought arms and external support that the OAU might provide. After months of negotiations a formal agreement was signed on December 13, 1972 in Kinshasa.

This agreement seemed more promising than previous unity efforts because it provided a structure for political and military collaboration between the MPLA and the FNLA. A Supreme Council for the Liberation of Angola was created to coordinate a unified military command and a political council. Cadres of both movements met to negotiate the implementation of the agreement, but they made no progress. The MPLA had not gained its principal objective—access to northwest Angola across the Zaire border—and its militants were still subject to arrest within Zaire. Even more serious for MPLA was the internal dissent precipitated by the unsuccessful negotiations.

Daniel Chipenda and the other MPLA leaders on the eastern front felt that they had not been adequately consulted regarding the agreement with FNLA so they attacked Neto's political leadership. Then, when Neto withdrew the best troops from the east to take advantage of the anticipated access to the northwest, they condemned his military leadership. The Neto and Chipenda factions in Zambia broke into open conflict and finally the dissidents formed the "Eastern Revolt." So this supreme effort by the OAU resulted in a further division within MPLA rather than the unity of Angolan nationalism.

Competition for International Alliances

The conflicts within Angolan nationalism were caused not only by such domestic factors as regionalism, personal ambitions, cultural differences, and ideology but also by competition for international alliances and support. Journalists frequently exaggerated the dependence of the movements on specific allies and simplistically identified MPLA with the Soviet Union, FNLA with the United States, and UNITA with China. The picture was much more complex. In their more candid moments, spokesmen for all the movements admitted that they would accept aid from any source as long as it was given without unacceptable conditions. Agostinho Neto, in trying to destroy the image of undue dependence on one foreign ally, declared: "No country or organisation could claim a monopoly on aid to the Angolan struggle."[56] In 1962, he traveled to Washington with Bishop Ralph Dodge to put his case before the American government and press and to remove pro-communist coloring from his movement's image.[57] Evidently he had some success because a U.S. embassy official in Leopoldville was quoted as saying, "U.S. policy is not, repeat not, to discourage the MPLA [Neto-Andrade faction] move toward the West and not to choose between these two movements."[58]

The Soviet Union gave the most consistent support to MPLA, but even that was not uninterrupted. In 1973, the Soviet Union, concerned with the internal strife within the movement, withdrew its support. The MPLA also actively sought Chinese aid as Neto visited North Vietnam, North Korea, and China in 1971.[59] During the same period, Agostinho Neto toured the Scandinavian countries and they contributed to "certain activities" of MPLA, FRELIMO, and PAIGC in 1972-73.[60]

The FNLA, which reputedly depended exclusively on the United States, also negotiated with many countries to receive assistance. Holden Roberto in 1963 met with Chinese Foreign Minister Chen Yi during Kenya's independence celebrations

(December 12, 1963) and with Soviet and Cuban representatives at the United Nations and then announced that he had been assured of "whatever we need in arms and money."[61] The fact that -such assistance was not actually delivered at that time was not due to the potential donor's reluctance to give or to any ideological scruples on FNLA's part about receiving aid from the socialist nations, but rather to Mobutu's requirement that all material assistance to the movement or to the government-in-exile had to be channeled through the Congolese Government."[62]

Ten years later (December 1973), Holden Roberto led an FNLA delegation to China and returned to Kinshasa with a promise of substantial Chinese aid. Almost immediately he flew to Bucharest and signed a joint declaration of cooperation and friendship between the Rumanian Communist Party and the FNLA. Back in Zaire at the thirteenth anniversary of the outbreak of the war, and only a month before the coup in Lisbon that ended the anticolonial struggle, Roberto announced that this "very special aid" from China and Rumania would give the Angolan struggle a "new thrust."[63]

UNITA, which did not even exist when the other two movements were negotiating for foreign assistance from 1961 to 1966, received only limited aid from China. The frequent journalistic association of UNITA and China did not represent significant dependence, but simply the fact that the People's Republic of China was the only government to publicly contribute to UNITA's support. UNITA, however, prized the tenuous tie with China and at its Third Congress in August 1973 extended its "gratitude to the People's Republic of China for its continuous support of our struggle for national liberation" and saluted China's entry into the United Nations as a "resounding victory" for "oppressed people of the world."[64]

The movements sought arms and diplomatic support from governments, yet their operations were so small that even the minor assistance offered by voluntary organisations could provide significant "humanitarian" aid which the movements turned to political advantage by satisfying some of the needs of their followers. In Western Europe and North America, nongovernmental organisations and small voluntary associations gave support to all three Angolan liberation movements. The most prominent and effective association in Europe was the Angola Comité, founded in Amsterdam in 1961, which gave ardent support to the MPLA and to its CONCP partners, FRELIMO and PAIGC. In North America, the Liberation Support Movement (LSM), organised in 1966, sent medical supplies, tents, and food to MPLA,[65] but its most significant contribution was the publication of eyewitness accounts of the fighting in Angola by LMS leaders and by MPLA military officers.[66]

The World Council of Churches also responded to the Angolan nationalist movements' requests for assistance by establishing the Special Fund of the Programme to Combat Racism in 1969. From 1970 through 1974, the program made grants totaling $1,050,000 "to organisations of oppressed racial groups or organisations supporting victims of racial injustice whose purposes are not inconsonant with the general purposes of the World Council." Of the total of $656,000 that was granted to Southern Africa liberation movements, the Angolan movements received $176,000: MPLA $78,000, FNLA $60,500, and UNITA $37,500.[67]

Opposition to Aid to Portugal

The Angolan nationalist movements complemented their efforts to receive international aid by campaigns to reduce the assistance going to the enemy, Portugal. During World War II, Portugal had maintained a strained neutrality between sympathy for the anticommunism of the Nazi and Fascist forces and the ties with its traditional ally Britain and other western European neighbours. Recognising that the war was going against the Axis Powers, and under pressure from Britain, Portugal tilted its neutrality toward the Allies by agreeing to embargo wolfram exports to Germany and by negotiating with Britain and the United States for use of the Lages Airfield on the Azores Islands in the North Atlantic. The strategic advantage of the Azores base loomed large in 1949 as Portugal was admitted to the North Atlantic Treaty Organisation (NATO) although its Iberian partner, Spain, was not welcomed. A bilateral agreement was signed by the United States and Portugal during World War II and renewed periodically.

American Response to the Angolan Armed Rebellion

When the agreement was renewed in 1951, the United States began to give Portugal military aid. By 1953, the total U.S. military assistance of $71.5 million actually exceeded the Portuguese defense expenditure from their own domestic receipts—$70.5 million.[68] From that high, the aid decreased and by 1960 it was less than $10 million.

When the war broke out in northern Angola in 1961, the United States made some moves indicating that it might take a stand for the independence of Angola in spite of its ties with Portugal. The United States voted in favour of the March 15 United Nations resolution calling on Portugal to introduce reforms in conformity with the resolution on the granting of independence to colonial countries and peoples. Ambassador Adlai E. Stevenson made a speech which Portugal and the African nations interpreted as supportive of Angolan liberation, saying:

"The United States would be remiss in its duties as a friend of Portugal if it failed to express honestly its conviction that step-by-step planning within Portuguese territories and its acceleration is now imperative for the successful political and economic and social advancement of all inhabitants under Portuguese administration—advancement, in brief, toward full self-determination."[69]

American Committee on Africa

Supporters of African liberation, such as the American Committee on Africa, worked to convince American public opinion and the U.S. government to cut off aid to Portugal even if they were not prepared to give full-fledged support to the Angolan liberation movements. The course of U.S. policy toward Angola, however, took the opposite direction. After voting for Resolution 1742 in January 1962, reaffirming the right of the Angolan peoples to self-determination, deploring "repressive measures," and calling for reform and for no support and assistance to Portugal, the United States turned around in the United Nations and voted with Portugal on all major issues involving the Portuguese colonies. Consistent with this new turn was the appointment by President John F. Kennedy of Admiral George W. Anderson, Jr., as ambassador to Portugal; he showed his sympathy with Portugal's "civilising presence" in Africa as he visited Angola and Mozambique in 1964.

In 1969, the Nixon Administration strengthened the U.S. support of Portugal on the basis of National Security Study Memorandum 39. This memorandum presented Five options for U.S. policy in Southern Africa and, if not formally, at least in practice, the Nixon Administration adopted Option 2, which took as its premise: "The whites arc here to stay and the only way that constructive change can come about is through them. There is no hope for the blacks to gain the political rights they seek through violence, which will only lead to chaos and increased opportunities for the communists."[70]

American–Portugal Bilateral Agreement

In 1962, Portugal had refused to enter an agreement for American use of Lages air base in the Azores because of its resentment of the U.S. anticolonialist stand. For nine years, the United States used the airfield without a formal accord. Then in December 1971, the United States and Portugal renewed their agreement on Lages Field. The new accord and the closer relations between the United States and Portugal were given greater visibility by a meeting at the Azores base between President Richard Nixon, Prime Minister Marcelo Caetano, and President Georges Pompidou of France. In return for the continued use of the air base the United States offered a grant of $1 million for educational projects, $5 million in nonmilitary surplus equipment, and Public Law 480 credits of $30 million for the export of surplus agricultural commodities. Export-Import Bank credit of $400 million was also made available to Portugal for projects to be approved.

An Angolan liberation leader condemned this United States support for Portugal on the grounds that, "President Nixon has come to Portugal's rescue with the new economic aid agreement in exchange for America's Azores bases. American aid will equal the entire amount of Portugal's military budget for a year. American credits will free Portuguese funds for pursuit of war aims. American aid is the main factor that keeps the Portuguese from pulling out of Africa.[71]

The Azores base proved strategically valuable for the United States in 1973 when other NATO allies refused to allow the United States to use their air space to fly supplies to Israel in the October War. The United States refueled C-5A and C-141 cargo planes at the Azores base, but the Portuguese permission was bought at a high price, according to reports: the Administration pledged to work against an anti-Portuguese amendment to the foreign aid bill being considered by the U.S. Congress.[72]

The Angolan nationalists and their friends in Western Europe were no more successful in decreasing British, French, and German aid to Portugal during the anticolonial war than they were in cutting off American aid. In Great Britain, missionaries of the Baptist Missionary Society inspired the Baptist Union of Great Britain and Ireland to start a public protest against British support of Portugal. The protest climaxed in a petition with 37,524 signatures, presented to the House of Commons on July 5, 1961 which viewed "with grave concern the continuing harsh and oppressive policy of the Government of the Republic of Portugal towards many of its subjects in its African territory of Angola" and humbly prayed "that no military supplies should be allowed to be sent from the United Kingdom of Great Britain and Northern Ireland to the Republic of Portugal and its overseas territories in Africa... while such repressive policy is continued."[73] Such protests, which were joined by liberation support groups and Portuguese opposition groups in London, did not weaken the centuries-old Anglo-Portuguese alliance.

After supporting the 1961-62 United Nations Resolutions critical of Portuguese colonial rule of Angola, Great Britain either abstained or opposed subsequent resolutions designed to put pressure on Portugal to free its African colonies. Britain also supplied frigates for the Portuguese navy, light aircraft for the air force, and jeeps to the army. Both Great Britain and the United States required assurances from Portugal that military assistance would be used only "to meet Portugal's NATO obligations."

France's support of Portugal was given without any political inhibitions and with no official restriction as to where it could be used. The Alouette helicopter supplied by France became particularly important in the latter years of the anticolonial war when the fighting became a duel between the Portuguese helicopters and the guerrillas' land mines.

West Germany, not being a member of the United Nations until 1973, was under less pressure to restrict its support of Portugal. During the colonial war. West Germany became the most important supplier of imports to Portugal, including large amounts of arms and aircraft. The West German Air Force acquired use of an air base in Beja, Portugal, which was constructed with German aid. The German military mission in Lisbon, which coordinated military relations between the two countries, was the largest foreign advisory group in Portugal.

NATO and Angolan Nationalism

This continued support of Portugal by the United States and Western Europe was called by Angolan nationalists the "Natoisation" of the war: "The napalm that burns our children is 'made in USA,' the planes that bomb us are 'made in Italy,' the defoliants that destroy our harvests are 'made in Germany,' and the helicopters that transport the Portuguese commandos are 'made in France.' This is what we call the 'NATO-isation' of the war in Angola. We are certain that halting this military assistance to Portugal would hasten the end of the war."[74]

The war did not come to an end because external military assistance to Portugal was halted. Rather, internal dissension within Portuguese nationalism overthrew the regime which was prosecuting the war. In retrospect, we can trace the military opposition to the regime, as we have above, but very few persons inside Portugal or outside were aware of the tremors that finally issued in the coup d'état of April 25, 1974.

Portuguese Coup d'Etat

Two months before the coup, all of Portugal and much of Europe was awakened to the strength of the opposition by the publication of a best selling book by the most charismatic of the Portuguese military officers, General Antonio de Spinola. *Portugal and the Future,* published on February 22, 1974, articulated criticisms of the regime which the political, economic, religious and military opposition had been formulating, each in its own sphere, but had not expressed publicly.

Politically, Spinola, who had instituted people's congresses in Guinea,[75] advocated free debate of all issues and equal opportunity of access to positions of political power—i.e., the parliamentary democracy that opposition candidates had proposed at each election. Economically, the general, who was close to the major capitalists, used the Europeanists' arguments proposing a rapid increase in industrialisation and integration into the Common

Market as the necessary means to achieve the desired prosperity for Portugal. Religiously, Spinola recognised that the authority of the Church in the future must be based on the principal that "to govern is to serve the community."[76] Finally, the deputy chief of staff of the armed forces affirmed that to try to win a guerrilla war militarily meant certain defeat. He agreed with the Movement of the Armed Forces (MFA) that the role of the military is only to create and conserve the security conditions that would permit sociopolitical solutions.

Prime Minister Caetano himself might have accepted the platform presented in *Portugal and the Future,* but the succumbed to pressure from the reactionary military hierarchy and dismissed both Spinola and the Chief of Staff, General Costa Gomes. The dismissals strengthened the MFA by providing possible standard bearers for the junior officers and rallying support of some business interests as well of the general public. Before the publication of the book, Costa Gomes was considered the most likely choice of the MFA for president of Portugal. The enthusiastic response to *Portugal and the Future* made Spinola a more attractive possibility for the top post.

The public acceptance of the book and the more open criticism of the regime led the MFA to attempt an ill-prepared coup d'état on March 16, 1974. The coup collapsed when it was discovered by forces loyal to the government and the regime assumed that by arresting and rusticating some of its leaders, the MFA had been effectively destroyed. Such complacency allowed the movement to work clandestinely and make more careful plans for a second try during the week of April 20, 1974.

On April 25, five short weeks after the abortive coup, the MFA overthrew in an almost bloodless coup d'état the police state which had ruled Portugal for forty-eight years. At twenty minutes after midnight, the announcer on the Catholic radio station read the chorus of a prohibited song:

Grandola, dusky village, Land of Liberty
The People are the rulers within you, O city.

At this signal, the MFA detained the commanders of the barracks and occupied the government radio-television stations without resistance. Simultaneously, the young officers took control of the key highways leading to the capital, the national bank, and the international airport.

By 4:20 A.M. the MFA broadcast an appeal to all inhabitants of Lisbon to stay in their houses and keep calm. Commands were given to the police, national guard, and other militarised units that were not part of the MFA to avoid any confrontation with the armed forces. The only violent confrontation on April 25 was between the MFA and the political police, the *Direccao Geral de Seguranca* (DGS), in which five persons were killed: two DGS agents, two civilians, and one off-duty soldier.

The population of the capital did not obey the appeal, but out of curiosity filled the streets and soon began to show enthusiastic support for the revolutionary forces. As the coup proceeded peaceably, except for the shots exchanged around the DGS headquarters, the public gave flowers to the soldiers who patrolled the streets in their military vehicles, and a red carnation stuck in the mouth of a rifle became the symbol of the coup.

The Portuguese did not know just who or what the MFA was, but within twenty-four hours they were convinced that the old Salazar-Caetano regime had been overthrown. At 8:00 P.M. the government announced the surrender of Caetano to Spinola. Just twenty-four hours after the coup began, the Junta of National Salvation appeared on national TV and pledged to govern Portugal according to the program of the MFA.

On April 26, all the newspapers carried the program of the MFA. The very first phrase of the document referred to the colonial situation: "Considering that after 13 years of war in the overseas territories, the regime in power had not succeeded in defining concretely and objectively an overseas policy which would lead to peace among the Portuguese of all races and creeds...."

Reaction in Angola

The news of the April 25 coup reached Angola, but its significance was not immediately clear. Although, the first reason for the coup was given as the unsuccessful colonial policy, the news was received with much more uncertainty in Angola than in the metropole. With the departure of Caetano, Tomas, and the rest of the Cabinet and the capture of the Secret Police headquarters, no one in Portugal doubted that a revolution had started, but in Angola the same officials continued in power.

The contrast between General Spinola's image in Portugal and that in Angola was one cause of the difference in Portugal's and Angola's reactions to the coup. In the metropole, Spinola had become the best-known spokesman for the political opposition with the publication of *Portugal and the Future.* Among Angolans, he was known as an arrogant colonialist riding in a military jeep with monocle and swagger stick. Spinola's record in Angola as a hard-line officer from 1961 to 1964 was different from the fame he established as a relatively liberal general in Guinea from 1968 to 1973.

In his first speech to the nation, Spinola pledged himself and the Junta of National Salvation to guarantee the survival of Portugal as a "pluricontinental" nation. This phrase and the argument for a Portuguese federation in Spinola's book did not sound to the Angolan nationalists like the rhetoric of independence.

The governor-general of Angola, Santos e Castro, who was a close friend of Cactano, was removed from office April 27 and replaced temporarily by Colonel Scares Carneiro. At a press conference on May 3, Carneiro conceded that although the Angolan people were happy with the change of government in Lisbon, there still prevailed a climate of unrest because no political decisions had been made regarding the future of Angola. Even those Angolans who were optimistic about the future noted certain inconsistencies. In Portugal the hated political police was immediately abolished, but it continued in Angola. Even Sao Jose Lopes, who had been its director since it was established in the colony in 1957 and had disappeared on April 25, returned to his post in Luanda a few days later.

General Francisco Costa Gomes, the first member of the Junta Nacional de Salvacao to visit Angola, did not clarify the new Lisbon government's colonial policy. He appealed to the liberation movements for a cease-fire and recognised that the war still continued. However, Portuguese troops were staying in their barracks and soon tension and boredom was reported among the soldiers.[77]

On May 19, the Portuguese commander-in-chief of the 50,000 troops in Angola ordered suspension of all military operations to allow the guerrillas to come out into the open peacefully in the hopes that a cease-fire could be signed.

The uncertainty about what April 25 meant in Angola was heightened on June 11 at the investiture of the new governor-general of Angola, Silvino Silverio Marques, who had been a hard-line governor-general of Angola from 1962 to 1966. His reappointment cast further doubt on the intentions of the Lisbon government to grant independence to Angola. At the ceremony in which Spinola installed Silverio Marques, the president said that immediate independence for the colonies would be the most blatant negation of the democratic ideal.[78]

The equivocal actions and statements of the Lisbon government caused more doubts and consternation in Angola than in Mozambique and Guinea-Bissau. In May, negotiations between PAIGC and Portugal began in London. In June, Mario Scares, the Portuguese foreign minister, went to Lusaka, Zambia, to initiate negotiations with FRELIMO. Portugal was pressed to negotiate with Guinea-Bissau and Mozambique by the effective military operations which had been mounted by PAIGC and FRELIMO, and neither of those movements had any serious competition as it claimed to speak exclusively for its country.

MPLA and FNLA repeatedly affirmed that they would enter negotiations only alter Portugal agreed to immediate independence for Angola. Jonas Savimbi was reported to have declared that the population of Angola was not prepared for immediate independence.[79] Then, on June 17, UNITA agreed to a cease-fire with Portugal.

By the end of July, MFA pressure had forced Spinola to promise freedom to the African territories.[80] Although, MPLA and FNLA had bitterly criticised UNITA for signing a cease-fire with the Portuguese, they followed suit in October.

The April 25 coup released much pent-up political energy in Angola. Within weeks, a score of political organisations had sprung up among both black and white communities. The prospects of an election or referendum in Angola prompted these new organisations to formulate platforms that would attract a constituency. Although, the sudden proliferation of these parties was impressive, they did not gain significant followings in their short lives.

As soon as each of the three movements had negotiated a cease-fire with the Portuguese government, it set up offices in all the population centers of the country and began political activities. MPLA was the last to set up its offices, in late October 1974. It became obvious that none of the post-coup political parties could compete with the movements which had been fighting the anticolonial war and had solid regional constituencies. Therefore, the parties that had burst on the scene in May and June disappeared just as rapidly in October and November when the three movements stepped up their political campaigns. The announcement in late November of a summit meeting of the three movements was the final blow to the new parties and from that time any Angolan, black or white, who wished to participate actively in the political process was forced to align himself with the MPLA, FNLA, or UNITA.

The rush of supporters to the three headquarters began soon after April 25. MPLA sympathizers and militants Hew off to Brazzaville to affirm their loyalty, as did FNLA supporters to Zaire. The UNITA adherents filled the trains going from Lobito, Nova Lisboa, and Silva Porto to the headquarters south-west of Luso. Such visits resulted in military recruitment, which enlarged the armed forces of each movement as well as creating political enthusiasm in adherents who could return to their homes and organise local party groups.

At a summit meeting in Mombasa, Kenya, January 2-5, 1975, the three movements recognised each other as independent parties with equal rights and responsibilities. All other parties were to be excluded from the negotiations that would prepare for Angolan independence. They also agreed, following the example of FRELIMO, that they were not ready to take over immediately, but that a period of transition was necessary. During the transition period the three movements would work together with the Portuguese in order to lay the basis for an independent Angolan state. At Mombasa they also proclaimed that the territorial integrity of Angola was to be maintained with its colonial borders, rejecting any separatist claim. According to the Mombasa agreement, every inhabitant of Angola regardless of race could become a citizen of the new country.

Transitional Government

Ten days later, at Alvor in Southern Portugal, the three movements and Portugal signed an agreement which spelled out in greater detail the general principles accepted in Mombasa. November 11, 1975, was set as the date for the proclamation of independence and full sovereignty of Angola. Until that date, all power would be exercised by a Portuguese high commissioner and a transitional government to be inaugurated January 31, 1975.

The presidents of the movements did not take posts in the transitional government; rather, they named trusted lieutenants to the presidential college. FNLA named Johnny Eduardo, who had held posts as president of FNLA's youth section and representative of the Front in North Africa, as well as being the Front's secretary for external relations. The second presidential colleague, Lopo do Nascimento, had been an active militant of MPLA since its inception in 1956. He was arrested by the Portuguese in 1959 and 1963 and since 1974 had been secretary of MPLA's Politburo. The UNITA president, Jose N'Dele, a Cabindan, had been secretary general of the National Union of Angolan Students and later was UNITA's secretary for youth.[81]

Beside the thirteen civil ministries in the transitional govern-ment, the Alvor Agreement established the National Defense Commission, which was to command an integrated army to be formed by 8,000 combatants from each of the movements and 24,000 Portuguese troops. The agreement also instructed the transitional government to hold elections for a constituent assembly by the end of October 1975.

Angolans were euphoric when the transitional government was inaugurated on January 31, 1975. The anxieties and uncertainties that had reigned in Angola since the April 1974 coup d'état seemed to vanish. Portugal's colonial policy had been clarified as the talk of federation and referendum ended and a definite date for independence had been accepted by all parties. The myriad political associations that appeared immediately after the coup disappeared, leaving the political field to the three movements which had fought against Portugal in the war of liberation. The whole Angolan population, black and white, accepted the fact that to be politically active meant to align oneself to one of the movements. Angolans were heartened by the presence in the government of men who had accumulated academic qualifications and experience in Portugal and internationally. The plan for integrated armed forces also gave the Angolans hope that law and order could be preserved without the intervention of foreign troops.

Angolans wanted to believe that they were on a smooth path to independence and unity. In retrospect, it can be seen that the euphoria of January-March 1975 was precariously based on the principle of peaceful competition for power laid down at Alvor. The agreement would have been workable only under one of two conditions: cither genuine consensus among the movements in keeping to the rules of procedure agreed upon, or the presence of an authority capable of enforcing these rules.[82] In a few weeks, events proved that neither condition prevailed.

The Angolan liberation movements had been formed as illegal, guerrilla organisations and during the war of liberation had acquired no experience of operating by consensus or of abiding by legal provisions. Even while facing a common enemy, the movements were unable to reach political or even strategic accommodations to present a united front against Portugal. When the self-interest of African states pushed the movements to agree to unity declarations during the war, they were always denounced or violated before they could be implemented. The movements were not able to break this pattern even when their activities were legitimated in the transitional government.

Yet, Angolans were hopeful as the movements *seemed to* undertake seriously their new responsibilities defined by the Alvor agreement. Each movement inaugurated intensive political campaigns to mobilise as large a part of the population as possible. The preindependence elections seemed to be an accepted goal and the parties utilised mass meetings, posters, wall inscriptions, local organisations, and the mass media to increase their constituencies. All three movements had women's and youth leagues to organise and lead rallies and carry on grassroots propaganda. It appeared that the movements had indeed adopted methods appropriate to a representative, multiparty democracy.

However, from the beginning of the post-Alvor period the movements had to divide their energies three ways: to staff and execute the transitional government, to organise partisan political campaigns, and to assume administrative, judicial, and police functions. It was the addition of this third responsibility that most seriously threatened the success of the Alvor plan.

Beginning of Civil Strife

If the Portuguese had been willing and able to carry out the civil and paramilitary functions necessary to keep the country operating, the nationalist movements might have moved toward a working consensus as they cooperated in the transitional government and presented their programs to the public. However, the colonial administrative machinery was paralysed, so the Portuguese invited the liberation movements to set up their own administrative offices in each provincial capital and allowed military units of each movement to police the areas where they had substantial popular support. A skeleton police force augmented by Portuguese army patrols was supposed to maintain overall order. The weakness of this divided authority was shown on February 1, 1975, in Luanda, just a day after the inauguration of the transitional government. In the MPLA-controlled Lixeira *musseque* a minor misunderstanding erupted into a shoot-out between FNLA and MPLA guerrillas. Seven persons, including two officers in a Portuguese patrol who had come to restore order, were killed.

Violence escalated in mid-February as the MPLA tried to "neutralize" the Chipenda faction or Eastern Revolt, resulting in twenty deaths.[83] As weeks passed, the conflicts between the movements increased in frequency and violence. At the end of March, Portugal's foreign minister, Major Ernesto Melo Antunes, and the minister for overseas territories, Dr. Antonio do Almeida Santos, rushed from Lisbon to Luanda to bring the leaders of the movements together. The Angolan leaders and the ministers agreed to end the fighting. They also repeated the Alvor pledge to integrate the movements' military units with the Portuguese armed forces. The Portuguese ministers had hardly returned to Lisbon when conflicts broke out again in Luanda between FNLA and MPLA. A curfew was ordered in the capital, but this did not bring peace to the city and the surrounding African townships. Small clashes continued to disturb Luanda and at the end of April another major combat between MPLA and FNLA forces shook Luanda. Lisbon papers estimated the casualties at more than 500 dead and 700 wounded.

The Portuguese high commissioner, General Silva Cardoso, warned the leaders of the movements and the population of Luanda that if the "fratricidal struggle for power" continued, the integrated armed forces would use force against any unauthorised armed groups. Perhaps, if he had been able to carry out his threat, law and order could have been maintained. Since that was not done, the two movements rushed to increase their own military strength and this became their primary concern, having their governmental and political responsibilities in a secondary position. FNLA received materiel from Zaire. MPLA's aid came mostly from Eastern Europe, which presented both logistic and political problems. A communique of the National Commission of Defense, dated April 29, 1975, prohibited the unloading of military supplies destined for MPLA from the Yugoslav ship *Postoyna,* but the commission was not able to enforce its own decrees.[84]

The escalation of military activities reduced the importance attributed to the political process. Also, the prognostications of the electoral results made the MPLA and FNLA doubt that they should trust their futures to the political process. The MFA and the OAU visiting delegation estimated in mid-1975 that in any popular plebiscite UNITA would win a plurality, followed by MPLA and FNLA.

The FNLA still believed in mid-1975 that it had the greatest military force, and it was not willing to have its future decided by ballots, where the result would be certain defeat. At the beginning of 1975, FNLA disposed an estimated 15,000 troops, which were relatively well equipped and well trained on a low technological level. The Chipenda forces were officially integrated into the FNLA forces in March 1975 but in fact maintained a semiautonomous status. They had their headquarters in Menonguc in the south of Angola.

The MPLA, combining ideological conviction with the solid support of the socialist bloc, was confident that it could gain power in Angola either by political maneuvers or by military strength. MPLA had about 3,000 guerrilla troops after the Chipenda breakaway. However, MPLA quickly recruited and trained several thousand men from its political constituency, mainly in the Luanda area. The USSR and Eastern European countries supplied the necessary arms for the expanding MPLA force. MPLA also armed its Poder Popular, the local units of political militants, which became an aggressive militia.

UNITA was the only movement ready to give itself wholeheartedly to the electoral process since that was its only hope to achieve power. Its trained military forces were small and its history of fighting from inside Angola had restricted its diplomatic contacts so it could not count on the sure support of any nation or bloc. Jonas Savimbi, in the midst of the first major FNLA-MPLA confrontation, declared the neutrality of UNITA.[85] It did stay out of the conflict from February to July of 1975. UNITA campaigned strenuously on the political front and projected the image of the movement most likely to bring peace and unity to Angola.

By the end of May 1975, the FNLA and MPLA were no longer responding to local isolated incidents as they clashed, but were setting the stage for a nationwide struggle in which each was preparing itself to gain exclusive power. This preparation required the increase of outside aid, including materiel and advisors. UNITA proposed a summit conference to avoid a direct confrontation between MPLA and FNLA and the two movements agreed. However, the agreement seemed to be motivated more by a desire to gain time for the military showdown than by a commitment to the peaceful resolution of their differences.

The Nakuru Agreement

The summit meeting of Holden Roberto, Agostinho Neto, and Jonas Savimbi in Nakuru, Kenya from June 16 to 21, 1975, did not halt the rapid escalation of the civil strife into a civil war. It did, however, produce a succinct analysis of the "causes for the deterioration of the situation in Angola":

1. The introduction of great quantities of arms by the liberation movements after the 25th of April and especially after their move to Luanda. This race for arms is due to the fact that the liberation movements have maintained their mutual lack of confidence resulting from their political and ideological differences and their divergences in the past.
2. The lack of political tolerance which manifests itself in violence in the activity of the liberation movements and their militants.
3. The existence of the so-called zones of influence and of regions of supposed military superiority.
4. The arming of the civilian population.
5. Military clashes among the liberation movements and their tendency to regionalise which in addition to causing numerous innocent victims, aggravates the situation by tending to increase tribalism, regionalism and racism.
6. The presence of reactionary agitation and of elements foreign to the process of decolonisation.

The seventeen-page Nakuru agreement elaborated on these causes and proposed solutions to reverse the trend of events in Angola by preparing "a peaceful transference of powers at the moment of independence." Yet, even as the leaders were meeting in Kenya, the movements were stepping up the race for arms; the much-publicised handshakes and hugs among the leaders, presided over by President Jomo Kenyatta, had not changed the "mutual lack of confidence."

The transitional government did face the key issue of a united Angolan army after the Nakuru meeting, but again the result was only accurate analysis unaccompanied by practical solutions. Rui Monteiro, the minister of information in the transitional government, after saying that the government hoped to have an integrated army before Angola gained its independence in November, went on to comment: "It will be difficult because our country is not used to democratic processes and it is hard explaining to them the concept of non-partisan and integrated military units."[86]

In July, the MPLA evidently decided that instead of following the agreement at Nakuru to eliminate the "zones of influence and regions of supposed military superiority" it would aggressively establish complete control of its zone—Luanda-Malange. By the beginning of August, the capital, the whole Kimbundu corridor, and the Lunda district were cleared of all FNLA military and political personnel. The only area in which the FNLA successfully resisted the MPLA was north of Luanda, where the FNLA zone dipped within a few miles of the capital.

Until July, UNITA had not engaged in the military clashes. Then MPLA began pushing south and "invading" the UNITA zone of influence. Cuanza-Sul became the first district of active confrontation between the MPLA and UNITA. By mid-August, UNITA was forced out of its "peacemaking" position and became one of the combatants again. The MPLA drove south along the coast, taking Porto Amboim, Novo Redondo, Lobito, and Benguela. It also sent its forces by an eastern route through Lunda and into Moxico. Although, UNITA formed an uneasy alliance with FNLA forces south of the Cuanza, they were not able to withstand the MPLA forces, which showed superiority in leadership and organisation as well as equipment.

The escalated fighting forced all sides to look for increased support from outside. MPLA's military successes due to Soviet and Communist bloc support was matched by more aid for FNLA and UNITA. In June 1974, China had sent an advance party of Chinese military instructors to the FNLA base at Kinkuzu. The remainder of the Chinese team, totaling 120, arrived in August together with materiel. For a year, China assisted FNLA, but after recognising that it could not successfully compete with the Soviets in an Angolan arms race, China withdrew its military instructors from Zaire in October 1975.

Also in 1975, the United States increased its aid to FNLA in Zaire and the Ford Administration sought to convince the American public that the national interest required a more substantial intervention to oppose communism in Angola. Overt and covert American aid to FNLA and UNITA increased in September.

There was no advantage, however, in sending more sophisticated equipment without skilled personnel to operate it. Events moved so swiftly toward independence on November 11 that there was no time for the advisors and technicians who had arrived from various countries to train the Angolans to use the new equipment. Therefore, each movement welcomed foreign forces. The Zairean troops could enter most easily across the-northern border to reinforce FNLA as it fought to hold its zone of influence in northwest Angola. Cuban forces arrived in October through Pointe-Noire in the Congo and Porto Amboirn to strengthen MPLA. In the same month, the Zulu column of white South African troops swept northward from Namibia. In three weeks they had recaptured Sa da Bandeira and the coastal cities of Benguela and Lobito, which the MPLA had taken in August and September. Two factors halted the drive of the Zulu column before it reached Luanda. First, the date of Angolan independence was fast approaching and all the movements wished to keep their foreign troops out of the headlines. Second, Cuban forces which had reached the Keve River by the first of November presented the first stiff opposition to the South African troops.

The strategic fact that Luanda was the center of the MPLA zone of influence had a dramatic, and perhaps decisive, effect in the first stage of the Angolan civil war. When the MPLA exerted exclusive military control over the Luanda-Malange districts in July 1975, the non-MPLA populations from the north and south fled the capital. The political leaders of the FNLA and UNITA felt particularly vulnerable without the military protection of their own troops so they also abandoned the capital. This meant the collapse of the transitional government, and on August 14 the acting Portuguese high commissioner in Angola, announcing the dissolution of the coalition regime, took over all executive powers.

However, the order dissolving the coalition provided for the Portuguese take-over of only those ministries "abandoned" by the FNLA and UNITA. The posts were actually being filled by MPLA officials although the arrangement was an informal one. This allowed the MPLA to extend its control over the whole Angolan administration while the Portuguese were still formally in authority. Such administrative control also gave a direct Financial advantage to the MPLA. All taxes paid in Angola came to the Luanda government, which was in the hands of the MPLA from August 1975 until independence.

Independence and Civil War

The proclamation of independence on November 11, 1975, was a subdued affair in most of Angola compared to the euphoric inauguaration of the transitional government nine months earlier. Only in Luanda did Angolans celebrate independence enthusiastically. The four other Portuguese African colonies had come to independence without major civil strife. The Portuguese government handed the reins of power to governments that were recognised as being representative of the people of Guinea-Bissau, Mozambique, Cape Verde, and Sao Tome and Principe.[87] The Lisbon regime could not decide what it would do in Angola, where the conflict between the three liberation movements was escalating with the approach of the independence date.

At the last minute, the Portuguese cabinet resolved that it would not recognise any of the competing movements. On November 10, the Portuguese high commissioner, Admiral Leonel Cardoso, announced in a brief ceremony in Luanda that he was transferring power to the "Angolan people," yet not a single Angolan was present. The Portuguese flag was lowered and some 2,000 Portuguese troops quietly boarded naval transports to return to Lisbon, retracing the route of Diogo Cao, who had arrived at the mouth of the Congo River almost five centuries earlier.

At midnight of November 10, thousands of Angolans gathered in the stadium near Luanda's city center to celebrate their independence and heard Agostinho Neto say: "In the name of the people of Angola, before Africa and the world, I proclaim the independence of Angola." Neto's forty-minute speech was punctuated by chants of "The struggle continues" and "Victory is certain." He acknowledged that the next phase of the struggle would be more arduous than the thirteen-year struggle against the Portuguese. Later in the day, Dr. Agostinho Neto was declared the president of the People's Republic of Angola (PRA).

The political struggle did continue. On November 11 the FNLA and UNITA proclaimed the independence of the Democratic People's Republic of Angola (UPRA). This loose anti-MPLA coalition formed a national council to act temporarily as the government with its capital in Huambo, the center of the UNITA zone of influence.

The military struggle also continued. At independence, the military power of MPLA and the anti-MPLA forces were in rough equilibrium. MPLA's forces were spearheaded by more than 1,000 Cubans,[88] who had at their disposal sophisticated Soviet weaponry such as T54 and T34 tanks. More effective for the MPLA than their other arms were the 122-millimeter rocket launchers (Stalin's Organs), which terrified the FNLA and UNITA soldiers and the general population.

The FNLA forces in the north with Zairean troops and 150 former Portuguese commandos[89] reached the Morro da Cal, twelve miles from Luanda, but on the eve of independence they failed to make the all-important breakthrough into the capital. The FNLA-UNITA troops in the south did little fighting, but gave support to the column of white soldiers organised and manned principally by South Africans who, for political and military reasons, were stalled on their push to the capital.

Independence was followed by a decisive shift in the military balance between the MPLA and the FNLA-UNITA coalition. The MPLA control of the capital not only provided the political and administrative advantages noted above, but also gave the MPLA the most strategic military position. It had internal lines of military communication and could move out from its base, which contained Angola's only international transportation and communications center.

The international allies of the MPLA were able with impunity to increase their aid in both materiel and personnel. Both the port and international airport of Luanda were available to the Russians and other socialist bloc nations, which rapidly increased the resources at MPLA's disposal. The Cuban combat troops tripled in the three weeks following independence, reaching at least 3,000 by the first of December.

Decline in American Military Support to the Angolan Revolution

On the other side, pressure mounted against those supplying materiel and personnel to the anti-MPLA forces. The Ford

Administration argued for increasing aid to the "anti-Marxist" forces, but the Vietnam backlash was very strong and congressional opposition against involvement in the Angolan civil war increased rapidly. In December, the U.S. Senate voted to prevent the Administration from continuing intervention in Angola. Although, this prohibition was only enacted into law when it was supported by the House of Representatives in February 1976, it was clear in November and December that the United States would not be able to balance the massive aid coming from the USSR and the socialist bloc to the MPLA.

The United States' inability or unwillingness to continue its military support of the anti-MPLA coalition had a cooling effect on France, Belgium, and other Western European countries which had also been supplying aid to UNITA and FNLA. The most direct military effect of the U.S. withdrawal was the pulling back of the South African personnel, who had led the FNLA/ UNITA columns and dislodged MPLA from the coastal cities in October and November. South Africa had assumed, on the basis of promises that are difficult to document, that the United States and other Western nations would give substantial support to the anti-MPLA coalition. South Africa was left out on a limb when the other aid to FNLA/UNITA decreased instead of equaling the greatly increased aid to MPLA.

South Africa and the Angolan Liberation Movement

South Africa also faced domestic opposition to its Angolan adventure. The governing Nationalist Party was unsuccessfully challenged by weak opposition parties accusing the government of failing to take the public into its confidence and to explain the actions and objectives of the South African troops in Angola. Some of the chief black leaders in South Africa also spoke out against the South African intervention.[90]

South Africa's withdrawal from Angola shifted the military balance decisively in favour of the MPLA. The South African presence had hurt the FNLA / UNITA more politically than it had strengthened them militarily. On November 27, Nigeria announced its recognition of the People's Republic of Angola. oiling South African intervention as the reason. Nigeria then made a financial contribution of $20 million lo the Luanda government.

The MPLA took advantage of its military and political advantage and launched a New Year's offensive in the north of Angola, led by Cubans and Katangese. By January 6, 1976, MPLA captured Uige, the FNLA's headquarters in Angola, and effectively eliminated any serious military threat in the north. This victory had political as well as military significance, since it took place on the eve of the meeting of the Organisation of African Unity (OAU) in Addis Ababa.

The OAU made the last international effort to reconcile the combatants in the Angolan civil war. The 1970 meeting was evenly divided between those nations supporting the Nigerian resolution to recognise the People's Republic of Angola and those voting for Senegal's resolution calling for a cease fire, withdrawal of foreign troops, and reconciliation of the three movements in order to form a government of national unity. The deadlock of twenty-two votes for each resolution was in fact a victory for the MPLA. More than had already recognised the MPLA regime in Luanda and not a single nation had recognised the FNLA/UNITA coalition government in Huambo. If the OAU had passed the Senegalese resolution, probably some nations would have recognised the Huambo government.

Returning politically victorious from Addis Ababa, the MPLA turned its military force southward, and if there had been any possibility of an MPLA-UNITA coalition it was then completely ruled out. Joao Filipe Martins, the Angolan minister of information, made it dear: "We have always staled that the FNLA and UNI TA are our enemies. There is only one movement in Angola and this is the MPLA."[91] The MPLA, with Cuban forces and Russian equipment, swept through the south almost as easily as they had the north. On January 25, defense Minister Pieter W. Botha told the South African parliament that South African troops were withdrawing from the front lines in Angola.

When MPI.A troops arrived within fifty miles of Huambo, the coalition forces with castward along the railway to Silva Porto, which had been the military headquarters of the UNITA forces dining the civil war. This strategic retreat did not strengthen the coalition's military position and within two weeks the MPLA had achieved its major military objectives.

Just three months after independence, the MPLA with the support of 10,000 Cuban troops and massive Russian aid took control of the major cities of Angola. February 11 can be taken as the date of the end of this phase of the Angolan struggle, which the MPI.A called the Second War of Liberation. On that date Huambo, the UNTA capital, and Sao Salvador, the last FNLA stronghold, were captured. The OAU recognised the People's Republic of Angola, and President Gerald Ford signed the bill prohibiting further U.S. aid to Angola.

The confrontation between Portuguese and Angolan nationalisms produced the political rhetoric of the anticolonial era, but the most decisive actions were the result of dynamics within each nationalism. The clash between the Salazar-Caetano regime and the Portuguese opposition issued in the coup on April 25, 1974. This, in turn, led to the end of Portuguese colonialism and the independence of Angola. Conflict within Angolan nationalism then generated a civil war which invited broad foreign intervention and led to the victory of the MPLA, which established the People's Republic of Angola.

NOTES AND REFERENCES

1. Basil Davidson, *In the Eye of the Storm: Angola's People* (Garden City, N.Y.: Doubleday, 1972), p. 242.

2. John A. Marcum, *The Angolan Revolution,* Vol. II: *Exile Politics and Guerrilla Warfare 1962-1976* (Cambridge, Mass.: The MIT Press, 1978), p. 178.
3. *Ibid.*, p. 161; and Jorge Alicerces Valentim, *Qui libere l'Angola?* (Brussels: Michele Coppens, 1969), pp. 40-42.
4. Letter of Jonas Savimbi, dated Sept. 21, 1965.
5. Marcum, II, 191-92.
6. *Ibid.*, p. 193.
7. *Ibid.*, pp. 194, 398n.
8. *Ibid.*, pp. 194, 398n.
9. *Ibid.*, pp. 194, 398n.
10. Carlos G. Nensala, "The Role of Fiscal Policy in the Economic Development of Angola" (M.A. dissertation. Catholic University of America, Washington, D.C., 1973), p. 24.
11. United Nations A/9623 (V): Report of Special Committee on the Implementation of the Declaration on the Granting of Independence to Colonial Countries and Peoples (1974), October 8, 1974, p. 6.
12. African Development, November 1973, p. 11.
13. United Nations A/9023 (III): Report of Special Committee on the Implementation of the Declaration on the Granting of Independence to Colonial Countries and Peoples (1973), October 11, 1973, p. 13.
14. United Nations A/AC 109/L. 842, February 28, 1973.
15. African World Annual, 1967-68, p. 29.
16. United Nations A/9023 (HI), p. 20.
17. F. Distler, "Angola: Preliminary Country Development Brief and Proposals for Technical Assistance" (mimeographed, December 4, 1974), p. 3.
18. Gerald J. Bender, "Portugal and Her Colonies Join the Twentieth Century: Causes and Initial Implications of the Military Coup," *Ufahamu, 4,* no. 3 (Winter 1974), 121.
19. *Ibid.*, p. 119.

20. *Ibid.*, p. 120.
21. *Idem.*
22. Oliveira Marques, II, 204.
23. *Eleicoes legislativas—subsidies para a historia da vida portuguesa 1945/1973* (Lisbon: Edicoes Delfos, 1973), pp. 9-10.
24. Oliveira Marques, II, 351.
25. *Ibid.*, p. 357.
26. *Ibid.*, p. 410.
27. *Africa Report,* 14 (Feb. 1969), 32.
28. Marcum, II, 180.
29. *Idem.*
30. Hugh Kay, *Salazar and Modern Portugal* (New York: Hawthorn, 1970), p. 360.
31. *Governmental Policy and the Church in the Portuguese Territories of Africa,* IDOC International No. 43 (Rome, 1972), pp. 29-30. The complete correspondence, including the reply of the Episcopal Conference, is found in A. F. Santos Neves, *Quo vadis, Angola)* (Angola: Editorial Coloquios, 1974), pp. 235-54.
32. In addition to *Quo vadis, Angola?,* A. F. Santos Neves published the lectures and papers of the Institute Superior Catolico de Nova Lisboa in various forms: Ecumenismo em Angola: do ecumenismo cristao an ecumenismn universal (Nova Lisboa-Angola: Editorial Coloquios, 1968); Liturgia, cristianismo e sociedade em Angola (Lisbon: Livraria Editora Pax, 1968); Negritude e revoluao em Angola (Paris: Editorial "Etc." 1974); and Para urn ecumenismo omnitotidimensional em Angola (Angola: Editorial Coloquios, 1975).
33. Arslan Hmnbaraci and Nicole Muchnik, *Portugal'.': African Wars: Angola, Guinea-Bissao, Mozambique* (Dar es Salaam: Tanzania Publishing House, 1974), p. 204.
34. *Idem.*
35. *Angola: Secret Government Documents on Counter-Subversion,* trans. and ed. Caroline Reuver-Cohen and William Jerman (Rome: IDOC, 1974), p. 119.

36. *Ibid.*, p. 115.
37. Moviniento Popular de Libertacao de Angola, Departamento de Educacaoe Cultura, *Ciencias naturias 3 classe* (Holland, 1972), pp. 103-6.
38. Avelino Rodrigues, Cesario Borga, and Mario Cardoso, O *movimento dos capitals e o 25 de Abril: 229 dias para derrubar o fascisms,* 3rd ed. (Lisbon: Moraes Editores, 1975), pp. 161-82.
39. *Ibid.*, p. 164.
40. *Ibid.*, p. 183.
41. *Ibid.*, p. 186.
42. Dinis de Almeida, *Origens e evolucao do mavimento de capitaes, subsidies para uma melhor compreensao* (Lisbon: Edicoes Sociais, 1977), p. 177.
43. *Ibid.*, p. 206.
44. Marcurn, II,201.
45. *Ibid.*, p. 219.
46. *Ibid.*, p. 220.
47. *Idem.*
48. "The War in Angola," Harvard-Raddiffe student booklet, 1973.
49. Marcum, II, 217.
50. *Idem.*
51. "The War in Angola," p. 4.
52. Marcum, II, 198.
53. *Idem.*
54. Marcum, II, 211.
55. *Idem.*

48. "The War in Angola," Harvard-Raddiffe student booklet, 1973.
49. Marcum, 11,217.
50. *Idem.*
51. "The War in Angola," p. 4.
52. Marcum, II, 198

53. *Idem.*

54. Marcum, II, 211.

55. *Idem.*

56. Marcum, II, 14.

57. *Idem.*

58. Marcum, II, 16.

59. *Ibid.*, p. 230.

60. *Ibid.*, p. 232.

61. *Ibid.*, p. 132.

62. *Ibid.*, p. 133.

63. *Ibid.*, pp. 230-31.

64. *Ibid.*, p. 230.

65. *Ibid.*, p. 238.

66. "Liberation Support Movement Interview—Daniel Chipenda," taped in Lusaka, Zambia, August 28, 1969, by Don Barnett; "Liberation Support Movement Interview on Angola—Spartacus Moniniainbu," taped in Dar es Salaam, Tanzania, March 21, 1968, by Don Barnett; Roy Harvey. *People's War in Angola: Report on the First Eastern Regional Conference of the MPLA* (Seattle: LSM Information Center, 1970); and "Interview in Depth MPLA—Angola #4," interview with Paulo Jorge, director of MPLA's Department of Information and Propaganda (DIP) (Richmond, B.C., Canada: LSM Information Center, 1973).

67. Elisabeth Adler, *A Small Beginning: An Assessment of the First Five Years of the Programme to Combat Rarism* (Geneva: World Council of Churches, 1974), pp. 15-17, 92-95.

68. William Minter, *Portuguese Africa and the West* (Middlesex: Penguin, 1972), pp. 45-46.

69. *Ibid.*, p. 78.

70. *The Kissinger Study of Southern Africa: National Security Study Memorandum 39 (Secret)*, ed. Mohamed A. El-Khawas and Barry Cohen (Westport, Conn.: Lawrence Hill, 1976), p. 105.

71. "America's Foreign Policy: Report of the First Africa-Based Conference of African and American Representatives, Lusaka, Zambia, Jan. 17-21, 1972" (New York, African-American Institute, 1972), p. 21.

72. *African News: An Information Service of the Southern Africa Committee*, 1, 36 (October 29, 1973), 1-2.

73. Len Addicott, *Cry Angola!* (London: SCM Press, 1962), pp. 101, 144, and *Angola: A Symposium—Views of a Revolt* (London: Oxford University Press, 1962), pp. 58-79.

74. Manuel Jorge, "Massive Aid Required to Hasten End of War and Assist National Reconstruction," *Objective: Justice,* 5, no. 1 (January-March 1973), 12.

75. Manuel Belchior, *Os Congressos do pavo da Guine* (Povoa de Varzin: Editora Arradia, 1973).

76. Antonio de Spinola, *Portugal e n future: Analise da conjuntura nacional,* 2d ed. (Lisbon: Arcadia, 1974), p. 38.

77. *New York Times,* June 5, 1974.

78. *Revista de Angola,* no. 313 (June 15, 1974).

79. *Idem.*

80. *New York Times,* July 28, 1974.

81. The transitional government inaugurated January 31, 1975 was made up as follows (M-MPLA, U-UNITA, F-FNLA, P-Portugal): Presidential Council—Lopo do Nascimento (M), Jose N'Dele (U), Johnny Eduardo (F); Ministry of Interior—Ngolo Kabanku (F), Secretaries of State, Geologo Henrique Santos (M) and Waiken (U); Ministry of Information—Manuel Rui Monteiro (M), Secretaries of State, Jaka Jamba (U) and Hendrick Vaal Neto (F); Ministry of Labour and Social Security—Antonio Dembo (U), Secretaries of State, Cornelio Caley (M) and Baptista Nguvulu (F); Ministry of Economy—Vasco Vieira de Almeida (P), Secretary of State for Industry and Energy, Augusto Lopes Teixeira (M), for Fisheries, Manuel Alfredo Teixeira Coelho (U), for Commerce and Tourism, Graca Tavares (F); Ministry of Planning and Finance—Saydi Mingas (M); Ministry of Justice—Diogenes Boavida (M); Ministry of Transportation and Communications—

Albino Antunes da Cunha (P); Ministry of Health and Social Matters—Samuel Abrigada (F); Ministry of Public Works, Housing and Urbanisation—Manuel Alfredo Rezende de Oliveira (P); Ministry of Education and Culture—Jeronimo Wanga (U); Ministry of Agriculture—Mateus Neto (F); Ministry of Natural Resources—Jeremias Kalandula Chitunda (U).

82. Heimer, *Social Change in Angola*, p. 48.

83. *Africa*, no. 43 (March 1975), p. 37.

84. *Didrio de Noticias,* May 5, 1975.

85. *Diario de Lisbon,* March 3, 1975.

86. *New York Times,* June 30, 1975.

87. The independence dates for these countries are: Guinea-Bissau, September 10, 1974; Mozambique, June 25, 1975; Cape Verde, June 5, 1975; Sao Tome and Principe, July 12, 1975; and Angola, November 11, 1975.

88. Marcum, II, 273.

89. Pedro Silva, Valdemar Moreira and Francisco Esteves, *Angola: Cnmandos especiais contra os cubanos* (Braga-Lisbon: Braga Editora, 1978).

90. *Washington Post,* January 24, 1976.

91. *The Times* (London), January 20, 1976.

Bibliography

Abshire, D.M., 'From the Scramble for Africa to the "New State"', in D.M. Abshire and M.A. Samuels (eds), *Portuguese Africa: A Handbook* (London: Pall Mall Press, 1969).

—, "Minerals, Manufacturing, Power and Communications', in D.M. Abshire and M.A. Samuels (eds), *Portuguese Africa: A Handbook* (London: Pall Mall Press, 1969).

Adelman, K.L., 'Report from Angola', in *Foreign Affairs* (New York), Volume 53 No. 3, April 1975.

Africa (Lisbon).

Africa Confidential (London).

Africa Contemporary Record: Annual Survey and Documents 1974-1975 (London: Rex Collings, 1975).

Africa Contemporary Record: Annual Survey and Documents 1975-1976 (London: Rex Collings, 1976).

Africa Contemporary Record: Annual Survey and Documents 1976-1977 (London: Rex Collings, 1977).

Africa Contemporary Record: Annual Survey and Documents 1977-1978 (New York: Africana Publishing, 1979).

Africa Digest (London).

Africa Research Bulletin (London).

Aguiar, L., *Livro Negro da Descolonizacao* (Lisbon: Intervencao, 1976).

Albright, D., *Soviet Policy Toward Africa Revisited* (Washington, DC: CSIS, 1987).

Angola: A Tentativa de Goipe de Estado de 27 de Maio de 77 (InformacSo do Bureau Polftico do MPLA, Edicoes Avante, 1977).

Angola, Rumo a Independencia. O Governo de Transicao: Documentose Personalidades (Luanda: Livrangol, 1975).

Baghel, Indu, "Angolan Liberation Movement and the Colonial Administrative Structure", *Indian Africanists,* Vol. I & II, New Delhi, 2007.

—, *Local Administation in Angola During the Portuguese Colonial Rule,* unpublished Ph.D. Thesis, University of Delhi, New Delhi, 2005.

Barber, J. and Barratt, J., *South Africa's Foreign Policy: The Search for Status and Security 1945-1988* (Cambridge: Cambridge University Press/SAIIA, 1990).

Barnet, D. and Harvey, R., *The Revolution in Angola: MPLA, Life Histories and Documents* (Indianapolis, Ind.: Bobbs-Merrill, 1971).

Bender, G., 'Kissinger in Angola: anatomy of failure', in R. Lemarchand (ed.), *American Policy in Southern Africa: The Stakes and the Stance* (Washington, DC: University Press of America, 1978a).

—, 'Angola, the Cubans and American anxieties', in *Foreign Policy* (Washington/New York), No. 31, 1978b.

—, Angola under the Portuguese: The Myth and the Reality (London: Heinemann, 1978c).

—, 'American policy toward Angola: a history of linkage', in G. Bender, J. Coleman and R. Sklar (eds), *African Crisis Areas and US Foreign Policy* (Berkeley, California: University of California Press, 1985).

—, 'The eagle and the bear in Angola', in *The Annals of the American Academy of Political and Social Science* (Philadelphia, Pa.), Volume 489, January 1987.

Benot, Y., 'The Impact of Stalinism on Radical African Socialism', in P. Gutkind and P. Wateman (eds) *African Social Studies* (London: Heinemann, 1977).

Birmingham, D., 'The twenty-seventh of May: an historical note on the abortive 1977 coup in Angola', in *African Affairs: Journal of the Royal African Society,* Volume 77, No. 309, October 1978.

Bowker, M. and Williams, P., *Superpower Detente: A Reappraisal* (London: Sage Publications/RIIA, 1988).

Braganca, A. de and Wallerstein, I. (eds), *The African Liberation Reader*, Volume I (London: Zed Books, 1982).

Brandenburg, P., 'Development, finance and trade', in D.M. Abshire and M.A. Samuels (eds), *Portuguese Africa: A Handbook* (London: Pall Mall Press, 1969).

—, "Transport systems and their external ramifications', in D.M. Abshire and M.A. Samuels (eds), *Portuguese Africa: A Handbook* (London: Pall Mall Press, 1969).

Bridgland, P., *Jonas Savimbi: A Key to Africa* (London: Hodder & Stoughton, 1986).

Brown, K., 'Angolan socialism', in C. Rosberg and T. Callaghy (eds). *Socialism in Sub-Saharan Africa: A New Assessment* (Berkeley, California: Institute of International Studies, 1979).

Burchett, W., *Southern Africa Stands Up* (New York: Urizen Books, 1978).

Campbell, B., *Liberation Nationale et Construction du Socialisme en Afrique* (Montreal, Quebec: Nouvelle Optique, 1977).

Campbell, K.M., *Southern Africa in Soviet Foreign Policy*, IISS Adelphi Paper 227 (London), Winter 1987/8.

Castro, A., O *Sistema Colonial Portugues em Africa* (Lisbon: Editorial Caminho, 1980).

Chabal, P., 'People's war, state formation and revolution in Africa: a comparative analysis of Mozambique, Guinea-Bissau and Angola', in *Journal of Commonwealth and Comparative Politics*, Volume XXI, No. 3, 1983a.

Chabal, P., *Amtlcar Cabral: Revolutionary Leadership and People's War* (Cambridge: Cambridge University Press, 1983b).

Chaliand, G., 'The Political Strategy of Guerrilla Warfare', in P. Gutkind and P. Waterman (eds) *African Social Studies* (London: Heinemann, 1977).

—, *Revolution in the Third World: Myths and Prospects* (Hassocks, Sussex: Harvester Press, 1977).

Chazan, N., Mortimer, R., Ravenhill, J. and Rothchild, D., *Politics and Society in Contemporary Africa* (London: Macmillan Education, 1988).

Chilcote, R.H., *Emerging Nationalism in Portuguese Africa: Documents* (Stanford, California: Hoover Insitution Press, 1972).

Clapham, C., *Third World Politics: An Introduction* (London: Routledge, 1985).

Clarence-Smith, G., *The Third Portuguese Empire 1825-1975: Study in Economic Imperialism* (Manchester: Manchester University Press, 1985).

Cohen, R., 'Marxism in Africa: the grounding of a tradition', in B. Munslow (ed.), *Africa: Problems in the Transition to Socialism* (London: Zed Books, 1986).

Coker, C., *NATO, the Warsaw Pact and Africa* (London: Macmillan/ RUSI, 1985).

—, *High Noon in Southern Africa: Making Peace in a Rough Neighbourhood* (New York/London: W.W. Norton, 1992).

Davidson, B., *In the Eye of the Storm* (Harmondsworth: Penguin, 1975).

Davis, N., 'The Angola decision of 1975: a personal memoir', in *Foreign* Affairs (New York), Fall. 1978.

Dobrynin, A., In Confidence: Moscow's Ambassador to America's Six Cold *War Presidents (1962-1986)* (New York: Times Books, 1995).

Dominguez, J., *To Make a World Safe For Revolution: Cuba's Foreign Policy* (Cambridge, Mass.: Harvard University Press, 1989).

Dongen, I. van, 'Agriculture and other primary production', in D.M. Abshire and M.A. Samuels (eds), *Portuguese Africa: A Handbook* (London: Pall Mall Press, 1969).

Duffy, J., *Portuguese Africa* (Cambridge, Mass.: Harvard University Press, 1959).

Duncan, W.R., The Soviet Union and Cuba: Interests and Influences (New York: Praeger, 1985).

Duner, B., 'Proxy intervention in civil wars', in *Journal of Peace Research,* No. 4, Volume XVIII, 1981.

Durch, W.J., "The Cuban military in Africa and the Middle East: from Algeria to Angola', in *Studies in Comparative Communism* (University of South California), Volume XI, Nos 1 and 2, 1978.

Ebinger, C.K., 'External intervention in internal war: the politics and diplomacy of the Angolan civil war', in *Orbis: A Journal of World Affairs* (Philadelphia: Foreign Policy Research Institute), Volume 20, No. 3 Fall 1976.

Edmonds, R., *Soviet Foreign Policy 1962-1973: The Paradox of Superpower* (London: Oxford University Press, 1975).

—, *Soviet Foreign Policy: The Brezhnev Years* (Oxford: Oxford University Press, 1983).

Ekwe-Ekwe, H., Conflict and Intervention in Africa: Nigeria, Angola, Zaire (London: Macmillan, 1990).

Facts and Reports, press cuttings on Angola, Mozambique, Guinea-Bissau, Portugal and Southern Africa (Amsterdam: Angola Comite): (1974) Volume Four; (1975) Volume Five.

Falk, R., 'Intervention and national liberation', in H. Bull (ed.). *Intervention in World Politics* (Oxford: Clarendon Press, 1984).

Franco de Sousa, A., *Mukanda ao Meu Irmao Angolano* (Pamphlet, 10 December 1990).

Freire Antunes, J., *Os Americaws e Portugal Vol. 1: Os Anos de Richard Nixon 1969-1974* (Lisbon: Publicacoes Dom Quixote, 1986).

Freire Antunes, J., *Kennedy e Salaiar: o Leao e a Raposa* (Lisbon: Difusao Cultural, 1991).

Freitas do Amaral, D., O Antigo Regime e a Revolucao: Memorias Politicas *(1941-1975)* (Venda Nova: Bertrand/Nomen, 1995)

Gaddis, J. Lewis, "The tragedy of Cold War history: reflections on revisionism', in *Foreign Affairs,* Volume 73, No. 1, January/February 1994.

Gavshon, A., *Crisis in Africa: Battleground of East and West* (Harmondsworth: Penguin Books, 1981).

Geldenhuys, D., *South Africa's Searchlor Security since the Second World War* (Braamfontein: South African Institute of International Affairs, September 1978).

—, *The Diplomacy of Isolation: South African Foreign Policy Making* (Johannesburg: Macmillan SA/SAIIA, 1984).

Gil Ferreira, H. and Marshall, M.W., *Portugal's Revolution: Ten Years On* (Cambridge: Cambridge University Press, 1986).

Golan, G., The Soviet Union and National Liberation Movements in the Third *World* (Boston, Mass.: Unwin Hyman, 1988).

Grundy, K., *The Militarisation of South African Politics* (London: I.B. Taurus, 1986).

Guerra, H., Angola: Estrutura Economics e Classes Sociais (Lisbon: Edicoes 70, 1979).

Halliday, F., *The Making of the Second Cold War* (London: Verso, 1983).

—, *Cold War, Third World: An Essay on Soviet-US Relations* (London: Hutchinson Radius, 1989a).

—, 'Revolutions and international relations: some theoretical issues'. Paper presented at the BISA/ISA Conference, London, March 1989b.

Halperin, M., 'The Cuban role in Southern Africa in J. Seiler (ed.). *Southern* Africa Since the Coup (Boulder, Col.: Westview Press, 1981).

Heimer, F., The Decolonisation Conflict in Angola 1974-1976: An Essay in Political Sociology (Geneva: Institute Universitaire de Hautes Etudes Internationales, 1979).

Hodges, T., 'How the MPLA won in Angola', in *After Angola: The War Over Southern Africa,* 2nd edn (New York: Africana Publishing, 1978).

Hoffmann, S., 'The problem of intervention', in H. Bull (ed.). *Intervention in World Politics* (Oxford; Clarendon Press/OUP, 1984).

Hutchison, A., *China's African Revolution* (London: Hutchinson, 1975).

Isaacson, W., *Kissinger: A Biography* (New York: Simon & Schuster, 1992).

Jackson, H., *From the Congo to Soweto: US Foreign Policy Toward Africa Since 1960* (New York: William Morrow, 1982).

Khazanov, A., *Agostinho Neto* (Moscow: Progress Publishers, 1986).

Kissinger, H., *Diplomacy* (New York: Simon & Schuster, 1994).

Klinghoffer, A., *The Angolan War: A Study in Soviet Policy in the Third World* (Boulder, Col.: Westview Press, 1980).

Kolakowski, L., *Main Currents of Marxism,* Volume III (Oxford; Oxford University Press, 1978).

Laidi, Z., *The Third World and the Soviet Union* (London: Zed Books, 1988).

Laidi, Z., *The Superpowers and Africa: The Constraints of a Rivalry 1960-1990* (Chicago and London: University of Chicago Press, 1990).

Laquer, W., 'Communism and nationalism in tropical Africa', in H. Kebschull (ed.). Politics in Transitional Societies: The Challenge of Change in Asia, *Africa and Latin America* (New York: Appleton Century Crofts, 1968).

Larkin, B., *China and Africa 1949-1970* (Berkeley, California: University of California Press, 1971).

Lawson, E.K., 'China's policy in Ethiopia and Angola', in W. Weinstein and T. Henriksen (eds). *Soviet and Chinese Aid to African Nations* (New York: Praeger, 1980).

Leffler, M.P., "Inside enemy archives: the Cold War reopened', in Foreign *Affairs,* Volume 75, No. 4, July/August 1996.

Legum, C., The role of Western Powers in Southern Africa', and 'A study of international intervention in Angola', in *After Angola: The War Over Southern Africa,* 2nd edn (New York: Africana Publishing, 1978).

Legum, C., 'African outlooks toward the USSR', in D. Albright (ed.), *Africa and International Communism* (London: Macmillan, 1980).

Leogrande, W., 'Cuban-Soviet relations and Cuban policy in Africa', in C. Mesa-Lago and J. Belkin (eds), *Cuba in Africa* (Pittsburgh, Pa.: University of Pittsburgh Press, 1982).

Little, R., *Intervention: External Involvement in Civil Wars* (London: Martin Robertson, 1975).

Lucena, M. de, A Evolucao do Sistema Corporativo Portugues Volume I (Lisbon: P. & R., 1976). Macfarlane, S. Neil, *Intervention and Regional Security* (London: IISS Adelphi Papers, No. 196, Spring 1985).

Macfarlane, S. Neil, *Superpower Rivalry and Third World Radicalism: The Idea of National Liberation* (London: Croom Helm, 1985).

Macfarlane, S. Neil, The Soviet Union and Southern African security', in *Problems of Communism,* Volume XXXVIII, March-June, 1989.

McGowen Pinheiro, P., "Politics of a revolt', in *Angola: A Symposium* (London: Oxford University Press, 1962).

Mack, A., "The politics of asymmetric conflict', in *World Politics,* January 1975.

Marcum, J., 'Three revolutions', in Africa Report, November 1967. Marcum, J., The Angolan Revolution, Volume I: Anatomy of an Explosion *1950-1962* (Cambridge, Mass.: MIT Press, 1969).

—, 'Lessons of Angola', in *Foreign Affairs,* Volume 54, No. 3, April *1976. Marcum, J., The Angolan Revolution, Volume II: Exile Politics and Guerrilla Warfare 1962-1976* (Cambridge, Mass.: MIT Press, 1978).

—, 'Angola: perilous transition to independence', in G. Carter and P. O'Meara (eds), *Southern Africa: The Continuing Crisis,* 2nd edn (Bloomington, Ind.: Indiana University Press, 1982).

Matumona, A., "Angolan disunity', in *Angola: A Symposium* (London: Oxford University Press, 1962).

Mayall, J., *Africa: The Cold War and After* (London: Elek Books, 1971).

Maxwell, K., *The Making of Portuguese Democracy* (Cambridge: Cambridge University Press, 1995).

Minter, W., *Portuguese Africa and the West* (Harmondsworth: Penguin, 1972).

Modelski, G., "The international relations of internal war', in J. Rosenau (ed.), *International Aspects of Civil Strife* (Princeton, NJ: Princeton University Press, 1964).

Morris, R., "The proxy war in Angola: the pathology of a blunder', in *New Republic* (Washington, DC), 31 January 1976.

MPLA, *1970* (Liberation Support Movement pamphlet).

MPLA, *Programa* (pamphlet).

MPLA, Centra; *Committee Plenary, 23-29 October 1976* (London: MAGIC).

MPLA, *First Congress Central Committee Report, 4-10 December 1977 (London:* MAGIC).

Neto, A., Cabral, A. and Mondlane, E., 'A Voz dos Povos cm Luta. *Declaracoes & Voz. da Liberdade* (Algiers: PPLN pamphlet, 1969).

Newitt, M., *Portugal in Africa: The Last Hundred Years* (London: C. Hurst, 1981).

Okuma, T., *Angola in Ferment* (Boston, Mass.: Beacon Press, 1962).

Oliveira e Castro, L. de, 'Situacao Econ6mica de Angola no ano de 1962', for *Ultramar,* Nos 13/14, 1963.

Oliveira Marques, A.H. de. *History of Portugal Vol. II: From Empire to Corporate State* (New York and London: Columbia University Press, 1972).

Oliveira Marques, A.H. de, *Hisioria de Portugal Vol. Ill: Das Revolucoes Liberals aos Nossos Dias* (Lisbon: Palas Editores, 1981).

Ottaway, D. and M., *Algeria: the Politics of a Socialist Revolution* (Berkeley, California: University of California Press, 1970).

Ottaway, D. and M., *Afrocommunism* (London: Holmes & Meier, 1981).

Paige, J., *Agrarian Revolution* (New York: Free Press, 1975).

Peking Review (Peking).

Pezarat Correia, P., *Descoloniwcao de Angola: A Joia da Coroa do Imperio Portugues* (Lisbon: Editorial Inquerito, 1991).

Porch, D., *The Portuguese Armed Forces and the Revolution* (London: Croom Helm, 1977).

Porter, B.D., *The USSR in Third World Conflicts: Soviet Arms and Diplomacy in Local Wars 1945-1980* (Cambridge: Cambridge University Press, 1984).

Queiroz, A., *Angola do 25 de Abril ao 11 de Novembro: A Via Agreste da Liberdade* (Lisbon: Biblioteca Ulmeiros, 1978).

Resolutions and Decisions of the Security Council 1961 (New York: UN Official Records).

Rosenau, J., 'Internal war as an international event', in J. Rosenau (ed.). *International Aspects of Civil Strife* (Princeton, NJ: Princeton University Press, 1964).

Roxborough, I., *Theories of Underdevelopment* (London: Macmillan, 1979).

Samuels, M.A., 'The nationalist parties', in D.M. Abshire and M.A. Samuels (eds), *Portuguese Africa: A Handbook* (London: Pall Mall Press, 1969).

Schlesinger, A.M., *A Thousand Days: John F. Kennedy in the White House* (Boston: Houghton Mifflin, 1965).

Seiler, J., "South Africa's regional role', in J. Seiler (ed.). *Southern Africa Since the Coup* (Boulder, Col.: Westview Press, 1981).

Shaw, T., 'South Africa, Southern Africa and the world system', in T. Callaghy (ed.). *South Africa in Southern Africa: The Intensifying Vortex of Violence* (New York: Praeger, 1983).

Shearman, P., *The Soviet Union and Cuba,* Chatham House Papers 38 (London: Routledge & Kegan Paul/RIIA, 1987).

Simpson, M., *The Soviet Union and Afro-Marxist Regimes: The Path to the Treaties of Friendship and Cooperation,* PhD thesis (University of London, 1989).

Scares, M., *Democratizacao e Descoloniwcao: Dez Meses no Govemo Provisorio* (Lisbon: Publicacoes Dom Quixote, 1975).

Somerville, K., *Angola: Politics, Economics and Society* (London: Frances Pinter, 1986).

—, *Foreign Military Intervention in Africa* (London: Pinter, 1990).

Sorenson, T., *Kennedy* (London: Hodder & Stoughton, 1965).

Spihola, A. de, *Portugal and the Future* (Johannesburg: Perskor Publishers, 1974).

Staniland, M., "Africa, the American intelligentsia, and the shadow of Vietnam', in *Political Science Quarterly,* Volume 98, No. 4, Winter 1983-84.

Stevens, C., The Soviet Union and Angola', in *African Affairs: Journal of the Royal African Society,* Volume 75, No. 299, April 1976.

Stevens, C., 'The Soviet role in Southern Africa', in J. Seller (ed.). *Southern Africa Since the Coup* (Boulder, Col.: Westview Press, 1981).

Stockwell, J., *In Search of Enemies: A CIA Story* (New York: W.W. Norton, 1978).

Szulc, T., 'Lisbon and Washington: behind the Portuguese revolution', in *Foreign Policy* (New York), No. 21, Winter 1975-76.

Themido, J.H., *Dei Anos em Washington 1971-1981* (Lisbon: Publicacocs Dom Quixote, 1995).

Therborn, G., 'From Petrograd to Saigon', in *New Left Review* No. 48.

Ulyanovsky, R., *National Liberation: Essays on Theory and Practice* (Moscow: Progress Publishers, 1978).

UNITA (Kwacha Unita Press, 1984).

United Nations Yearbook 1960 & 1961 (New York: UN).

Valdes, N., 'Revolutionary solidarity in Angola', in C. Blasier and C. Mesa-Lago (eds), *Cuba in the World* (Pittsburgh, Pa.: University of Pittsburgh Press, 1979).

Valenta, J., "The Soviet-Cuban Intervention in Angola 1975', in *Studies in Comparative Communism* (University of South California), Volume XI, Nos 1 and 2, 1978.

Weissman, S., "The CIA and US policy in Zaire and Angola', in R. Lemarchand (ed.), *American Policy in Southern Africa: The Stakes and the Stance* (Washington, DC: University Press of America, 1978).

Wheeler, D.L., 'Origins of African nationalism in Angola: Assimilado protest writings, 1859-1929', in R.H. Chilcote (ed.). *Protest and Resistance in Angola and Brazil: Comparative Studies* (Berkeley, California: University of California Press, 1972).

—, 'Portuguese withdrawal from Africa, 1974-1975: the Angolan case', in J. Seiler (ed.). *Southern Africa Since the Coup* (Boulder, Col.: Westview Press, 1981).

Wheeler, D.L. and Pelissier, R., *Angola* (London: Pall Mall Press, 1971).

White, G., 'Revolutionary socialist development in the Third World: an overview', in G. White, R. Murray and C. White (eds). *Revolutionary Socialist Development in the Third World* (Brighton: Wheatsheaf, 1983).

Windsor, P., 'Superpower intervention', in H. Bull (ed.). *Intervention in World Politics* (Oxford: Clarendon Press, 1984).

Wohlgemuth, P., "The Portuguese territories and the United Nations', in *International Conciliation* (New York), No. 545, November 1963).

Yadav, Surya Narain, *African Politics and Government: Post-Cold War Challenges,* Jnanada Prakashan, New Delhi, 2009.

—, *Ethnicity, National Security and Democracy,* Jnanada Prakashan, New Delhi, 2009.

Yadav, Surya Narain and Indu Baghel, *Democracy, Development and Human Rights,* Jnanada Prakashan, New Delhi, 2009.

Index